Pro Objective-C Design Patterns for iOS

Carlo Chung

Apress®

Pro Objective-C Design Patterns for iOS

Copyright © 2011 by Carlo Chung

ISBN-13 (pbk): 978-1-4302-3330-5

ISBN-13 (electronic): 978-1-4302-3331-2

Printed and bound in the United States of America 9 8 7 6 5 4 3 2 1

President and Publisher: Paul Manning
Lead Editor: Douglas Pundick
Technical Reviewer: James Bucanek
Editorial Board: Steve Anglin, Mark Beckner, Ewan Buckingham, Gary Cornell, Jonathan Gennick, Jonathan Hassell, Michelle Lowman, Matthew Moodie, Jeff Olson, Jeffrey Pepper, Frank Pohlmann, Douglas Pundick, Ben Renow-Clarke, Dominic Shakeshaft, Matt Wade, Tom Welsh
Coordinating Editor: Corbin Collins
Copy Editors: Mary Ann Fugate, Mary Behr
Compositor: MacPS, LLC
Indexer: BIM Indexing & Proofreading Services
Artist: April Milne
Cover Designer: Anna Ishchenko

Distributed to the book trade worldwide by Springer Science+Business Media, LLC., 233 Spring Street, 6th Floor, New York, NY 10013. Phone 1-800-SPRINGER, fax (201) 348-4505, e-mail orders-ny@springer-sbm.com, or visit www.springeronline.com.

For information on translations, please e-mail rights@apress.com, or visit www.apress.com.

Apress and friends of ED books may be purchased in bulk for academic, corporate, or promotional use. eBook versions and licenses are also available for most titles. For more information, reference our Special Bulk Sales–eBook Licensing web page at www.apress.com/info/bulksales.

The source code for this book is available to readers at www.apress.com.

Contents at a Glance

Contents

About the Author

 **Carlo Chung** is a computer scientist, tinkerer, and amateur photographer. He earned a master's degree in computer science, specializing in computer vision (a branch of artificial intelligence). Any idea about putting A.I. and any small gadgets together can get him excited. He likes daydreaming about making the iPhone more "intelligent" and "humanoid." He applied his knowledge of computer vision to the iPhone platform and created several apps, two of which have been featured on the front page of the App Store, with one on the top-paid list in the Photography category. When he is away from his keyboard, you may see him playing a part in a drum circle or out in the field prospecting for gold.

About the Technical Reviewer

James Bucanek has spent the past 30 years programming and developing microcomputer systems. He has experience with a broad range of technologies, from embedded consumer products to industrial robotics. James is currently focused on Macintosh and iPhone software development. When not programming, James indulges in his love of the arts. He earned an associate's degree from the Royal Academy of Dance in classical ballet and occasionally teaches at Adams Ballet Academy.

Acknowledgments

"You know what, this is a really tough book to write." That is the warning I got from one of the acquisitions editors at Apress when we first spoke on the phone. With his trust and faith in me to pull this book off, I started this writing journey in the summer of 2010.

My gratitude goes out to Corbin Collins, coordinating editor, for helping the whole team stay focused. Thanks to Douglas Pundick, development editor, for all his suggestions during the editorial review process to help make this a great book. Thanks to Michelle Lowman, acquisitions editor, for her support and patience. Thanks to James Bucanek, technical reviewer, for his critical comments until the last minute before the book went to press. Thanks to Mary Ann Fugate and Mary Behr, the copy editors, for their impeccable copy editing efforts to make this book look wonderful. Thanks to all of the wonderful people at Apress—this book would not be possible without all their help in making it all happen.

I want to acknowledge and give my many thanks to Michael Fredrickson and Sreenivasa Busam, who helped review my chapters from the perspective of their domain of knowledge. Last but not least, I want to thank Mike Hambleton for his expertise in technical writing, precision, and patience in helping to review my chapters

Preface

With over 200,000 apps (and counting every second) available for download at the whim of its users, Apple's App Store affects all walks of life. The effect of Apple's "There is an app for that" catchphrase definitely cannot be ignored. Believe it or not, I had been using my iPad to finish many parts of this book while sitting on my couch during the course of four months.

Every day there is a growing number of iOS developers who want to jump on the bandwagon and get rich with their next killer apps in mind. As of this writing, there are more than 50,000 iOS developers around the world, and the number is growing rapidly. If you are one of those who are serious about iOS development and want to make your development effort more productive with good software design principles, then this is the book for you.

I am an iOS developer and understand well the many pains and gains from developing an app. Learning a new programming language is never easy. Finally the lightbulb flickers on and we start developing apps. When we look at the Cocoa Touch framework, it is very easy for even a seasoned developer to realize its elegance in design and organization. Its elegance comes from the thoughtfulness of its designers by putting different well-known (or not yet known) design patterns in various framework infrastructures, which makes it scalable and flexible to use by third-party developers like you and me. Much of the framework reuses the same types of patterns again and again; any new elements added later to the framework can easily be absorbed by other application developers without taking a steep learning curve again.

Understanding the patterns that are used in the Cocoa Touch framework is just part of the picture. If you don't spend time on your project's design and just start coding as soon as you get your killer app ideas, it will become a giant mothball as you add more features to it later. The worst-case scenario is that it will become unmanageable and you (or other developers in the team) will be totally lost in your code. You might end up spending more time fixing coding flaws (bugs) instead of focusing on new improvements.

To fully take advantage of the framework, one should have a good grasp of design patterns and apply them appropriately during implementation. This book was inspired by the original classic *Design Patterns: Elements of Reusable Object-Oriented Software*, written by Erich Gamma, Richard Helm, Ralph Johnson, and John Vlissides, often referred to as the Gang of Four. In each chapter of this book, I reference any details of a pattern to its original definitions.

Today we understand the importance of using design patterns in many software projects. Most of the Cocoa Touch framework was written in Objective-C and, as of this writing, there is no other book that explains implementation of design patterns in the Objective-C language on the market. This book's aim is to be the first definitive guide on how to implement the classic design patterns in Objective-C language for Cocoa Touch development on the iOS platform.

You do want to make your life easier as an iOS developer, right? Without knowing best practices in application software design, the development process would be frustrating or even fruitless in the end. Also, reusing what you have already developed that is proven to work is the key to catching up with the frenetic pace of change in the App Store or software market in general.

With a little patience to understand the materials in this book and effort to apply them to your real projects whenever you can, you will soon experience the benefits from design patterns!

I have developed a web site for this book at www.objective-c-design-patterns.com, where you can find other information related to the book. On the web site, you are also welcome to share your success stories and any hurdles you encountered while using design patterns in your projects. Source code for this book is available at www.apress.com.

Happy coding!

Carlo Chung
March 2011

Part **I**

Getting Your Feet Wet

Chapter 1

Hello, Design Patterns!

Almost every computer programming book starts with a "Hello, World!" chapter to introduce the topic. Since this book is all about design patterns, let's start with "Hello, Design Patterns!"

As you've already picked up this book, you are probably familiar with the notion of design patterns in object-oriented programming. A design pattern is useful as an abstraction tool for solving design problems in other fields like engineering and architecture. The notion was borrowed by software development for a similar purpose. A design pattern is a template for an object or class design that solves a recurring problem in a particular domain.

This chapter provides a brief history of design patterns and their relationships with the Cocoa Touch technologies. It discusses issues that can affect a design, talks about object notation used in the book, and explains how design patterns are organized.

What This Book Is

This book is for any professional or aspiring iOS developer who wants to take advantage of design patterns to make his or her software development efforts more productive and more fun! The purpose of this book is to show you how to put design patterns into action in iOS application development. I will focus on applicability of various design patterns with the Cocoa Touch framework and its related technologies.

Although some of the principles and notions may also be applicable to Cocoa Touch's big brother, Cocoa for Mac OS X, there is no guarantee that they will work perfectly with the full-blown Cocoa. You can use this book as a quick reference to design patterns in Objective-C.

What you'll learn:

- The basic concepts of various design patterns.

- How to apply them to your code based on different design scenarios.

- How design patterns can strengthen your apps.

The website for this book is www.objective-c-design-patterns.com or
www.objectivecdesignpatterns.com. Feel free to share your success stories and hurdles
on using design patterns in your projects.

The source code is available at www.apress.com

What You Need Before You Can Begin

Just like any other iOS application development book, you'll need a copy of Xcode and
iOS SDK to run the sample code in this book. The sample projects for this book were
compiled and tested using Xcode version 3.2.5 and iOS SDK 4.2, so any newer versions
should also work well. There are many free/paid tools available for developing iOS
applications on platforms other than Mac OS X, but there's no guarantee that any of the
samples from this book will work as they should if they are created on those other
platforms.

This book also covers some aspects of designing an iOS application. You may want to
download/purchase some software tools to help build wireframes and UI layouts for
practicing or designing real applications. The wireframes in this book were created using
OmniGraffle (www.omnigroup.com/products/omnigraffle/). The website also provides an
area where you can download various free stencils or wireframe templates.

Class and object diagrams were used extensively in this book, but the choices of
software tools for modeling class and objects are very limited. As of this writing, most of
them are based on some standard notations that are only applicable to other object-
oriented programming languages such as C++, Java, and C#. Objective-C has some
special language features that are hard to represent with standard notations, such as
categories and extensions (anonymous categories). For this reason, I have invented
some notations just for the special features; they are explained in the "Objects and
Classes Used In This Book" section later in this chapter. You can use a graphic
authoring tool of your choice to draw Objective-C classes and objects based on the
invented notations. Hopefully, there will be a set of standardized object modeling
notations for Objective-C coming out soon.

What You Need to Know Before You Can Begin

This book is in a pro series, so it's not "iOS development 101" or "Start using Objective-
C in 24 hours." I assume that you, the reader, have basic knowledge of the iOS SDK (the
Cocoa Touch framework). Further, you should feel comfortable with the Objective-C
programming language. Otherwise, you will miss many of the insights and advanced
techniques and tricks presented in this book.

Although this book is targeted at intermediate and advanced developers, you don't need
to have in-depth knowledge of design patterns in order to pick up their concepts. If you
were exposed to some design patterns somewhere in your career path, you will still
benefit from the explanations in this book. Every pattern chapter uses some everyday

analogies to assimilate the theme of the design pattern. Also, there are tips and notes to dispel any confusion where applicable.

Are you ready? Let's roll!

Design Déjà-vu

As a developer, you have likely had the feeling that "I've solved this problem before but don't know exactly where or how." This happens all the time, especially when you're working on particular types of projects repeatedly. For example, every database application has features like database access so that your application can store and retrieve its data. If you do a good job recording the details of the problems and how you solved them, you can easily reapply the strategies instead of reinventing them.

The experiences of some of the most common design déjà-vu scenarios as well as strategies applicable to them were first authoritatively described and cataloged in *Design Patterns: Elements of Reusable Object-Oriented Software*, by Erich Gamma, Richard Helm, Ralph Johnson, and John Vlissides (Addison-Wesley Professional, 1994). It captured design experiences in designing object-oriented software in a form that people could use effectively as design patterns. Ironically, the predecessor of Cocoa (Touch) frameworks, NEXTSTEP, was designed with many elegant, reusable object-oriented software design patterns and it played a major role as a source of inspiration for the original "Gang of Four" (a popular nickname for the authors of the above book).

According to *Design Patterns: Elements of Reusable Object-Oriented Software*,

A design pattern is a description of communicating objects and classes that are customized to solve a general design problem in a particular context.

In short, a design pattern is a customized solution to a problem in a context. The context is a recurring situation in which the problem occurs. The problem is the goal you are trying to achieve in this context. The same problem in a different context may have different constraints and challenges. And the customized solution is a design that achieves the goal in a particular context and resolves the constraints that come with it.

A design pattern abstracts the key aspects of a particular object-oriented design problem or issue that has proven to be effective over time. It expresses important insights on object-oriented designs. Some principles of design influence design patterns. These principles are rules of thumb for constructing reusable and maintainable object-oriented applications, such as "favor object composition over class inheritance" and "program to an interface, not an implementation."

For example, if you encapsulate and isolate some parts of a program that vary by defining interfaces for them, they can vary independently of other parts of the program because they are not tied to any specifics. You can then change or extend those variable parts without affecting the other parts of the program. The program consequently becomes more flexible and robust to change because you eliminate dependencies and reduce couplings between parts. These benefits make design patterns important when you want to write reusable software.

Programs (and the objects and classes within) that adapt and use design patterns in their design will be more reusable, more extensible, and easier to change in the future. Moreover, programs that are based on design patterns tend to be more elegant and efficient than other programs that aren't, as they require fewer lines of code to accomplish the same goal.

The Origin of Design Patterns - Model, View, and Controller (MVC)

The Model-View-Controller design pattern (MVC) and its variants have been around at least since the early days of Smalltalk. The design pattern is fundamental to many mechanisms and technologies in Cocoa Touch.

Objects in a MVC design patterns are segregated into one of three roles in an application: model, view, or controller. The MVC pattern also defines the way objects communicate with each other across abstract boundaries of their roles. MVC contributes important factors to a good Cocoa Touch application design. A major step in designing an application is to choose one of these three groups an object or a class should fall into. It should be relatively painless to use any technologies packaged from the Cocoa Touch framework if the application has a well-defined MVC segregation.

The pattern itself is not an absolute pattern of its own; rather, it is compound pattern in that it comprises several other elemental patterns. Those elemental patterns are discussed in detail throughout the pattern catalog of this book.

Many objects in MVC applications are more easily extensible and reusable than other applications that are not based on MVC, as their interfaces tend to be better defined. What's more, many Cocoa Touch technologies and architectures are built upon the MVC pattern and require your applications and objects play by the rules set for the MVC roles.

The following sections describe how each of the MVC roles plays a part in the architecture.

Encapsulating Data and Basic Behaviors In Model Objects

Model objects maintain an application's data as well as define the special logic that manipulates it. They are reusable because they represent knowledge that is applicable to a specific problem domain. For example, a model object might represent a complex data structure for what the user has drawn on the screen—or be as simple as an item in a to-do list application.

Once any data that contains persistent information of the application is loaded, it should be put in the model objects. In an ideal situation, a model object should not have any explicit association with any user interface used for presenting and editing it.

Presenting Information to the User with View Objects

A view object can respond to user actions and knows how to present itself onscreen. A view object usually presents data obtained from model objects from the application. It can work with a portion of a model object, a complete model object, or even multiple different model objects. Often, in conjunction with user actions, it allows modifications to that data.

Despite the close relationship between a view object and a model object, view objects are not coupled with model objects in an MVC application. Except for performance reasons (such as when a view needs to cache data), the view should not be used for storing the data it is presenting.

Since view objects can work with many different model objects, they tend to be reusable and consistent across different applications. The UIKit framework offers a variety of collections of view classes that you can reuse in your own applications.

Tying up the Model to the View with Controller Objects

A controller object acts like a middleman between view and model objects. As a middleman or mediator, it can establish a communication channel through which its views can acknowledge and respond to changes in the models.

Besides the mediating role, controller objects can perform other operations for an application, such as managing the life cycles of other objects, performing setup, and coordinating tasks for the application.

For instance, a value that's a result of a user action through a view object, such as entering a value in a text input box, can be passed to a controller object. The controller object may also tell the view object to change its appearance or behavior based on the same user action, such as disabling a text input box.

Depending on the required design, controller objects can be either reusable or non-reusable (concrete).

MVC as a Compound Design Pattern

MVC is not a bottom-line design pattern by itself. It contains several more relatively primitive design patterns, which are discussed in the pattern catalog throughout this book. The elemental design patterns in MVC work together to define functional collaborations that are characteristic of an MVC application.

The Cocoa (Touch) version of MVC comprises the Composite, Command, Mediator, Strategy, and Observer patterns.

- *Composite (Chapter 13)*: The view objects forms a view hierarchy in a coordinated manner. The view components in the hierarchy can range from compound views (such as table views) to individual views (such as text boxes or buttons). Each of the view nodes at any level can respond to user actions and draw itself onscreen.

- *Command (Chapter 20)*: This is a target-action mechanism in which view objects can defer an execution on other objects, such as controllers, until certain events have occurred. The mechanism incorporates the Command pattern.

- *Mediator (Chapter 11)*: A controller object plays a middleman role that adopts the Mediator pattern; it forms a bi-directional conduit for the flow of data between model and view objects. Changes in model are communicated to view objects through the controller objects of an application.

- *Strategy (Chapter 19)*: A controller can be a "strategy" for any view object. A view object isolates itself in order to maintain its sole duty as a data presenter and delegates all application-specific decisions of the interface behavior to its "strategy" object (the controller).

- *Observer (Chapter 12)*: A model object keeps interested objects such as controllers updated with any changes to its internal state.

Figure 1–1 shows how these patterns work together in a fictitious scenario.

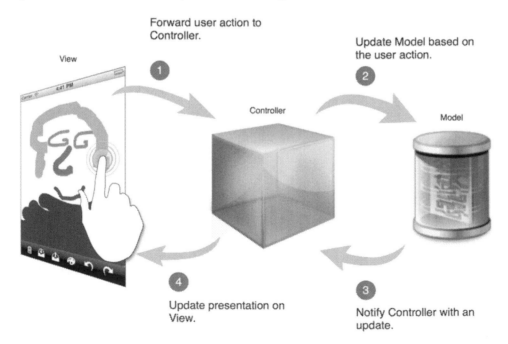

Figure 1–1. *An illustrative example on how Model, View, and Controller interact as a group of different entities*

This is what's happening in Figure 1–1:

1. The user creates a touch event by touching or dragging her finger across the canvas view. The actual view (layer) being touched is right at a particular level in a view composite. The canvas (view) forwards the touch information to its view controller.

2. The controller object receives the touch event and its related information. It then applies a strategy to change the state of a model and/or request the view object to update its behavior or appearance based on the same event.

3. Once a change has occurred and has been updated in the model object, the model object notifies all registered observer objects such as controllers.

4. The controller acts as a mediator to communicate any changed data from the model to the view(s), so they can update their appearances accordingly.

Issues That Can Affect Your Design

Design patterns can certainly improve your system designs in many ways. But there are a few design principles that can also affect your designs. Some of them are for software designs in general but some are specific to Objective-C and Cocoa Touch. I will discuss each of them in the following sections.

Programming To An Interface, Not An Implementation

Many software developers understand object-oriented concepts like classes, objects, inheritance, polymorphism, and interfaces. But what's the difference between class inheritance and interface inheritance (subtyping)? An interface defines a type, and interface inheritance (subtyping) allows you to use an object in place of another. On the other hand, class inheritance is a mechanism for defining an object's implementation and type by reusing functionality in parent class or just simply sharing code and representation. Class inheritance allows you to define a new kind of class rapidly by inheriting most of what you need from existing classes for free. In fact, there is a close relationship between class and type. The contrast, though, is that an object can have many types while objects of different classes have the same type.

Defining families of classes with identical interfaces is important because polymorphism depends on the interfaces! Other object-oriented programming languages like Java allow developers to define a type of "interface" (compared to a class) that defines a "contract" between clients and concrete objects being used. Objective-C has a similar kind of thing called protocol. A *protocol* also acts like a contract of objects but can't be instantiated as an object itself. Implementing a protocol or inheriting from an abstract class let objects share the same interfaces (I'll discuss some issues relating to using protocol versus abstract base class in the next section). So all objects of the subtypes can respond to the requests in the interface of the protocol or abstract class.

There are two benefits from the practice:

- As long as the objects conform to the interface that clients expect, the clients shouldn't be aware of the exact types of objects they use.

- Clients only know about the protocol(s) or abstract class(es) defining the interface, so the clients don't know anything about the objects' classes.

This leads to the principle of reusable object-oriented software design according to the Gang of Four book:

Program to an interface, not an implementation.

A common practice in client code is not to declare variables of particular concrete classes' objects. Instead, use only an interface defined by a protocol or an abstract class. You will see this notion and theme throughout this book.

@protocol vs. Abstract Base Class (ABC)

So it's better to program to an interface, not an implementation. But what kind of interface should it be? In Objective-C, you can use a language feature called protocol (@protocol as its syntax). A protocol doesn't define any implementation; instead it only declares methods that determine how conforming classes should behave. So a protocol is an "interface" that only defines abstract behavior. Classes that implement the protocol define actual implementation for those methods to perform real operations. Another way to define a high-level abstract type is to define an abstract base class (ABC). With an abstract base class, you can create some default behavior that other subclasses can share. An abstract base class is like other regular classes but it leaves out some behavior that can or should be overridden by subclasses.

If you decide to change a protocol that you have defined in the past, you will probably break the other classes that implement it. A protocol (or an interface) is like a contract between an abstract type and concrete types. When the contract changes, everything that follows needs to change as well. The only exception is when you only change some of the protocol methods to become "optional" with a @optional directive. An abstract base class, on the other hand, is little more flexible than protocol in terms of interface changes. You are free to add new methods to an abstract base class without breaking the rest of the inheritance chain. Also, you can freely add, remove, or factor default behavior in some stubbed-out methods that could be used by subclasses.

For clients that want to use objects of the type defined in a protocol, let's say you have a protocol called Mark, and the clients need to refer any object of that kind with the following syntax:

```
id <Mark> thisMark;
```

If Mark is declared as an abstract base class, then the syntax should be just like other classes, like so:

```
Mark *thisMark;
```

In a method that accepts a Mark protocol object as a parameter, it would look like this:

```
- (void) anOperationWithMark:(id <Mark>) aMark;
```

Likewise, for a Mark abstract base class it goes like this:

```
- (void) anOperationWithMark:(Mark *) aMark;
```

Which one looks better? It's apparent that the Mark protocol reference seems a little awkward to use. Then why should you still keep protocols around anyway? One of the main reasons is that Objective-C is unlike other object-oriented languages, such as C++, that support multiple-inheritance. So if one of your classes needs to be a subclass of UIView, but at the same time it also needs to be a custom abstract type of yours, then you definitely need that abstract type to be a protocol rather than an abstract base class. For classes that don't need to subclass another class other than your abstract type, you can let them subclass your abstract base class directly.

But perhaps you might change the design later to support classes of your abstract type that can also be subclasses of, for example, UIView. Can you have the best of both world? A flexible solution for this situation in general is first to have an abstract base class for classes that don't need to subclass other classes, and then you can later define a protocol of the same name for other classes to implement including your abstract base class. You can find a similar strategy in the Cocoa Touch framework in which NSObject base class conforms to NSObject protocol.

Object Composition vs. Class Inheritance

Class inheritance or subclassing allows you to define an implementation of a class in terms of another's. Subclassing is often referred to as *white-box reuse* because the internal representation and details of parent classes are often visible to subclasses.

Object composition is an alternative to class inheritance. Object composition requires that the objects being composed have well-defined interfaces and that they are defined dynamically at runtime through references acquired by other objects. So you can compose objects within other ones to create more complex functionality. Since no internal details of objects are visible to others, they appear as "black boxes" and this style of reuse is called *black-box reuse*.

Both white-box and black-box reuses with class inheritance and object composition have their advantages and disadvantages. Some of the pros and cons about class inheritance are summarized next.

Pros:

- Class inheritance is straightforward to use because the relationship is defined statically at compile-time.

- It makes it easier to modify the implementation being reused.

Cons:

- Because class inheritance is defined at compile-time, you can't change the inherited implementations from parent classes at runtime.

- Part of the representation in subclasses is often defined in parent classes.

- Subclasses are exposed to details of parent classes' implementation, so it breaks encapsulation.

- Any change in the parent's implementation will force its subclasses to change as well because their implementations are so tied up together.

- You need to rewrite the parent class or the inherited implementation because the inherited implementation becomes obsolete or inappropriate for new problem contexts.

Reusing a subclass can be problematic due implementation dependencies. One solution for this is to inherit (subtype) only from protocol(s) or abstract (base) class(es), as they usually have little or, in a protocol, no implementation.

Object composition lets you use one object with many others as each expects the others' interfaces to work. For this reason, they require carefully designed interfaces to make them work properly in a system. However, object composition also has some pros and cons to consider.

Pros:

- You don't break encapsulation because objects are now accessed only through their interfaces.

- There are substantially fewer implementation dependencies, as the object's implementation is defined in terms of the interfaces.

- You can replace any object at runtime with another of the same type.

- It helps keep a class encapsulated so it can focus on one task.

- Your classes and their hierarchies will remain small. They will be less likely to grow into something unmanageable.

Cons:

- The design will tend to have more objects.

- The behavior of the system will depend on the relationships of different objects instead of being defined in one class.

- Ideally, there is no need to create new components to achieve reuse. It is quite rare that you should be able to get all the functionality you need just by assembling existing components through object composition. In practice, the set of available components is never quite rich enough.

Despite the cons, object composition can provide many benefits on system design. Those cons can be counter-balanced by using class inheritance in certain areas as it helps make it easier to make new components from old ones.

So when you *favor object composition over class inheritance,* it doesn't mean that you shouldn't use class inheritance at all. You need to make a clear judgment on how to reuse classes and objects in certain situations. Class inheritance and object composition can work together if you design them properly for your systems. A natural way to think before you design a class is more towards object composition. You can then refine the design by looking for redundant behavior; if found, it may be a sign that's begging for class inheritance there. You will see object composition in the design patterns discussed in this book.

Objects and Classes Used in this Book

I use different diagrams and graphics in the book to illustrate some important ideas of the patterns. Sometimes I'll use screenshots or other visual representation to showcase, for example, the structure of a composite tree object. But I needed something more formal and clear to denote relationships and interactions between classes and objects alike. Most commonly used notations throughout the patterns in the book are class and object diagrams. I borrowed the OMT (Object Modeling Technique) notation and modified it to fit my needs. This section is going to describe the notations used for class and object diagrams.

Class Diagram

A class diagram illustrates classes, the static relationships between them, and their structure. In Objective-C, you can define a protocol, (abstract) class, and a category in your applications.

Protocol, Abstract Class, Concrete Class, and Category

In general, a round rectangular box denotes a class entity with its name in bold type at the top and operation names in the lower part of the box. If you are reading an electronic version of this book, you'll see that the background color of the protocol's title bar is pink and the other class entities' title bars have a light blue background. Names for abstract anything are in italics. So a protocol and an abstract class appear in bold and italics. A protocol name is enclosed in a pair of angle brackets. Instance variables are put in the very bottom part of the box. Samples of different class entities are illustrated in Figure 1–2.

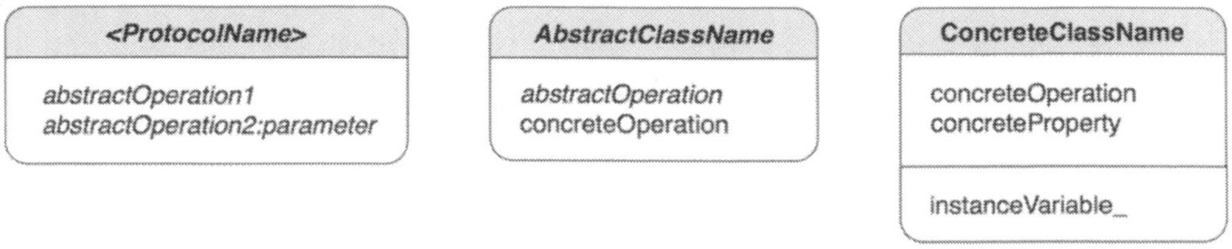

<ProtocolName>
abstractOperation1 *abstractOperation2:parameter*

AbstractClassName
abstractOperation concreteOperation

ConcreteClassName
concreteOperation concreteProperty
instanceVariable_

Figure 1–2. *A protocol with abstract operations on the left; an abstract class with both abstract and concrete operations at the center; and a concrete class with a concrete operation, concrete property, and an instance variable on the right*

Denoting a category is a little tricky because the original OMT doesn't support category as of this writing. A category is an extension of a class, but is not a subclass of that class. So it might be been confusing if I used arrows to illustrate the relationship. I've come up with the notation of augmenting a class box as shown in Figure 1–3.

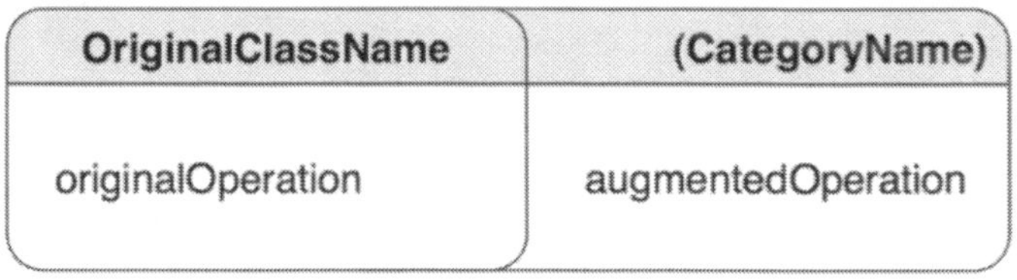

OriginalClassName	**(CategoryName)**
originalOperation	augmentedOperation

Figure 1–3. *The original class is on the right and its category is augmented on the right.*

The original class box is on the left and there's a similar rectangular box attached to it. The category name is enclosed in parenthesis and its augmented operations are put in the lower part of the box just like other classes. This notation may not be the most flexible notation especially if you have 100 categories in your design. But it is good enough for the illustrations used in this book.

In a class or object diagram, there can be some other roles that are part of the design. Those roles could be an abstract entity, such as a client, or some other classes within or outside the scope of the design. A grayed out round rectangular box denotes an implicit role that is part of an interaction but isn't essential to the discussion. Otherwise, a participant class will be denoted as round rectangle with a solid black border. If this is an ebook, the background color of a participant class box is light blue while the implicit one's background is clear or white (see Figure 1–4).

Figure 1–4 *An implicit class on the left and a participating class on the right*

Instantiation

When I want to illustrate a class creating another class, I use a dashed line with an arrowhead to indicate that relationship. This is called the "creates" relationship. The arrow points to the class that is instantiated, as shown in Figure 1–5.

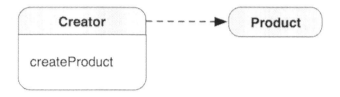

Figure 1–5. *A class instantiates another class.*

Inheritance

The OMT notation for class inheritance is a hollow triangle connecting a subclass to its parent class. Figure 1–6 shows this type of relationship with ConcreteClass being a subclass pointing its inheritance arrow to its parent class, AbstractClass. For interface inheritance (subtyping or conformance), I use a similar type of arrow to denote that kind of relationship but the arrowhead is associated with a dashed line instead. Figure 1–6 illustrates that kind of relationship also.

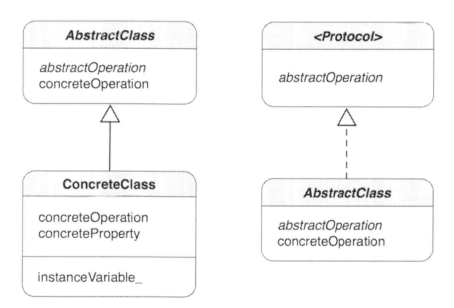

Figure 1–6. *On the left, a concrete class inherits an abstract class to show a class inheritance relationship. On the right, a class subtypes (conforms to) a protocol to show an interface inheritance relationship.*

Acquaintance

I use a solid arrow pointing from a class to another to indicate an acquaintance relationship. This relationship and the other one called aggregation are crucial to the object composition principle (I'll talk about aggregation next). Figure 1–7 shows the relationship in that ConcreteClass has a reference to an AnotherClass object, but it doesn't "own" the life of the AnotherClass object and the reference can be shared by other objects. Or simply, ConcreteClass "knows" AnotherClass.

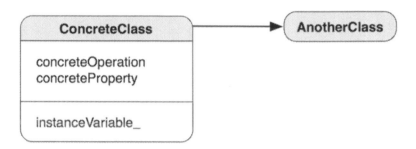

Figure 1–7. *ConcreteClass forms an acquaintance relationship with AnotherClass.*

Aggregation

Like the acquaintance relationship, I use an arrow to indicate a reference to another object except that there is a diamond at the base of the arrow. But the relationship of the reference is somewhat different. Figure 1–8 shows that ConcreteClass has an aggregation relationship with AnotherClass. ConcreteClass owns AnotherClass as part of ConcreteClass, so both ConcreteClass and AnotherClass are an aggregate. The diagram of the figure also demonstrates another attribute of a reference. I use a double-headed arrow to mean "more than one." So, in the case of ConcreteClass, it contains multiple instances of AnotherClass as instanceVariable_.

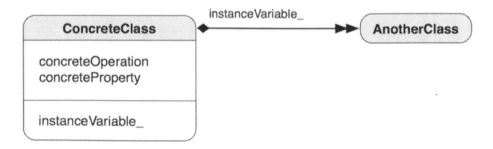

Figure 1–8. *ConcreteClass forms an aggregation relationship with multiple references to AnotherClass.*

Pseudocode

Sometimes a pattern can be better illustrated with pseudocode to sketch out the implementations of some operations. The body of a pseudocode annotation is put in a rectangular, dog-eared note box, as shown in Figure 1–9.

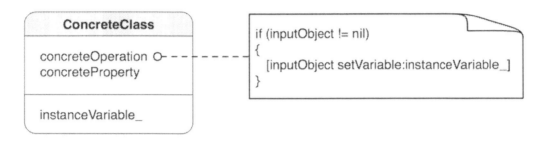

Figure 1–9. *Pseudocode annotation*

Object Diagram

An object diagram is only used for showing relationships between objects. It provides an idea of how objects can interconnect with each other in a design pattern. The names of objects are using a format of "aSomeClass" where SomeClass is the class of the object. A symbol for an object is very similar to one used for class diagrams. Each object is put in a round rectangular box with two compartments separating the object name from its object references. The background of the title bar of an object is also light blue in color. Solid arrows with a round circle base are used for pointing to the other objects being referenced. Figure 1–10 shows a sample object diagram.

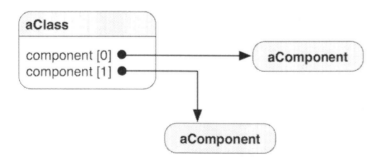

Figure 1–10. *An object diagram shows arrows with a round circle base indicating object references from an aClass object.*

How the Patterns are Organized

This edition covers 21 design patterns. They are organized into eight functional parts based on their practical themes or domains of usage: Object Creation, Interface Adaptation, Decoupling of Objects, Abstract Collection, Behavioral Extension, Algorithm Encapsulation, Performance and Object Access, and State of Object.

Summary

I've introduced the background, history, and benefits of design patterns as well as issues that would affect the architectural design of an application. I do hope that this chapter has been a good warm-up for the real flesh in the upcoming chapters.

Chapter 2

A Case Study: Designing an App

Just like the next top-paid app in the app store, we need some good ideas to start with. The good idea we are going to use for this book example is a drawing app. We call it TouchPainter. It is simple yet comprehensive enough to showcase many design patterns and best practices.

We will go through several design phases, and during each process we will come up with some requirements, use cases, and problems related to our design. Along the road, we will explore different design patterns that can solve the design problems to satisfy the requirements.

There are three main milestones in our design process:

- Conceptualizing the ideas
- Designing the look-and-feel
- Architectural design

From conceptualizing the ideas, we will collect some basic requirements and use cases about our TouchPainter app, such as somehow the user should be able to use the app, and the user's experience when using it.

Once we have a pretty good idea about what we are going to put in the app, we will move forward to have a basic look-and-feel laid out. The look-and-feel design process gives a developer a chance to explore what UI elements can be grouped together in a logical way. Not only can the process provide a developer a big picture of what looks good or bad in the first place, it can also possibly eliminate unnecessary UI elements so it simplifies and enhances the user experience. This is an iterative process, so the design should be open for changes easily. Many developers use pencils and paper to sketch what different views can be put together. Once the sketches look satisfying, developers/UI designers can start using some software to put together wireframes with more realistic-looking widgets to refine the design. If things don't look as expected, you may want to go back to the paper design or make some changes onscreen with the widgets. We are going to explore this process when we put some wireframes for the look-and-feel and requirements together in that section.

When the look-and-feel is ready, it'll be time to define some technical problem domains that can affect the architecture of the application. A problem domain can go like, "How can the user open a scribble?"

Ready? Let's go!

Conceptualizing the Ideas

Any type of software development needs some sorts of requirements, and this one is no exception. But we don't need to define every detail at the beginning. All we need is the most basic one to start with. What should be our first requirement?

- A drawing pad allows scribbling with the user's finger.

I don't think any user of our app will be satisfied with just a black and white drawing experience. It would be nice to have some options for setting different colors and stroke sizes. Then we have another requirement:

- It allows the user to change stroke colors and sizes.

But just allowing the user to scribble is not enough; we should also allow the user to save it. So we have another requirement for that:

- It allows the user to save a scribble.

It wouldn't make sense if the user couldn't open a saved scribble again and modify it. So here we go:

- It allows the user to open a saved scribble.

What if the user doesn't like his or her masterpiece, and wants to get rid of it and start over?

- It allows the user to delete the current scribble.

It would be nice to allow the user undo and redo what he or she has drawn. So here comes another requirement:

- It allows the user to undo and redo scribbling.

The list can go on and on, but for now we have some basic requirements to kick-start our design with. But before we dive into a design phase, we should make sure we have the look-and-feel of it so we can get a pretty good idea about what the app should look like. Let's summarize our first-ever requirements for our wonderful drawing app:

- A drawing pad allows scribbling with the user's finger.
- It allows the user to change stroke colors and sizes.
- It allows the user to save a scribble.
- It allows the user to open a saved scribble.

- It allows the user to delete the current scribble.

- It allows the user to undo and redo scribbling.

Designing the Look-and-Feel

Do you remember the last time you were asked or you decided to make last-minute changes on the user interface and/or user experience for your app? Moments like that aren't fun. So a better practice, at least in iOS development here, is to design the entire look-and-feel as well as user experiences that are close to the final product as early as possible. I call it Look-and-Feel–driven design. We have heard about data-driven design, event-driven design, and test-driven design. But they all deal only with technical details. However, Look-and-Feel–driven design can let us focus on the user experience at a very early stage. Not only can it save us some crunch time before it's released, but it also makes sure stakeholders and developers are on the same page down the road. Even in development, with the look-and-feel of the application and UI design ready, developers who are busy cutting their code will have some good visual clues about what exactly they are working on. It can increase productivity, as many possible hard-to-find bugs or design flaws can be found at an early stage.

Let's move on to the look-and-feel of our drawing app. How should we get started? A pen and a piece of paper or, if you prefer, graphical stencils drawn on a computer should be a good start. Here is the first look of our app in Figure 2–1.

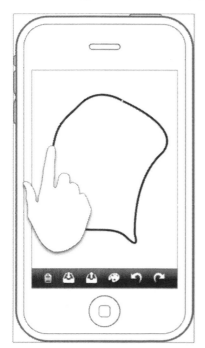

Figure 2–1. *The first wireframe as a main canvas view for our first requirement*

In our first draft of the look-and-feel, it shows that the user can use his or her finger to scribble lines (or whatever shape the user wants) on the screen. So that should fulfill our first requirement: *a drawing pad allows scribbling with the user's finger.* We feel OK about this part.

At the bottom of the view, there is a toolbar that contains six buttons—from left to right, deleting, saving, opening a saved scribble, selecting different stroke colors and sizes, and undoing/redoing what's drawn onscreen.

The wireframe just looks like a typical iPhone app that does allow the user to draw something with a finger. It also allows the user to change other settings that are related to the session. We are happy with the look for now. Let's move on to the next wireframe for our other requirements in Figure 2–2.

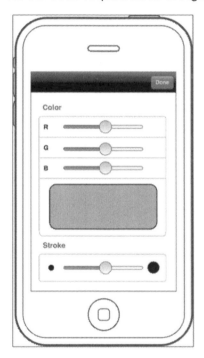

Figure 2–2. *The wireframe of a palette view that can fulfill our second requirement*

In this wireframe, the user can adjust the stroke color and size by varying various color component sliders. The grayish box in the middle of the page will show the current stroke color based on the selected RGB values. Adjusting the slider at the bottom section of the page can set the stroke size. This wireframe fulfills our second requirement: *it allows the user to change stroke colors and sizes.* Tapping the Done button will take us back to the main canvas view, as shown in Figure 2–1.

Up to this point, we are pretty confident that the wireframes we've got so far can fulfill four out of five requirements, except the fourth one, which allows the user to open a saved scribble. Our first question about that requirement is, how does the user know what scribble to open in the first place? So definitely we need some sort of browser so the user can browse through a whole bunch of them and pick the one he or she wants. We can picture it as a thumbnail view.

Our rough wireframe for a thumbnail view is shown in Figure 2–3.

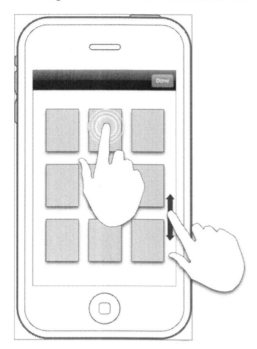

Figure 2–3. *The wireframe of a thumbnail view that can fulfill our fourth requirement*

Once the user hits the palette button on the main canvas view, it will bring up the thumbnail view as shown in Figure 2–3. The user can scroll through a list of scribble thumbnails by swiping the page upward and downward. The user can also tap any one of them to open it on the canvas view, so the user can continue to work on it. Otherwise, the user can go back to the main canvas view by hitting the Done button.

We can refine the design later if needed, but we are pretty happy with the look-and-feel of the wireframes. Let's move on to the next stop—architectural design.

Architectural Design

As we know, this book is about design patterns in Objective-C and iOS development, so I guess a lot of you can't wait to ask yourself this question: what patterns should I use for this app? Well, I believe a lot of people have a habit of finding patterns first and then spending a lot of time trying to "fit" them in a project so it looks "professional," although the patterns may not resolve the problems correctly.

Before we think about resolving solutions, we need to have problems first. In the last section, we've already come up with some basic requirements for the app from some primitive use cases. A use case describes "who" can do "what" with an app. We can elaborate some design problems out of those requirements (or use cases), so we can find some possible ways to solve them later.

We are going to lay out and examine some problem domains elaborated from the original requirements. Each of them has some refined, specific features or sub-problems related to the principle domain. We come up with four major domains and their specific features as follows :

- View Management
  - Transition from one view to another
  - Using a mediator to coordinate view transitions
- Scribble representation
  - "What" can be drawn onscreen
  - Representing marks with a composite structure
  - Drawing a scribble
- Representation of a saved scribble
  - Capturing the state of a scribble
  - Restoring the state of a scribble
- User operations
  - Browsing a list of scribble thumbnails
  - Undo/redo scribbling
  - Changing stroke colors and sizes
  - Deleting the current scribble on the screen

View Management

The Model-View-Controller pattern is discussed in Chapter 1. A model represents the data that is presented by a view. A controller stands between a view and a model to coordinate them. So each controller "owns" a view and a model. In iOS development, that kind of controller is referred to as a view controller. From the wireframes we have in the previous section, we have an idea of what the TouchPainter app should have. There are three views, and each of them should be maintained by a corresponding controller. So we have three controllers based on our initial UI design:

- `CanvasViewController`
- `PaletteViewController`
- `ThumbnailViewController`

CanvasViewController contains our main canvas view on which the user can scribble with a finger, as illustrated in Figure 2–1. PaletteViewController maintains a bunch of user control elements so the user can adjust the color and size of a stroke, as in Figure 2–2. Any new settings will be forwarded to the model of the CanvasViewController. The ThumbnailViewController showcases all previously stored scribbles as thumbnails, so the user can browse through all of them until he or she taps one to open it, as illustrated in Figure 2–3. All necessary information about that scribble will be forwarded to the CanvasViewController to display the scribble on the canvas view.

There are some interactions between different view controllers. They are tightly dependent on each other. Things can become chaotic, especially if we want to add more view controllers to the application later.

Transition from One View to Another

When the user taps the palette button on the CanvasViewController, the view will be replaced by the PaletteViewController's view. Likewise, a hit on the button that opens a thumbnail view on the CanvasViewController will bring up the view of the ThumbnailViewController. When the user taps the Done button on the navigation bar to finish his or her business, it will take the user back to the view of the CanvasViewController. Figure 2–4 illustrates their possible interactions.

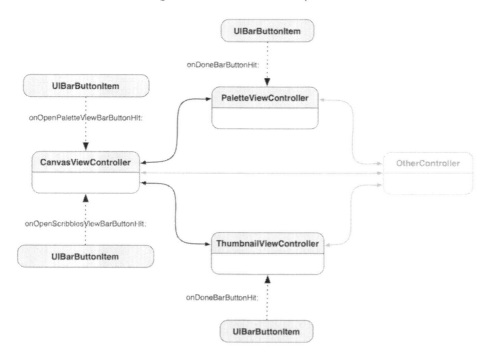

Figure 2–4. *A diagram shows dependencies among* CanvasViewController, PaletteViewController, *and* ThumbnailViewController *in a typical iOS application design.*

When you look at the diagram Figure 2–4 and you think, "There is nothing wrong with it. I have been doing it and it works all the time," then you may want to know why it may not be a good design in most applications. In a typical iOS application, view transitions like the one shown in Figure 2–4 don't look very complex, even though there are certain dependencies among those controllers. The application can't scale well if views and their controllers are dependent on each other. Also, if we modify the way the views change, code changes in each of them are almost unavoidable. In fact, the dependencies are not just among the view controllers but the buttons as well. Those buttons are indirectly related to particular view controllers. If the app grows larger and more complex, the dependencies could be out of control, and a bunch of hard-to-understand view transition logics will follow. We need a mechanism to reduce interactions between different view controllers and buttons, so it will make the whole structure less coupled but more reusable and extensible. A kind of coordinating controller just like a view controller should help, but its role is not to coordinate a view and a model; it needs to coordinate different view controllers for proper view transitions.

Using a Mediator to Coordinate View Transitions

The Mediator pattern (Chapter 11) suggests an object that encapsulates the logic of how a set of objects interacts. A mediator promotes loose coupling among different objects by keeping them from referring to each other explicitly. So their interactions can be varied in a centralized place, and their dependencies can be reduced. A structure for their new interaction patterns is illustrated in Figure 2–5.

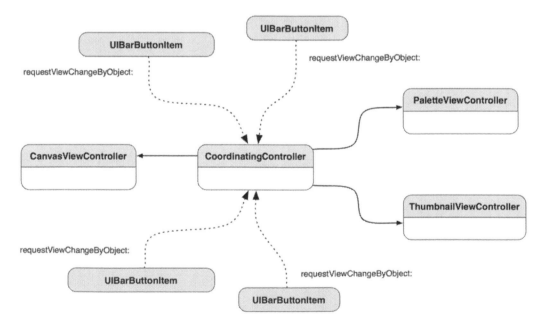

Figure 2–5. *A diagram shows fewer dependencies among the view controllers and their buttons with the introduction of* CoordinatingController *as a mediator.*

With the introduction of our new member, CoordinatingController, to our architecture, any further changes to the architecture later will be a lot easier. The CoordinatingController encapsulates logic that coordinates the traffic of view-changing requests fired off from different controllers and buttons alike. Interactions are not just limited to view transitions, but they could be information forwarding and operation invocation. Should those interactions need to be modified later, the only place that we need to go to is in CoordinatingController, not any other view controllers. With this structure, the CoordinatingController knows everyone on the interaction map. A button tap will trigger a call to CoordinatingController to request a view transition. Based on the information stored in the button, such as a tag, CoordinatingController can tell what view the button desires to open. If we want to reuse any of those view controllers, we don't need to worry about how they should be connected in the first place.

Now the CanvasViewController, PaletteViewController, ThumbnailViewController, and their buttons perform just like different musicians in an orchestra. They don't depend on each other to perform a piece but just follow what a conductor tells them about when and what to do. Can you imagine an orchestra without a conductor?

Scribble Representation

When the user touches the canvas view, touch information will be collected, such as the location of the touch. We need to have some sort of data structure to organize touches onscreen, so that all touches can be conglomerated and managed as a single entity. Especially when we need to parse the data later (e.g., draw it on the screen), the data structure needs to be highly organized and predictable.

"What" Can Be Drawn Onscreen?

Before we think of any possible data structure that can be used to hold the touch data, let's take a look at how we should define a stroke.

If the user first touches the screen and then moves his or her finger, it creates a stroke. However, if the finger doesn't move but finishes the touch at the same location where it started, that should be considered a dot. These are illustrated in Figure 2–6.

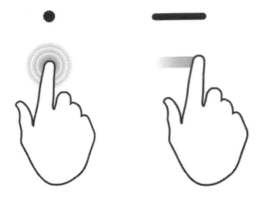

Figure 2–6. *A dot created by a single touch vs. a line by dragging it on the screen*

It's intuitive to think of a dot as just a single location, while a stroke has multiple locations along the path. A stroke is an entity by itself that contains a series of touch locations. The challenge here is how to manage both types of entities as if they were a single type. Can we think of a stroke that *has* multiple dots? If a stroke has an array to hold all the dots, then can we just use a stroke structure to represent both the dot and stroke? But then for the case of a dot, we will waste memory for having an array that is just a dot in a stroke. The best case is we can have a design pattern to let us have our cake and eat it too.

Before we examine how we can make use of a data structure to represent strokes and dots, let's think about how we can draw a point and line on the screen. The Cocoa Touch framework has a framework called Quartz 2D, which provides an API to draw 2D glyphs on a UIView, including lines and different polygons.

To draw anything on a UIView, we need to get ahold of a drawing context provided by the runtime. For instance, if we want to draw a dot, then we pass in the drawing context and the size of the dot as a CGRect that contains the width and height as well as the location information to a Quartz 2D function, CGContextFillEllipseInRect(). For drawing a line, we need to first let the context move to the first point with a function call, CGContextMoveToPoint(). After the first point is set to the context, we will add the rest of the points that are supposed to be part of a line to a series of function calls to CGContextAddLineToPoint(). When the last point is added, we will close the line by calling CGContextStrokePath(). Then the points are connected as a line and drawn on a UIView. A visual representation of the process is illustrated in Figure 2–7.

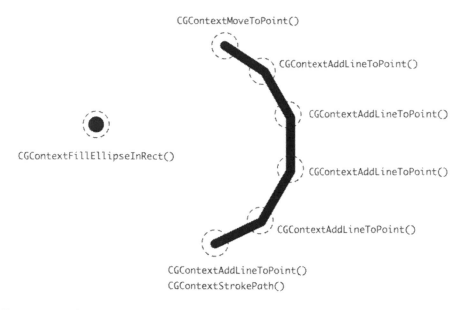

Figure 2–7. *A visual representation of drawing a dot and a stroke with Quartz 2D*

Representing Marks with a Composite Structure

We can, of course, use whatever primitive data structures we know of for storing strokes, dots, and whatnot. However, if we use, let's say, a multi-dimensional array to store everything, we need a lot of type-checking to use and parse, plus it would take a lot of debugging to make the structure robust and consistent. One object-oriented way of thinking about a kind of structure that can keep independent dots as well as strokes that have other dots (vertices) as children is a tree. A representation of a tree allows complex object relationships like our strokes and dots scenario to be organized and localized in one place. A design pattern that solves this kind of structural problem is called the Composite pattern (Chapter 13).

With the Composite pattern, we can compose our strokes and dots into a tree structure so that we can treat each of the nodes uniformly. A visualized structure of strokes, dots, and vertices is illustrated in Figure 2–8.

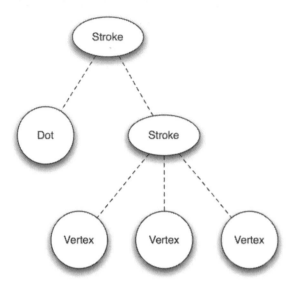

Figure 2–8. *A diagram showing a composite structure for both* Dot *and* Stroke.

A dot is a leaf node, which is fine on its own. A stroke is a composite that can contain other dots as vertices; at the same time, it can also contain other composites as strokes. They are quite different entities. If we want each of them to represent the same type, then we need to generalize them into a common interface. Therefore, no matter what concrete type each component actually is, the generic type is still the same. With that scheme, we can treat each of them uniformly when we use them.

If the component is just a single dot, then it will be rendered as a filled circle to represent a "dot" onscreen. But if it's a series of dots (vertices) with which they are supposed to be connected together as a group of entities, then they will be plotted as a connected line (stroke). That is the distinction between them.

Either a stroke or a dot is, in fact, a kind of "mark" on a medium, which is the screen in our case so we add a Mark as a parent type for Vertex, Dot, and Stroke. Their relationships are illustrated as a class diagram in Figure 2–9.

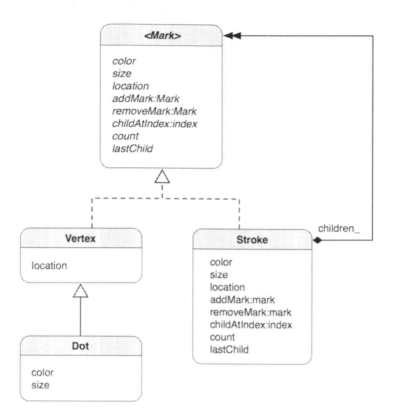

Figure 2-9. *A class diagram for the* Mark *model as a composite structure with* Dot *and* Stroke *as concrete classes*

The parent type Mark is a protocol. A protocol is an Objective-C feature that defines a contract of behavior without implementation. Concrete classes implement the interface a Mark protocol declares. Vertex, Dot, and Stroke are all concrete classes of Mark. Both Vertex and Dot need location information, but Dot also needs color and size as extra attributes, so Dot inherits Vertex as its subclass.

Mark defines attributes as well as methods for all the concrete classes. So any of them can be treated uniformly when the clients operate each of them based on the interface. There are methods for a Mark object to add other Mark objects as children and behave like a composite. Stroke implements the method for adding other Mark objects as its children. There are some other operations related to child management defined in the Mark protocol, such as removing children, returning a particular child based on an index, and returning the number of children as well as the last child in a children list.

Drawing a Scribble

Now we have a data structure set up that allows the app to manage points created by the user's touches in a logical way. The location information of touches plays a vital role when we present it onscreen. But the composite structure that we have examined in the last section doesn't have an algorithm to draw itself on the screen.

We know the only way to put any custom drawing on a `UIView` is to override its `drawRect:` instance method. That method will be called upon when an update on the view is requested. For example, we can send a message of `setNeedsDisplay` to a `UIView`, and then it will invoke the `drawRect:` method that defines any custom drawing code. We can then use a current graphics context as `CGContextRef` to draw whatever we want within the same method call. Let's look at how we can use the mechanism to draw a composite structure.

We can add a drawing operation like `drawWithContext:(CGContextRef)context` to the `Mark` protocol so every node can draw itself according to its specific purpose. We can pass a graphics context obtained in the `drawRect:` method to the `drawWithContext:` method, so a `Mark` object can draw in it. A possible implementation of the `drawWithContext:` method for `Dot` would go like the one in Listing 2–1.

Listing 2–1. *drawWithContext:* *Implementation in* Dot

```
- (void) drawWithContext:(CGContextRef)context
{
  CGFloat x = self.location.x;
  CGFloat y = self.location.y;
  CGFloat frameSize = self.size;
  CGRect frame = CGRectMake(x - frameSize / 2.0,
                            y - frameSize / 2.0,
                            frameSize,
                            frameSize);

  CGContextSetFillColorWithColor (context,[self.color CGColor]);
  CGContextFillEllipseInRect(context, frame);
}
```

With an active context, an ellipse (a dot) can be drawn in the context with location, color, and size.

As for a vertex, it provides only a particular location in a stroke. So a `Vertex` object will add a point to a line only in the context (well, in terms of Quartz 2D, we add a line to a point) with its own location (coordinates), as shown in Listing 2–2.

Listing 2–2. *drawWithContext:* *Implementation in* Vertex

```
- (void) drawWithContext:(CGContextRef)context
{
  CGFloat x = self.location.x;
  CGFloat y = self.location.y;

  CGContextAddLineToPoint(context, x, y);
}
```

For a `Stroke` object, it needs to move the context to the first point, pass the same `drawWithContext:` message and graphics context to each child, and set its stroke color. Then it wraps up the whole line drawing operation with the Quartz 2D functions `CGContextSetStrokeColorWithColor` and `CGContextStrokePath`, as shown in Listing 2–3.

Listing 2–3. *drawWithContext: Implementation in Stroke*

```
- (void) drawWithContext:(CGContextRef)context
{
    CGContextMoveToPoint(context, self.location.x, self.location.y);

    for (id <Mark> mark in children_)
    {
        [mark drawWithContext:context];
    }

    CGContextSetLineWidth(context, self.size);
    CGContextSetLineCap(context, kCGLineCapRound);
    CGContextSetStrokeColorWithColor(context,[self.color CGColor]);
    CGContextStrokePath(context);
}
```

The primary challenge when designing the Mark protocol is to come up with a minimal set of operations to provide open-ended functionality. Performing surgery on the Mark protocol and its subclasses for adding new functionality is both invasive and error-prone. Eventually, the classes get harder to understand, extend, and reuse. So the key is to focus on a sufficient set of primitives for a simple and coherent interface.

Another way to extend the behavior of a composite structure like Mark, we can use another design pattern called the Visitor pattern. The Visitor pattern (Chapter 15) allows us to define any external behavior that can be applied to a composite structure as a "visitor." Visitors "visit" each node in a complex structure to perform particular operations based on the actual type of a visited node.

Representation of a Saved Scribble

The representation of a scribble in memory is a single composite object that has a recursive structure of dots and strokes. But how can we save the representation in the file system? Representations in both places should be compatible, which means each of the representations can convert to the other without any problem.

Without using any structured and elegant mechanism to save our objects, the code could end up in complete chaos, especially if it's hard-coded in a single place. We can break down a general object-saving process into multiple steps:

1. Serializing an object structure into a structured file blob

2. Constructing a path in the file system where the blob will be saved

3. Saving the blob just like a regular file

As for loading the same blob from the file system and resurrecting it back to its original object structure, it should take similar steps to perform but in a somewhat reversed order:

1. Reconstructing the path where the blob was saved in the file system

2. Loading the blob from the file system just like a regular file

3. Deserializing it and restoring its original object structure

If we put all these steps into a giant function to handle all those chores, it will be very difficult to manage and reuse. Also, sometimes we are interested in saving not only the whole object structure but also a portion of it (e.g., only the last changes). We definitely need some sort of encapsulated operations to handle the different types of anomalies of saving the state of a scribble.

Let's not be concerned about constructing paths and such, but focus on capturing the state of a complex object in memory and turning it into an encapsulated representation, so that we can save it in the file system and restore it later.

We can use a design pattern called Memento to solve this kind of problem. Memento allows an object to save its own state however (or as complex as) it wants as an object, which is called a memento object, according to the pattern. Then some other object, such as a caretaker object, safeguards the memento object somewhere, often in the file system or memory. The caretaker object doesn't know the format of any details about the memento object. Sometime later, when it is requested, the caretaker object passes the memento object back to the original object to let it restore its state based on the saved information in the memento. Figure 2–10 illustrates their interactions in sequence.

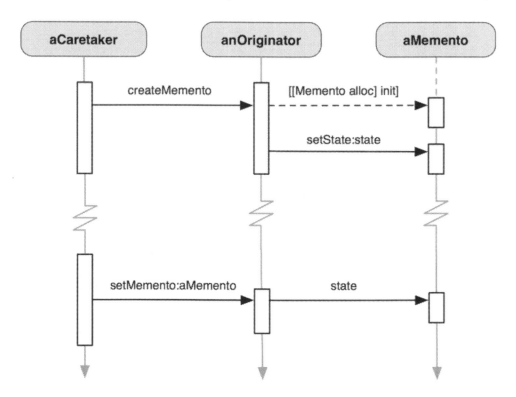

Figure 2–10. *A sequence of how* anOriginator *object is instructed by* aCaretaker *to capture its own state as* aMemento—aCaretaker *manages* aMemento *and passes it back to* anOriginator *sometime later to let* anOriginator *restore its state.*

Capturing the State of a Scribble

Based on our problem, we need to separate the original object structure from its own captured state. But before we dive into any details, we need to figure out what we need to archive and unarchive later. In Figure 2–3, we drafted a user interface that allows the user to browse through all thumbnails of previously saved scribbles. Beyond the fact that we need to save Mark objects, we also need to save the corresponding snapshot image of the canvas view during the saving process.

Also, we may decide to archive more elements, such as a canvas and some other attributes that could be applicable to a drawing. Things can evolve when we keep releasing new versions of the app later. For the sake of flexibility, we decide to create another class that manages all these bells and whistles. We call the new class Scribble. A Scribble object encapsulates an instance of Mark composite object as its internal state. Scribble acts like a model in the Model-View-Controller paradigm, as explained in Chapter 1. In this problem domain, we need a Scribble object to be part of the capturing and restoring process with its Mark composite state instead of using Mark directly. Mark is very difficult to use directly, as it provides only primitive operations on a composite structure.

Besides Scribble being the model in the system, we also need a caretaker to save the state of a Scribble object. Let's add another class to play that role and call it ScribbleManager. An actual process of saving a scribble could be very complicated and involve a lot of other objects and such, so we will discuss only saving the internal state of a Scribble object in the rest of the section.

As illustrated in Figure 2–11, CanvasViewController initiates a call to ScribbleManager to save a scribble. ScribbleManager then asks the Scribble object that was passed in to create a memento. The Scribble object in turn creates an instance of ScribbleMemento and saves its internal Mark reference to it. At this stage, ScribbleManager can either keep the returned memento object in the memory or save it in the file system. In this "saving a scribble" process, we want the ScribbleManager to save the memento object in the file systems so the ScribbleMemento object needs to encode itself into a form of data, which is an instance of NSData. The ScribbleManager doesn't know anything about the data but just stores it in the file system with a path that only ScribbleManager has knowledge about. The overall process is like passing a black box of memento objects around, in that only the originating object can wrap and unwrap it. Everything starts from a simple message call of saveScribble:scribble from CanvasViewController to ScribbleManager.

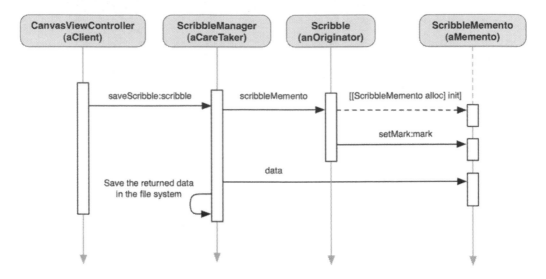

Figure 2–11. *A sequence diagram shows how the state of a* Scribble *can be saved as a* ScribbleMemento *object.*

There are at least two benefits when we use the Memento pattern as our object-archiving solution:

- The details of the internal structure of a ScribbleMemento object are not exposed to the outside world. If later we decide to change what and how a Scribble object needs to save about its state, we don't need to change other classes in the app.

- The ScribbleManager doesn't know how to access the internal representation of a ScribbleMemento object (as well as its encoded NSData object). Instead, it just passes the object along in its own internally defined operations to store it in either the memory or file system. Any changes in the way to save a memento don't affect other classes.

Restoring the State of a Scribble

OK, now we know how to save the state of a Scribble object as a memento object. Then how can we resurrect a Scribble object with the same mechanism? The loading part is pretty much like the saving process in reverse gear. A client (in this case, it may not be the original CanvasViewController, though) tells an instance of ScribbleManager what particular Scribble to load, which could be identified by an index. Then the ScribbleManager object reconstructs the path that was used for saving the old ScribbleMemento object and loads it from the file system as an instance of NSData. The ScribbleMemento class decodes the data and regenerates an instance of ScribbleMemento. The ScribbleManager passes the memento to the Scribble class. The Scribble class uses the memento to resurrect the original instance of Scribble with the

`Mark` reference stored in the memento. The resurrected `Scribble` object that was previously archived will be returned to the client. The cycle is then complete, as illustrated in Figure 2–12.

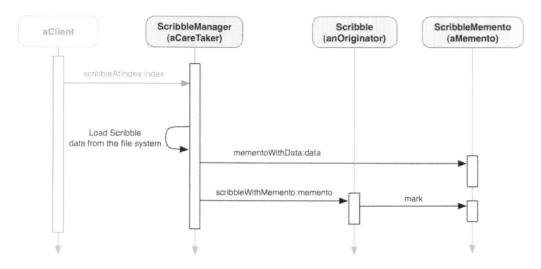

Figure 2–12. *A sequence diagram shows how a* `Scribble` *object can be restored with a* `ScribbleMemento` *object.*

At this point, we probably have a question about the loading process. How does the client know what scribble to open in the first place? So our next step is to set up a view so that the user can browse through all thumbnails of previously saved scribbles. When the user taps, one of them will open it back on the `CanvasView` through its controller, `CanvasViewController`, with a corresponding index of the thumbnail to tell `ScribbleManager` what scribble to open.

User Operations

We have discussed some foundational or architectural problem domains in the previous sections. There are some other problem domains related to the user's experience or expectations of the application—things like how to browse a list of scribble thumbnails, undoing/redoing any scribbles, changing stroke colors and sizes, and deleting the current scribble on the screen. The following subsections will go through each of the domains.

Browsing a List of Scribble Thumbnails

We know now how to save scribbles and their thumbnails. How can we browse through all of them so we can open any one of them? Let's flash back to the UI wireframe of a thumbnail view in Figure 2–3; the thumbnail view populates all saved scribbles as individual thumbnails for browsing. When there are a lot of thumbnails fighting each other to display on the view as fast as possible, it makes us think that they could bog down the main thread of the application. It could then slow down the responsiveness for any user actions.

Instead of taking the chance of letting the main thread handle tons of image loading operations one after the other, we should take the better approach of letting each individual thumbnail load its real image in a background thread. That can improve responsiveness while a bunch of thumbnails are busy doing their business independently. But here is a question, though—what would happen to some thumbnails with their own threads waiting in line for the others to finish? When should the user expect to see them? We need some kind of placeholder image for each of them to display while it's waiting for a chance to load the actual image. When the real images are completely loaded, they will show in place of the placeholder images. It makes for a consistent and predictable user experience. Figure 2–13 illustrates the thumbnail view in action, in which it is partially filled with loaded scribble images.

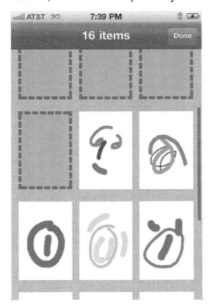

Figure 2–13. *The thumbnail view filled with placeholder images and fully loaded scribble thumbnails*

How can we design a class to do that? Well, in fact, there is a design pattern called the Proxy pattern (Chapter 22). A proxy is a placeholder or a surrogate of a real resource or object. One aspect of the Proxy pattern is to have a virtual proxy to help lazy-load heavy-weighted resources when it's requested to do so.

We need to create a thumbnail proxy class that returns a default placeholder image while it's doing some sort of lazy-loading for an actual image in the background. A typical example application on iOS is Mail. Every attachment in an e-mail is shown as a rectangular placeholder image. Until you tap it, it will load the actual attachment in the background. Instead of taking extra time to load potentially bulky email messages due to the size of the attachments, it displays a placeholder image for each attachment so the user can read the content immediately without waiting for the whole thing to be downloaded. Figure 2–14 illustrates the concept of the design.

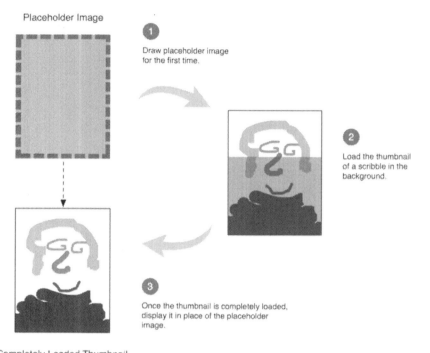

Figure 2–14. *A thumbnail proxy for a scribble is first showing a placeholder image and then loading a real thumbnail in the background. When the loading process is completed, the proxy shows the real image in place of the placeholder image.*

We can create a proxy class called `ScribbleThumbnailProxy`. Since it knows how to draw something on a view, `ScribbleThumbnailProxy` should be a subclass of `UIView`. A `ScribbleThumbnailProxy` object represents a thumbnail image. Each of the thumbnails does the following things when it is first loaded on the thumbnail view:

1. Since there is no real image available, it draws a default placeholder image in its `drawRect:rect` method.

2. It spawns a new thread that will load the real thumbnail image with a provided location in the file system.

3. When the real image is loaded, the thread will ask itself to redraw itself and the `drawRect:rect` will be invoked again.

4. At this time, a real image is available, so it draws the real image instead.

The user can browse through the whole thumbnail view to select which one to open. By tapping one of them, the real scribble represented by the thumbnail will be opened on the canvas view again, as shown in Figure 2–15.

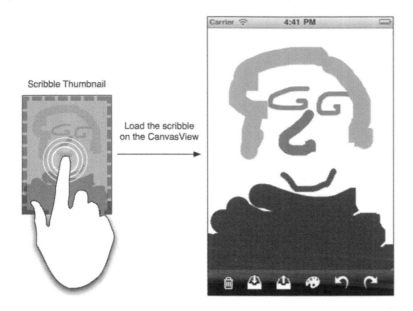

Figure 2–15. *An illustrative diagram shows that a scribble thumbnail can be used as a button to invoke loading the real scribble on the canvas view.*

Undo/Redo Scribbling

One of our requirements is to allow the user to undo or redo what is drawn on the screen so each stroke or dot can be undone, or if it's necessary, redone. We've already put two buttons for these purposes in the original wireframe in Figure 2–1. The left-turning button is for undoing and the right-turning one is for redoing, as illustrated in Figure 2–16.

Figure 2–16. *The undo and redo buttons on the canvas view's toolbar*

In order to achieve the undo capability, we need to somehow keep track of what has been drawn so we can remove it from the view, one at a time. At the same time, what has been removed from the view can also be replayed onscreen. For these reasons, it would be very difficult, if not impossible, to put any drawing mechanism in instance methods or functions. There is almost no way to reuse those functions and methods for keeping a history of drawing commands effectively. We need to put a drawing command into an object, so it can be kept in a history, as shown in Figure 2–17.

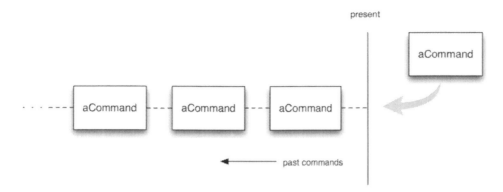

present

aCommand

aCommand ---- aCommand ---- aCommand

◀──────── past commands

Figure 2–17. *Each command object is added to a list of command history. By iterating through the list, one can undo/redo particular commands.*

Each command has methods to "execute" an operation and "undo" to reverse the action. By enumerating the list, we can ask any one of the commands to undo/redo its operations. We can use an index to keep track of the current command. Moving the index in the direction toward the commands invoked in the past, we can undo each command one at a time. Likewise, moving the index forward up to the present command allows us to redo each of them. A design pattern that can help solve this kind of design problem is called the Command pattern (Chapter 20).

There are a few framework classes available in the Cocoa Touch framework for you to implement the Command pattern—for example, an object of NSInvocation encapsulates a command in the form of a target-selector entity. An NSUndoManager instance maintains a list of NSInvocation objects in its undo and redo stacks. Once an NSInvocation object is pushed in the NSUndoManager's undo stack, it can be popped and invoke its registered undo operation. Any popped NSInvocation object from the undo stack will be pushed to a redo stack. Then the undo/redo cycles can continue. The details of implementing the Command pattern are explained in Chapter 20.

Changing Stroke Colors and Sizes

The Command pattern (Chapter 20) is not only for implementing an undo/redo infrastructure but can also be used for implementing any deferred-command mechanism. In the sense of traditional desktop applications, each menu item of the main menu encapsulates a command object. When the user activates the menu item, the embedded command will be invoked. The command is first assigned to each menu item when the application is loaded, but an invocation of the command is deferred until the menu item is activated later. One of the benefits of using the Command pattern in a menu design is that the commands used in menu items can be reused in other areas, such as keyboard shortcuts or some other user interface elements for the same commands.

Based on our requirements for our PaletteViewController, the user can change stroke sizes and colors that will be used for the next stroke/dot creation in

CanvasViewController. We need some commands to change stroke colors and sizes for that reason and purpose. PaletteViewController has three sliders to let the user adjust the color of a stroke by setting each color component—red, green, and blue—individually. Instead of creating separate commands that operate on individual color components, we rather create one single command that deals with the overall color change.

Let's say we create a SetStrokeColorCommand class just for that. According to the wireframe in Figure 2–2, there are three sliders and each of them is for adjusting one particular color component. After we hook them up with a SetStrokeColorCommand object, it will do its job in its execute operation to update the color of the next stroke and the color palette view located right below the sliders. The color palette reflects the current stroke color based on the values from the RGB sliders. The SetStrokeColorCommand object becomes a liaison for them. The SetStrokeColorCommand object notifies other observing components of any color changes made by moving the RGB sliders. For some reason, we need to have more than one component to monitor color changes; we can let SetStrokeColorCommand maintain a list of multiple observers. SetStrokeColorCommand can notify its observers when color changes occur, so they can perform appropriate operations. The observe-notify or publish-subscribe model is known as the Observer pattern (Chapter 12). Making a command object notify observers is an example of using compound design patterns for solving design problems. Likewise, we can create a similar class, SetStrokeSizeCommand, for updating the size of the next stroke created on the canvas view.

Figure 2–18 illustrates how SetStrokeColorCommand and SetStrokeSizeCommand objects interact with various UISlider controls as well as the small color palette view on the PaletteViewController and CanvasViewController.

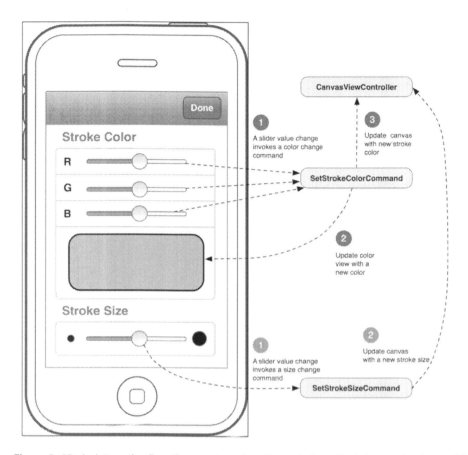

Figure 2–18. *An interactive flow diagram shows how the controls on the* PaletteViewController *interact with various command objects and their targets (i.e.,* PaletteViewController *and* CanvasViewController*).*

Should we need to change the UI elements to present a different way to change stroke colors and sizes, we can still reuse what's in SetStrokeColorCommand and SetStrokeSizeCommand objects. We can, for example, use a circular color selection wheel instead of separate RGB sliders to change the stroke color with the same SetStrokeColorCommand object.

Deleting the Current Scribble Onscreen

We can use the same idea to create another command class and use its object to delete the current scribble onscreen. A toolbar button is bound to the delete command. When the button is tapped, the command will be executed and the embedded instructions to delete the current scribble data will be carried out. When the canvas view is refreshed by the command, the original scribble will be gone, and the user can start drawing a new one again.

Reviewing the Patterns Used

It's a very hefty chapter. You should give yourself a pat on the back for making it this far! We've explored various design patterns through our design process for our TouchPainter app. Some of them were used as stand-alone solutions while others were consolidated as a group of compound patterns. A lot of times, we don't even recognize them when we use them in our projects. Here, I've compiled a list of design patterns that I have used or mentioned in the chapter so far. Let's see how many of them you can recognize; otherwise feel free to thumb back to the previous pages and rediscover them:

- Mediator
- Composite
- Visitor
- Proxy
- Memento
- Command
- Observer

Summary

We went over some warm-ups, and now you should feel pumped to move to the next chapters to explore deeper into design patterns so you can use them for your next top-selling or award-winning iOS projects.

In the rest of the book, we will explore the details of each of the 21 design patterns. We will elaborate examples that we have used in this chapter as well as new examples for some other patterns that have yet to be explored. We will also discuss how the Cocoa Touch framework has adapted some of the design patterns, so we can reuse them for free rather than reinventing the wheel.

Part II

Object Creation

Chapter 3

Prototype

Back in the old days when printing wasn't common, people used to use some sort of wooden stamps (later they became rubber stamps) to print some commonly used graphics and text on paper. Many years later, people realized that by combining different commonly used stamps, it could be one of the easiest ways to mass reproduce the same information on paper. Without using the same stamps for printing the same glyphs on paper, distribution of information and knowledge would be much more expensive and time-consuming.

In many object-oriented applications, there are objects that are just too expensive or complex to create. It would be a lot easier if we could recreate the same object with slight changes only. A typical example could be cloning a composite structure (e.g., a tree structure). It's very difficult to construct another tree composite from scratch. Rather we reuse the one that is available with slight modification to fit a particular situation in the program.

If we can turn some objects into rubber stamps and tell them to create a clone of themselves, it can save a lot of effort to build them. It's highly reusable and more maintainable than creating different individual classes with very few differences from the parent class.

The pattern that applies to the "clone" operation is called the Prototype pattern. Cloning is to manufacture a line of products with the same mold. An item that a mold is based on is a prototype. A prototype determines what a final product should be. Some attributes, like color and dimensions, could be slightly different despite the fact that the products are copied from the same mold. Despite the small differences, they are still of the same kind.

In this chapter, we are going to discuss some issues related to object cloning in general and then how to implement the Prototype pattern for cloning complex objects in Objective-C.

What Is the Prototype Pattern?

The Prototype pattern is one of the simplest design patterns. A client knows an abstract `Prototype` class. At runtime any object that is a subclass of the abstract `Prototype` can be cloned at the client's will. So the client can make multiple instances of the same type without creating them manually. A class diagram that shows their static relationships is illustrated in Figure 3–1.

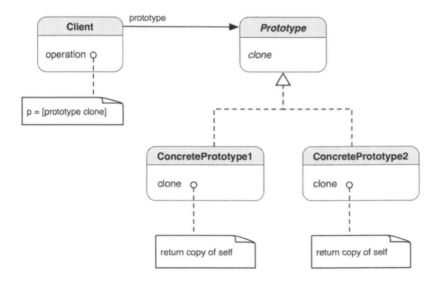

Figure 3–1. *A class diagram of the Prototype pattern*

`Prototype` declares an interface for cloning itself. `ConcretePrototype` as a subclass of the `Prototype` implements the `clone` operation for cloning itself. The client here creates a new object by asking a prototype to clone itself.

> **THE PROTOTYPE PATTERN:** Specify the kinds of objects to create using a prototypical instance, and create new objects by copying this prototype.*
>
> * The original definition appeared in *Design Patterns,* by the *"Gang of Four"* (Addison-Wesley, 1994).

When Would You Use the Prototype Pattern?

We may think about using the Prototype pattern when

- We need to create objects that should be independent of what they are and how they are created.

- Classes to be instantiated are determined at runtime.

- We don't want to have a hierarchy of factories for a corresponding hierarchy of products.

- The differences between instances of different classes are just a few combinations of state. Then it's more convenient to clone a corresponding number of prototypes rather than instantiating them manually.

- Classes are not easy to create, such as composite objects in which each component can have other components as children. It'd be easier to clone existing composite objects and modify the copies.

> **NOTE:** A common misconception about using the Prototype pattern is that a prototype object should be an archetypal object and, typically, one that is never actually used. That misconception focuses on a particular way to implement the pattern. From a functional point of view, a prototype object can be *any* object that should be better off cloning itself than getting instantiated manually. There are two particularly common situations where we would naturally think about using the pattern
>
> 1) You have many related classes whose behavior is slightly different, and they mostly differ in internal attributes, such as name, image, etc.
>
> 2) You need to use a composite (tree) object as a basis for something else, e.g., use a composite object as a building block to build another composite object.
>
> There are a lot more situations where you'd apply this pattern in the real world. Using design patterns is more art than science. Break some rules, be creative, and work smarter!

The bottom line for this pattern is to make a *true copy* of an object so we can use it as a basis (prototype) for something else related in the same context. So our next stop is to discuss issues related to copying objects.

Shallow Copying vs. Deep Copying

If an object has a pointer as a member variable that points to some resource in memory, how would you make a copy of that object? Would you just copy that pointer value and pass it to a new object as a clone? The pointer is just a placeholder that stores an address of some resource in memory. In a cloning operation, if a pointer is just copied over to a new object (a clone), the underlying resource is still actually being shared by both instances, as illustrated in Figure 3–2.

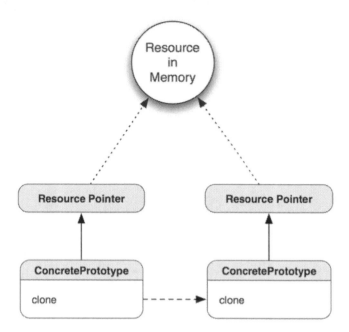

Figure 3–2. *An illustration depicts a scenario of cloning* ConcretePrototype1 *by just copying the value of the Resource Pointer 1, but the actual resource is not copied.*

In the clone operation of ConcretePrototype, it copies a pointer value of the Resource Pointer to a new clone. Even though the instance of ConcretePrototype made another instance of the same type as its clone, the pointers in both instances are still pointing to the same resource in memory. So the pointer value is cloned but not the *actual* resource. We call this shallow copying.

So what's deep copying then? Deep copying is to copy not just pointer values over but also the resources being referenced by the pointers. A deep copying version of the same clone operation is illustrated in Figure 3–3.

The clone operation is to not just simply make a copy of the Resource Pointer to a new one but also to make a true copy of the actual resource in memory. So the pointer of the clone is pointing to a copy of the same resource (content) in memory but in a different location.

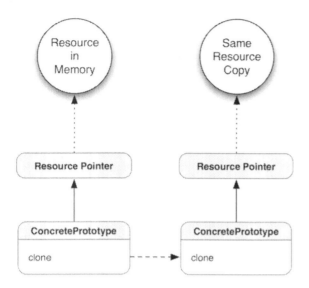

Figure 3–3. *This is a similar scenario as in Figure 3–2, but the actual resource in memory is copied during the cloning operation.*

Using Object Copying in the Cocoa Touch Framework

The Cocoa Touch framework provides a protocol for any NSObject descendent to implement deep copying. Any subclass of NSObject needs to implement the NSCopying protocol and its method, (id)copyWithZone:(NSZone *)zone. NSObject has an instance method called (id)copy. The default copy method calls [self copyWithZone:nil]. For subclasses that adopt the NSCopying protocol, that method needs to be implemented, otherwise it will raise an exception. In iOS, this method retains the newly cloned object before returning it. The invoker of this method is responsible for releasing the returned object.

Most of the time, an implementation for deep copying doesn't look very complicated. The idea is to copy any necessary member variables and resources, pass them to a new instance of the same class, and return the new instance. The trick is to make sure you do really copy the resource in memory and not just pointer values. It's more apparent when you need to deal with a composite structure like the one for the TouchPainter app in Chapter 2.

Implementing the Copy Method for the Mark Aggregate

In our original TouchPainter app, one of the most important data structures is the Mark aggregate object that contains all Dots and Strokes instances for a scribble. There are at least two situations that require the cloning of the whole structure:

■ Make a deep copy of it and archive it.

■ Reuse the same scribble as a "pattern template" (rubber stamp) to repeat the same pattern as the user draws.

For the first one, we need to make sure the copy won't be modified while it's being kept for archiving or other related processes as compared to just retaining a reference to the original aggregate (see Memento pattern in Chapter 23 for details).

If we allow the user to reuse the same scribble as a basis for other strokes, then we need to let the current scribble copy itself so it can be used as a "pattern template" feature.

We are going to adopt a composite structure (Composite pattern, Chapter 13) that contains the user's strokes in the TouchPainter app. The composite structure is illustrated in Chapter 2 as an integral part of the app. The parent of the structure called Mark is defined as an Objective-C protocol. Mark has three concrete classes (components) that define a composite object at runtime. Dot and Vertex define individual components while Stroke defines composite components that can also contain other Mark instances as children. Dot is a subclass of Vertex. The challenge here is to make an exact deep copy of the whole Mark aggregate structure without knowing how to parse the whole tree. A Stroke object can contain objects of Dots or its subclasses as well as other Stroke objects. We need to modify the original Mark and its implementing classes to have a "copy" method that will do the recursive deep copying trick. Figure 3–4 illustrates a class diagram of the Mark composite classes with a copy method.

There is not much change in the interfaces of Mark and its concrete classes except a copy method is added to each of them. There is a fictitious client that does savePattern with a currentMark as a copy called pattern for later use. How to use the copies depends on the application, but the rule of thumb is we ask objects to create themselves when it's too complicated to recreate by a client, like reconstructing an existing Mark composite object, for example.

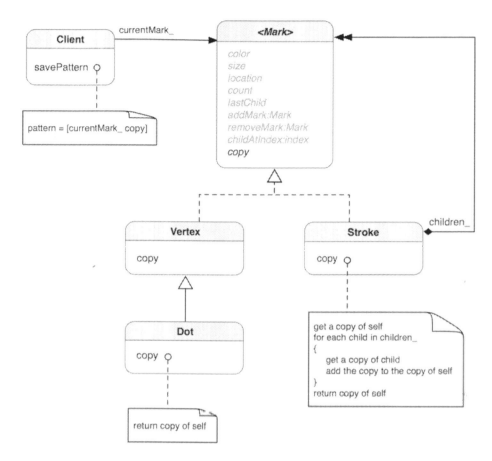

Figure 3–4. *A class diagram of the* Mark *composite classes implementing the Prototype pattern*

Now let's look at some code.

Listing 3–1 illustrates changes in the Mark protocol.

Listing 3–1. *Mark.h*

```
@protocol Mark <NSObject>

@property (nonatomic, retain) UIColor * color;
@property (nonatomic, assign) CGFloat size;
@property (nonatomic, assign) CGPoint location;
@property (nonatomic, readonly) NSUInteger count;        // number of children
@property (nonatomic, readonly) id <Mark> lastChild;

- (id) copy;

- (void) addMark:(id <Mark>) mark;
- (void) removeMark:(id <Mark>) mark;
- (id <Mark>) childMarkAtIndex:(NSUInteger) index;

@end
```

We have added a new copy method to the Mark protocol that returns an instance of an implementing class.

There are a few implementing classes that will implement the copy method. Classes of their objects that will be part of a Mark aggregate at runtime are Vertex, Strokes, as well as a subclass of Vertex, Dot. Dot objects are to represent a single dot drawn on the screen as opposed to a Stroke object. A Stroke object can be the grandparent of all types of Mark as well as just a simple parent that contains Vertex objects to form a complete stroke. Vertex doesn't do anything except maintain the location (coordinates) on the screen, so a rendering algorithm can draw them as a stroke (see Composite pattern in Chapter 13 and Visitor pattern in Chapter 15).

A visual diagram that depicts their relationships is illustrated in Figure 3–5.

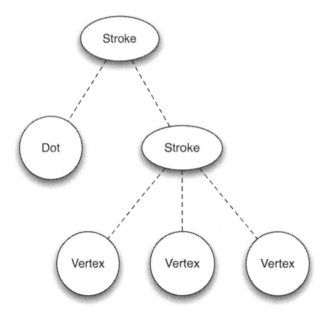

Figure 3–5. *The relationships between* Dot, Stroke, *and* Vertex *objects as a composite structure*

We will continue to implement the copy method for the implementing classes of the Mark protocol. The first one is Vertex in Listing 3–2.

Listing 3–2. *Vertex.h*

```objc
#import "Mark.h"

@interface Vertex : NSObject <Mark, NSCopying>
{
  @protected
  CGPoint location_;
}

@property (nonatomic, retain) UIColor *color;
```

```
@property (nonatomic, assign) CGFloat size;
@property (nonatomic, assign) CGPoint location;
@property (nonatomic, readonly) NSUInteger count;
@property (nonatomic, readonly) id <Mark> lastChild;

- (id) initWithLocation:(CGPoint) location;
- (void) addMark:(id <Mark>) mark;
- (void) removeMark:(id <Mark>) mark;
- (id <Mark>) childMarkAtIndex:(NSUInteger) index; // needs to be added to draft

- (id) copyWithZone:(NSZone *)zone;

@end
```

Wait a minute—why is there no copy method and copyWithZone: instead? And why is there a copy method in the Mark protocol but not the copyWithZone: method? The Mark protocol adopts the NSObject protocol while Mark's concrete classes adopt Mark and subclass NSObject class. The NSObject protocol doesn't have a copy method declared, but NSObject does. When a message of copy is invoked on a receiver of NSObject, NSObject will in turn forward the call to its subclass that adopts the NSCopying protocol. The subclass needs to implement the required copyWithZone:zone method defined in NSCopying to return a clone of itself. If the subclass doesn't implement the method, an instance of NSInvalidArgumentException will be thrown. That's why we need to let the Vertex class adopt the NSCopying protocol and implement its copyWithZone:zone method for the cloning process. However, the NSObject protocol doesn't have a method copy declared, so we also declared it in our Mark protocol to avoid compiler warnings. Vertex is a subclass of NSObject, so it implements that copyWithZone: method as in Listing 3–3.

Listing 3–3. *Vertex.m*

```
#import "Vertex.h"


@implementation Vertex
@synthesize location=location_;
@dynamic color, size;

- (id) initWithLocation:(CGPoint) aLocation
{
  if (self = [super init])
  {
    [self setLocation:aLocation];
  }

  return self;
}

// default properties do nothing
- (void) setColor:(UIColor *)color {}
- (UIColor *) color { return nil; }
- (void) setSize:(CGFloat)size {}
- (CGFloat) size { return 0.0; }

// Mark operations do nothing
```

```
- (void) addMark:(id <Mark>) mark {}
- (void) removeMark:(id <Mark>) mark {}
- (id <Mark>) childMarkAtIndex:(NSUInteger) index { return nil; }
- (id <Mark>) lastChild { return nil; }
- (NSUInteger) count { return 0; }
- (NSEnumerator *) enumerator { return nil; }

#pragma mark -
#pragma mark NSCopying method

// it needs to be implemented for memento
- (id)copyWithZone:(NSZone *)zone
{
  Vertex *vertexCopy = [[[self class] allocWithZone:zone] initWithLocation:location_];

  return vertexCopy;
}

@end
```

In the overridden copyWithZone: method, a new instance of Vertex is created with
[[self class] allocWithZone:zone] and initialized with the current location. [self
class] is used because we want its subclasses to be able to reuse this copy method as
well. If directly used [Vertex alloc], then its subclasses will just return a copy of Vertex
but not its own actual type. Vertex only implements the location property, so once the
new copy is initialized with the current location then vertexCopy is returned.

Vertex objects are used for composing strokes and don't contain any other information
such as color and size. But when there is a single point created on the screen by the
user, we need another type of data structure to contain color and size to represent that
dot. Besides color and size, location is also crucial to an individual dot. So we create a
subclass of Vertex called Dot as shown in Listing 3–4.

Listing 3–4. *Dot.h*

```
#import "Vertex.h"

@interface Dot : Vertex
{
  @private
  UIColor *color_;
  CGFloat size_;
}

@property (nonatomic, retain) UIColor *color;
@property (nonatomic, assign) CGFloat size;

- (id) copyWithZone:(NSZone *)zone;

@end
```

Similar to Vertex, it implements the copyWithZone: method to support copying in
conjunction with the protocol. Its implementation of the method is shown in Listing 3.5.

Listing 3–5. *Dot.m*

```
#import "Dot.h"


@implementation Dot
@synthesize size=size_, color=color_;


- (void) dealloc
{
  [color_ release];
  [super dealloc];
}

#pragma mark -
#pragma mark NSCopying delegate method

- (id)copyWithZone:(NSZone *)zone
{
  Dot *dotCopy = [[[self class] allocWithZone:zone] initWithLocation:location_];

  // copy the color
  [dotCopy setColor:[UIColor colorWithCGColor:[color_ CGColor]]];

  // copy the size
  [dotCopy setSize:size_];

  return dotCopy;
}


@end
```

The first initialization statement is almost the same as Vertex. Dot supports two more attributes types, so it also needs to set the color and size properties with its own color_ and size_ private variables on top of location. Both location and size can be assigned to a copy with zero concern. However, color needs some attention here. We need to make a copy of UIColor with an existing CGColor value in the color_ variable. Finally the method returns dotCopy.

Let's move on to the Stroke class as shown in Listing 3–6.

Listing 3–6. *Stroke.h*

```
#import "Mark.h"


@interface Stroke : NSObject <Mark, NSCopying>
{
  @private
  UIColor *color_;
  CGFloat size_;
  NSMutableArray *children_;
}
```

```
@property (nonatomic, retain) UIColor *color;
@property (nonatomic, assign) CGFloat size;
@property (nonatomic, assign) CGPoint location;
@property (nonatomic, readonly) NSUInteger count;
@property (nonatomic, readonly) id <Mark> lastChild;

- (void) addMark:(id <Mark>) mark;
- (void) removeMark:(id <Mark>) mark;
- (id <Mark>) childMarkAtIndex:(NSUInteger) index;
- (id) copyWithZone:(NSZone *)zone;

@end
```

Then let's see its implementation in Listing 3–7.

Listing 3–7. *Stroke.m*

```
#import "Stroke.h"


@implementation Stroke

@synthesize color=color_, size=size_;
@dynamic location;

- (id) init
{
  if (self = [super init])
  {
    children_ = [[NSMutableArray alloc] initWithCapacity:5];
  }

  return self;
}

- (void) setLocation:(CGPoint)aPoint
{
  // it doesn't set any arbitrary location
}

- (CGPoint) location
{
  // return the location of the first child
  if ([children_ count] > 0)
  {
    return [[children_ objectAtIndex:0] location];
  }

  // otherwise returns the origin
  return CGPointZero;
}

- (void) addMark:(id <Mark>) mark
{
  [children_ addObject:mark];
}

- (void) removeMark:(id <Mark>) mark
```

```objc
{
  // if mark is at this level then
  // remove it and return
  // otherwise, let every child
  // search for it
  if ([children_ containsObject:mark])
  {
    [children_ removeObject:mark];
  }
  else
  {
    [children_ makeObjectsPerformSelector:@selector(removeMark:)
                         withObject:mark];
  }
}

- (id <Mark>) childMarkAtIndex:(NSUInteger) index
{
  if (index >= [children_ count]) return nil;

  return [children_ objectAtIndex:index];
}


// a convenience method to return the last child
- (id <Mark>) lastChild
{
  return [children_ lastObject];
}


// returns number of children
- (NSUInteger) count
{
  return [children_ count];
}


- (void) dealloc
{
  [color_ release];
  [children_ release];
  [super dealloc];
}

#pragma mark -
#pragma mark NSCopying method


- (id)copyWithZone:(NSZone *)zone
{
  Stroke *strokeCopy = [[[self class] allocWithZone:zone] init];

  // copy the color
  [strokeCopy setColor:[UIColor colorWithCGColor:[color_ CGColor]]];

  // copy the size
```

```
  [strokeCopy setSize:size_];

  // copy the children
  for (id <Mark> child in children_)
  {
    id <Mark> childCopy = [child copy];
    [strokeCopy addMark:child];
    [childCopy release];
  }

  return strokeCopy;
}
```

@end

The Stroke class implements the same copyWithZone: method as the Vertex and Dot classes. But for Stroke, it needs to copy not only attributes that are defined in Mark but also its children (a for loop in the foregoing code). Each child in the children_ collection variable needs to make their own copy first, and then a Stroke object will add that cloned child to a cloned strokeCopy as a new child. When everything is cloned and set, it will return the strokeCopy as a clone of the original Stroke object.

You may have noticed that the location property that was declared in the Mark protocol is now defined as @dynamic in the @implementation scope of Stroke. A stroke doesn't keep its own location on a view but just returns the location of its first child, if there is one. There are two overridden accessor methods for the location property to handle the special case. setLocation: doesn't do anything, while location returns the screen coordinates of the stroke's first child. We use @dynamic to tell the compiler not to generate those accessor methods for us as opposed to using @synthesize because we create own version of them. The details of the composite structure are discussed in Chapter 13.

We know that a Stroke object can contain any Mark reference as a child. A particular type is the Vertex; its purpose is to provide the location information to a drawing algorithm. Vertex is a direct subclass of Dot. Dot already has that copyWithZone: method implemented, as shown in Listing 3–3.

Now we have all the copying hocus-pocus set up, so we are ready to discuss how to use the prototype pattern to implement the "Pattern Template" feature.

Using a Cloned Mark As a "Pattern Template"

Now each subclass of Mark is clonable and able to return a true copy of it. One important use of object copying is for saving the state of it. In other words, a snapshot of what the object is at the moment when it is cloned (copied). When does it need to be copied? Undo and redo. Before executing an operation, the state of an object (e.g., a document) needs to be saved in some way. Then the state is pushed to an undo stack. When an undo operation is requested, the last state of the object (document) will be restored back to the application. Most of the time, copying objects is complicated and error-prone. If clients handle the process, the client code may need to be changed every time there are some changes in a target class (e.g., document again). When we are talking about copying objects, we may be thinking only about some simple objects with just a few member variables and interfaces. However, things can go pretty wild when you need to deal with composite objects. It would be very complicated to clone a composite object just like that. A composite object could be very heavy-weighted and tricky to handle. You can picture traversing the whole structure and making new instances of each node with corresponding attributes. What's even worse is that we don't know the exact type of each node in the structure and that makes it even more complicated to create them externally. The implementation of prototype in the Mark family is not just a lifesaver for such situations but essential for the "Pattern Template" feature that we are going discuss in this section.

We want to reuse a particular stroke and make it as a "pattern template" to apply it to the CanvasView as a basis for drawing different things. The idea is to copy a particular Mark (either Stroke or Dot) and paste it on the CanvasView so the user can reuse the same pattern over and over again. A sample drawing based on that idea is shown in Figure 3–6.

Figure 3–6. *A pattern with both original and cloned strokes—a black stroke indicates the original stroke. Gray strokes are copies of the black one.*

The black stroke is the original stroke that was saved before as a pattern template. The gray ones are the clones of it. Both the black and gray strokes have the same shape. The cloned strokes may have different attributes in terms of color and location (or even transformation). The user can select whatever stroke onscreen and set it as a pattern template to be reused later. Each time the user applies the pattern, the application makes a copy out of the original and puts it on the CanvasView. Then the user can change the attributes, such as color, size, and location, of the stroke copies. A final structure that comprises the original stroke and the copies can be saved as another pattern template. The possibilities are unlimited.

We are not going too deep into this feature, but we will discuss the idea with some code snippets. I will leave this part for you to implement in the sample project as an exercise.

Let's assume that we have an instance of Mark that was selected by the user as a pattern template called selectedMark. We will make a copy of it and save it in a data structure called templateArray, as shown in the snippet here.

```
id <Mark> patternTemplate = [selectedMark copy];

// save the patternTemplate in
// a data structure so it can be
// used later
[templateArray addObject:patternTemplate];
```

At this time, we have no idea what the user exactly selected. All we know is it's an instance of Mark aggregate that could have just one Dot or multiple Strokes and each of them has multiple Vertex in it. With just a simple yet magical copy message sent to the selectedMark, we have a perfect copy of it. Now when the user wants to apply one of the previously saved pattern templates to the CanvasView, we will need to get it from the templateArray with a patternIndex provided by the user and append it to a current Mark composite. Then the new one will become part of the current one, as shown in the following snippet.

```
id <Mark> patternClone = [templateArray objectAtIndex:patternIndex];
[currentMark addMark:patternClone];
[canvasView setMark:currentMark];
[canvasView setNeedsDisplay];
```

After we set the canvasView with an updated Mark instance, we send a setNeedsDisplay message to it to draw the Mark on the screen.

Obviously we can't add a copy of a stroke on the screen just like that without at least modifying its location; otherwise it may cover the original one if it's still there. But the code snippets should be clear enough to showcase the idea of how to use the Prototype pattern that we have implemented in Mark to make this TouchPainter app more magical.

Summary

In this chapter, we have explored how to use the Prototype pattern to implement copying for the Mark composite structure in the TouchPainter app. A deep copying implementation is necessary for a Mark aggregate that contains a tree structure when we need to make a true copy of it. An example in the Memento pattern discussed in Chapter 23 keeps a copy of a complete Mark aggregate before saving it in a memento object.

The Prototype pattern is one of the simplest and easiest patterns for object creation. In the next chapter, you will see another object creation pattern that doesn't use a copy method to create the same type of object, but a method that decides what type of object to create.

Chapter 4

Factory Method

We have seen factory methods almost in every application written in an object-oriented language. The Factory Method pattern is an integral part of the Abstract Factory pattern in Chapter 5. Different concrete factories create their own products (objects) by using an overridden factory method that was defined in a parent abstract factory class.

An object factory is like real factories that manufacture tangible products; for example, a shoe manufacturer produces shoes and a cell phone manufacturer produces cell phones. Let's say you are asking the manufacturers to produce some products for you, and you send them a "produce product" message. Both the shoe and cell phone manufacturers are following the same protocol of "produce product" to start their production lines. At the end of the process, each manufacturer returns the specific type of products they produced. We call the magic word "produce" a factory method because it's a method to tell a creator (factory) to get what you want.

The creator itself may not necessarily be an abstract factory; it could be any class. The whole point is not to create objects directly but to use a factory method of a class/object to create concrete products for you that are returned as an abstract type. Why is it better? We are going to discuss it in more detail in the next sections.

What Is the Factory Method Pattern?

A factory method is also called a virtual constructor. It's applicable when a class can't anticipate the class of objects it must create and wants its subclasses to specify the objects it creates.

A static class structure of the Factory Method pattern is illustrated in Figure 4–1.

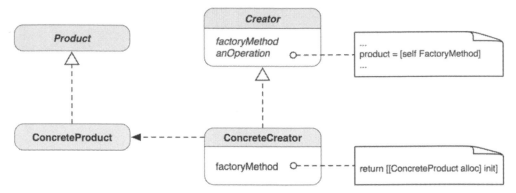

Figure 4–1. *A class diagram of the Factory Method pattern*

The abstract `Product` defines the interface of objects the factory method creates. The `ConcreteProduct` implements the `Product` interface. The `Creator` defines the factory method that returns an object of `Product`. It may also define a default implementation of the factory method that returns a default `ConcreteProduct` object. Other operations of the `Creator` may call the factory method to create a Product object. The `ConcreteCreator` is a subclass of the `Creator`. It overrides the factory method to return an instance of `ConcreteProduct`.

> **THE FACTORY METHOD PATTERN:** Define an interface for creating an object, but let subclasses decide which class to instantiate. Factory Method lets a class defer instantiation to subclasses. *
>
> * The original definition appeared in *Design Patterns,* by the "Gang of Four" (Addison-Wesley, 1994).

The original definition of the Factory Method pattern seems to focus on letting subclasses decide what objects to create. There is a variant that an abstract class uses a factory method to create objects of its private subclasses or any other classes. We will discuss this type of variant later in this chapter.

When Would You Use the Factory Method?

You'd naturally think about using the Factory Method pattern when

- The exact class of objects created can't be anticipated at compile time.

- A class wants its subclasses to decide what to create at runtime.

- A class has some helper classes as its subclasses and you want to localize the knowledge of which one to return.

The bottom line of using this pattern is that a factory method can give a class more flexibility to change what class of objects to return. A common example of using this architecture is NSNumber in the Cocoa Touch framework (or Cocoa in general). Even though you can create an instance of NSNumber with a typical alloc init two-step approach, it doesn't do much unless you use one of its predefined class factory methods to create a meaningful instance of it. For example, a message [NSNumber numberWithBool:YES] will get you an instance of NSNumber's subclass (NSCFBoolean) that contains the Boolean value provided to the class factory method. The Factory Method pattern is particularly useful for framework designers. We will discuss a little more about factory methods in the Cocoa Touch framework in a later section.

Why Is It a Safe Approach to Creating Objects?

It's considered a best practice to create objects with a factory method as opposed to creating new concrete objects directly. The Factory Method pattern allows clients to expect that objects that are created by a factory method share a common set of behavior. So any new introduction of new concrete products to the class hierarchy doesn't need any code changes to the client code, because the interface of any returned concrete object is the same as the old ones that the clients have been using.

Generating Different Canvases in TouchPainter

For the TouchPainter app that is discussed in Chapter 2, we needed to have a canvas view to let the user draw something with a finger. That canvas view incorporates with a drawing algorithm to render any scribble produced by touches (see the Composite pattern in Chapter 13 and the Visitor pattern in Chapter 15). The canvas class is called CanvasView, which is a subclass of UIView. We are going to use that class as a top-level abstract class and extend it with a couple more subclasses to provide more canvas types for the user. There will be two more canvas types to choose from, ClothCanvasView and PaperCanvasView. ClothCanvasView will have a cloth-style background, while PaperCanvasView will have a recycled paper-style background. Each of them would have some more behavior specific to the canvas. However, we will not go over the details of them; we will focus on using the pattern to generate them at runtime.

We know we are going to add two more canvas types to the original CanvasView. But we are not going to instantiate either one of them directly. Otherwise, every time we need to add more canvas types or even just to modify their initialization interfaces, we also need to modify the client code to reflect the changes. Instead we will let the client use some top-level classes for both CanvasView and CanvasViewGenerator to decouple with any specific CanvasView that will be returned.

An instance of a specific CanvasView is created by a factory method, canvasViewWithFrame:aFrame, defined in CanvasViewGenerator abstract class. There are two subclasses of CanvasViewGenerator. Each of them is responsible for creating an instance of a specific CanvasView by overriding the parent's canvasViewWithFrame: method. PaperCanvasViewGenerator will create an instance of PaperCanvasView while

ClothCanvasViewGenerator will create an instance of ClothCanvasView. Their relationships are illustrated in Figure 4–2.

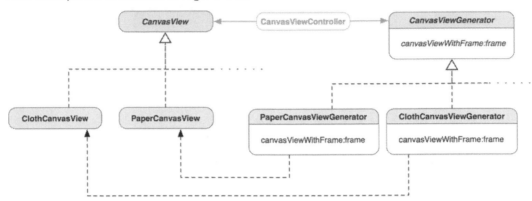

Figure 4–2. *A class diagram illustrates a parallel class hierarchy of* ClothCanvasView, PaperCanvasView, *and their corresponding generators.*

The controller of the CanvasView, CanvasViewController, will be the client of instances of both CanvasView and CanvasViewGenerator. The CanvasViewController will use an instance of CanvasViewGenerator to get a reference to a correct instance of CanvasView based on the user's preferences. Different types of CanvasViewGenerator can be used to generate different canvases for the CanvasViewController.

The top-level CanvasView defines what the default behavior of any CanvasView type should be. Subclasses of it present different textures with different images on screen and other possible specific behaviors. Code snippets for both the PaperCanvasView and ClothCanvasView are illustrated in Listing 4–1.

Listing 4–1. *PaperCanvasView.h*

```
#import <UIKit/UIKit.h>
#import "CanvasView.h"

@interface PaperCanvasView : CanvasView
{
   // some private variables
}

// some other specific behaviors
@end
```

Listing 4–1 shows the class declaration of PaperCanvasView with some omitted behavior and private member variables. Let's assume one of its particular behaviors is it has its own image view that has a paper texture image, as in Listing 4–2.

Listing 4–2. *PaperCanvasView.m*

```
#import "PaperCanvasView.h"


@implementation PaperCanvasView
```

```objc
- (id)initWithFrame:(CGRect)frame
{
  if ((self = [super initWithFrame:frame]))
  {
    // Add a paper image view on top
    // as the canvas background
    UIImage *backgroundImage = [UIImage imageNamed:@"paper"];
    UIImageView *backgroundView = [[[UIImageView alloc]
                                    initWithImage:backgroundImage]
                                    autorelease];
    [self addSubview:backgroundView];
  }

  return self;
}

// implementation for other behaviors

@end
```

@"paper" is the name of the image that has the texture of paper. It's assigned to backgroundView, which is an instance of UIImageView. Then the backgroundView is added to the main content view as a subview to show the paper image. Likewise, we have a declaration for ClothCanvasView as in Listing 4–3.

Listing 4–3. *ClothCanvasView.h*

```objc
#import <UIKit/UIKit.h>
#import "CanvasView.h"

@interface ClothCanvasView : CanvasView
{
  // some private variables
}

// some other specific behaviors

@end
```

Like PaperCanvasView, we have omitted some possible specific behaviors of ClothCanvasView here for brevity. ClothCanvasView also displays a different image texture as part of its unique behavior, as shown in Listing 4–4. Its texture image is called @"cloth" and is constructed almost the same way as in PaperCanvasView in Listing 4–2.

Listing 4–4. *ClothCanvasView.m*

```objc
#import "ClothCanvasView.h"


@implementation ClothCanvasView


- (id)initWithFrame:(CGRect)frame
{
  if ((self = [super initWithFrame:frame]))
  {
    // Add a cloth image view on top
```

```
        // as the canvas background
        UIImage *backgroundImage = [UIImage imageNamed:@"cloth"];
        UIImageView *backgroundView = [[[UIImageView alloc]
                                        initWithImage:backgroundImage]
                                       autorelease];
        [self addSubview:backgroundView];
    }

    return self;
}

// implementation for other behaviors

@end
```

Implementations for both `PaperCanvasView` and `ClothCanvasView` are very straightforward. They inherit the default behavior defined in the `CanvasView` class as well as possibly some other ones. Now we have our products defined. We also need to define a creator for each of them. The following code snippets demostrate the implementation of our abstract `CanvasViewGenerator` class in Listings 4–5 and 4–6.:

Listing 4–5. *CanvasViewGenerator.h*

```
#import "CanvasView.h"

@interface CanvasViewGenerator : NSObject
{

}

- (CanvasView *) canvasViewWithFrame:(CGRect) aFrame;

@end
```

Listing 4–6. *CanvasViewGenerator.m*

```
#import "CanvasViewGenerator.h"


@implementation CanvasViewGenerator

- (CanvasView *) canvasViewWithFrame:(CGRect) aFrame
{
    return [[[CanvasView alloc] initWithFrame:aFrame] autorelease];
}

@end
```

`CanvasViewGenerator` has one method, `canvasViewWithFrame:(CGRect) aFrame`. The default implementation of that method is just to create an instance of plain `CanvasView` and return it. Subclasses of this generator need to override this method to return the actual concrete type of `CanvasView`, such as `PaperCanvasViewGenerator`, as shown in code snippets in Listings 4–7 and 4–8.:

Listing 4–7. *PaperCanvasViewGenerator.h*

```
#import "CanvasViewGenerator.h"
#import "PaperCanvasView.h"
```

```
@interface PaperCanvasViewGenerator : CanvasViewGenerator
{

}

- (CanvasView *) canvasViewWithFrame:(CGRect) aFrame;

@end
```

Listing 4–8. *PaperCanvasViewGenerator.m*

```
#import "PaperCanvasViewGenerator.h"


@implementation PaperCanvasViewGenerator

- (CanvasView *) canvasViewWithFrame:(CGRect) aFrame
{
  return [[[PaperCanvasView alloc] initWithFrame:aFrame] autorelease];
}

@end
```

The PaperCanvasViewGenerator overrides the canvasViewWithFrame: method to return an instance of PaperCanvasView.

Another generator that returns an instance of ClothCanvasView is defined in Listings 4–9 and 4–10.

Listing 4–9. *ClothCanvasViewGenerator.h*

```
#import "CanvasViewGenerator.h"
#import "ClothCanvasView.h"

@interface ClothCanvasViewGenerator : CanvasViewGenerator
{

}

- (CanvasView *) canvasViewWithFrame:(CGRect) aFrame;

@end
```

Listing 4–10. *ClothCanvasViewGenerator.m*

```
#import "ClothCanvasViewGenerator.h"


@implementation ClothCanvasViewGenerator

- (CanvasView *) canvasViewWithFrame:(CGRect) aFrame
{
  return [[[ClothCanvasView alloc] initWithFrame:aFrame] autorelease];
}

@end
```

Using Canvases

The CanvasViewController is using the original CanvasView. In order to change that at runtime, we need to add a method in the CanvasViewController that uses a CanvasViewGenerator to get an instance of CanvasView, as shown Listing 4–11.

Listing 4–11. *CanvasViewController.h*

```
#import "CanvasView.h"
#import "CanvasViewGenerator.h"

@interface CanvasViewController : UIViewController
{
  @private
  CanvasView *canvasView;     // a canvas view
}

@property (nonatomic, retain) CanvasView *canvasView;

- (void) loadCanvasViewWithGenerator:(CanvasViewGenerator *)generator;

@end
```

CanvasViewController has a new method called loadCanvasViewWithGenerator:(CanvasViewGenerator *)generator that takes an instance of CanvasViewGenerator and asks it to return an instance of CanvasView to be used in the controller. The implementation of this method is shown in Listing 4–12.

Listing 4–12. *CanvasViewController.m*

```
#import "CanvasViewController.h"

@implementation CanvasViewController

@synthesize canvasView=canvasView_;

// Implement viewDidLoad to do additional setup after loading the view,
// typically from a nib.
- (void)viewDidLoad
{
  [super viewDidLoad];

  // Get a default canvas view
  // with the factory method of
  // the CanvasViewGenerator
  CanvasViewGenerator *defaultGenerator = [[[CanvasViewGenerator alloc] init]
                                                    autorelease];
  [self loadCanvasViewWithGenerator:defaultGenerator];

}

// Unrelated methods are removed for the sake of brevity

#pragma mark -
#pragma mark Loading a CanvasView from a CanvasViewGenerator

- (void) loadCanvasViewWithGenerator:(CanvasViewGenerator*)generator
```

```
{
  [canvasView_ removeFromSuperview];
  CGRect aFrame = CGRectMake(0, 0, 320, 436);
  CanvasView *aCanvasView = [generator canvasViewWithFrame:aFrame];
  [self setCanvasView:aCanvasView];
  [[self view] addSubview:canvasView_];
}

@end
```

First we ask `canvasView_` (a member variable that holds the current instance of `CanvasView`) to remove itself from its superview before we add a new one to it. Then we send a message of `canvasViewWithFrame:aFrame` with a specified frame size to `generator` for an instance of `CanvasView`. Based on the type of the generator, an appropriate instance of `CanvasView` is returned. We assign a newly returned `aCanvasView` to the member variable `canvasView_` through an accessor method `setCanvasView:`. Why? It's because the returned `aCanvasView` is autoreleased and we want to retain it in the controller. It's a good practice to set any member variable using an accessor method rather than sending a `retain` message manually. `retain` is defined as an attribute of the `canvasView` property, so we are good once `aCanvasView` is set with the property. Then we add the updated `canvasView_` (now it's `aCanvasView`) back to the controller's main view as a new subview.

So next time around, when the user selects a specific canvas type, the app will pass an instance of a concrete generator to the `loadCanvasViewWithGenerator:` method and the original canvas view will be replaced by a new one.

Using Factory Methods Within the Cocoa Touch Framework

Factory methods can be seen almost everywhere in the Cocoa Touch framework. We already know the common two-step object creation: `[[SomeClass alloc] init]`. Sometimes, we have noticed that there are some "convenience" methods that return an instance of the class. For example, `NSNumber` has numerous `numberWith*` methods; two of them are `numberWithBool:` and `numberWithChar:`. They are class methods, which means that you send `[NSNumber numberWithBool:bool]` and `[NSNumber numberWithChar:char]` to `NSNumber` to get an instance of `NSNumber` with different types you pass in as a parameter. The class factory methods of `NSNumber` take care of all the details about how to create an instance of a concrete subtype of `NSNumber`. In the case of `[NSNumber numberWithBool:bool]`, the method takes the `bool` value and initializes an instance of internal subclass of `NSNumber` that can reflect the provided `bool` value.

We have mentioned that there is a variant of the Factory Method pattern that is used for generating concrete subclasses by an abstract class. Those `numberWith*` methods in `NSNumber` are an example of the variant. They are not meant to be overridden by private subclasses of `NSNumber` but are convenient ways for `NSNumber` to create whatever is appropriate. In our foregoing TouchPainter app example, an instance of `CanvasViewGenerator` needs to be created by some other classes. For the case of

NSNumber, there are no other "number generators" to be generated elsewhere but methods that are bundled at the class level that serve a similar purpose. They are called class factory methods.

The Factory Method pattern we implemented in the TouchPainter example can be simplified with this type of variant by bundling a group of class factory methods to return different types of concrete CanvasView. The only problem is that the client (CanvasViewController) now needs to be aware of what exactly it wants (with exact class factory methods) but not a generator selected and returned by the user.

Summary

The Factory Method pattern is one of the most commonly used design patterns in object-oriented software design. Factory methods decouple application-specific classes from your code. The code only needs to deal with any abstract Product interface. So the same code can be reused to work with any user-defined ConcreteProduct classes in the application. We have used the Factory Method pattern to help us implement the TouchPainter app to support multiple types of CanvasView that would be selectable by the user.

In the next chapter, we are going to see another pattern for object creation that is closely related to the Factory Method pattern. Their resemblance is always confusing.

Chapter 5

Abstract Factory

A lot of people love pizzas. The structure of a typical pizza is pretty much standard, even though it could be prepared in different pizzerias. A standard pizza has toppings, cheese, sauce, and dough. There are so many styles of pizzas out there. For example, New York-style and Chicago-style have different characteristics of ingredients; thin crust dough vs. thick crust dough, marinara vs. plum tomato sauce, and Reggiano vs. mozzarella cheese. Let's say you go to a pizzeria. There are two pizza chefs who are from New York and Chicago respectively. They specialize in their own pizza styles. This time you order a New York-style pepperoni pizza. Then back in the kitchen, the chef from New York has started preparing ingredients for your order, like thin crust dough, marinara sauce, Reggiano cheese, and some pepperoni. The next time, you go to the same pizzeria and order the same pizza but in Chicago style. Then the chef from Chicago will prepare stuff, like thick crust dough, plum tomato sauce, mozzarella cheese, and pepperoni. Although you order the same type of pizza (pepperoni), the characteristics of the ingredients are somewhat different from style to style.

Even though they seem to be different pizzas, the bottom line is they have the basic characteristics a pizza should have. So a "pizza" is like a type of food from a high-level perspective—or you can just simply call it an abstract food type. That abstract pizza type has some basic requirements, such as toppings, dough, cheese, and sauce, no matter what exactly they actually are. Pizza chefs are like factories that produce the same kind of product, but the style and attributes of the actual products could be different. All pizza chefs share pretty much the same "generic" or "abstract" knowledge of baking pizzas, though the final style of the pizza depends on the actual chef who prepared it. Those chefs from New York and Chicago are "actual" or "concrete" pizza chefs. They produce their pizzas in their specific styles. We consumers don't care about "how" the delicious pizzas are made, as long as they are good pizzas.

In software design, if a client wants to create an object of a class manually, then the client needs to know the details of the class in question to create it. What'd be worse is that a group of related objects can be created differently based on different criteria at runtime, and then the client needs to know all the nitty-gritty in order to create them. We can solve that problem by using the Abstract Factory pattern.

An abstract factory provides a consistent interface for creating families of related or dependent objects without specifying their concrete classes or any details about how to create them. The client is decoupled from any of the specifics of concrete objects obtained from a factory. Possible relationships among a family of factories and their products are illustrated in Figure 5–1.

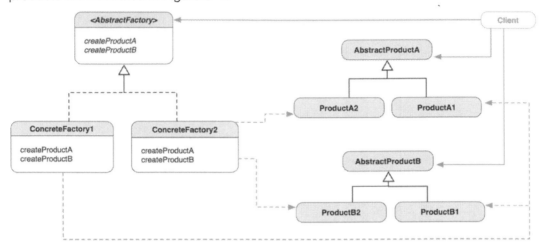

Figure 5–1. *A class diagram shows the relationships between a family of factories and their related products.*

As shown in Figure 5–1, the Client knows only AbstractFactory and AbstractProducts. The details of the structures and any actual operations are handled as a black box in each of the factory classes. Even the products have no idea who is going to be responsible for creating them. Only the concrete factories know how and what to create for the client. An interesting thing about this pattern is that a lot of times it's implemented with the Factory Method pattern (Chapter 5). A factory method defers the actual creation process to a subclass that overrides it. So in the diagram, the createProductA and createProductB| methods are factory methods. The original abstract methods don't create anything. This type of abstraction is so versatile and extensively used almost anywhere an abstract creation process is required. The Abstract Factory pattern is commonly used with other design patterns, such as the Prototype pattern (Chapter 3), the Singleton pattern (Chapter 7), and the Flyweight pattern (Chapter 21).

In this chapter, we are going to extend our TouchPainter app from Chapter 2 with the Abstract Factory pattern. Also we will discuss the pattern you will find commonly in the Cocoa Touch framework.

ABSTRACT FACTORY: Provides an interface for creating families of related or dependent objects without specifying their concrete classes.*

* The original definition appeared in *Design Patterns*, by the "Gang of Four" (Addison-Wesley, 1994).

ABSTRACT FACTORY VS. FACTORY METHOD

The Abstract Factory and Factory Method patterns are very similar in many ways. It's very confusing to many people when to use which one of them. Both of them can be used for the same purposes of creating objects without letting clients know what exact concrete objects are being returned. The following table is a side-by-side comparison between the Abstract Factory and the Factory Method patterns.

Abstract Factory	Factory Method
Abstract product creation through object composition	Abstract product creation through class inheritance
Creates families of products	Creates one type of product
The parent interface needs to be changed for supporting new products.	Subclass the Creator and override the factory method to create new products.

Applying the Abstract Factory to the TouchPainter App

Let's picture a scenario: the companies you are partnering with would like to have the same TouchPainter app that we did in Chapter 2 under their brand names and logos. In this section, we are going to white-label and brand the app for two companies: Sierra Corporation and Acme Corporation. Their brands are Sierra and Acme.

Apparently, we didn't keep any branding in mind when we first designed the app. Now the best place to brand it is a main view that has some design specific to a particular brand. Other UI elements may also be involved in the branding process, such as a main button that takes the user to the main app as well as a toolbar on the main canvas. It seems there are quite a few variations we need to put into the architecture.

THE GOLDEN RULE OF SOFTWARE DESIGN: Variation needs abstraction.

If you have multiple classes sharing common behavior but varying in actual implementations, then you may need to have some sort of abstraction type inherited as their parent. The abstraction type defines common behavior that all related concrete classes will share. For example, we know how a common pizza looks and what to expect when we order one. We say, "Let's go out for pizzas!"; "pizza" is an abstract type that defines common characteristics that a pizza should have. But we can get a slightly different style of the same, let's say, pepperoni pizza from different stores. Because there are so many different types of pizzas out there, we simply call them "pizzas" to refer to that particular type of food.

Back to our branding design, we have several variations in products and branding, so they need some sort of abstraction for all of them. We need two branding factories, and each one of them will produce three different UI elements by factory methods. There are customized UIView, UIButton, and UIToolbar elements for each brand. Their relationships are illustrated in a class diagram in Figure 5–2.

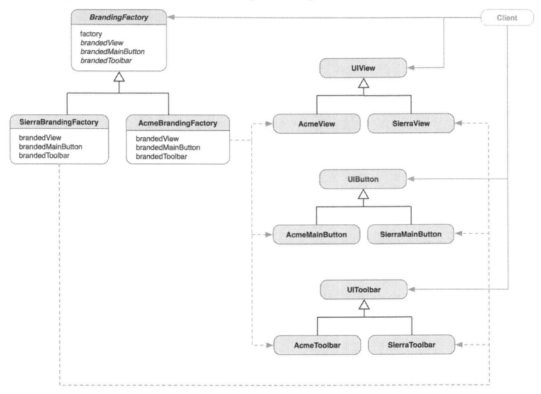

Figure 5–2. *A class diagram of the TouchPainter app that supports multiple UI elements in different brands with the Abstract Factory pattern*

The class structure in Figure 5–2 is similar to the one in Figure 5–1. Each of the products has its own product hierarchy and is supported by a factory method (the Factory Method pattern, Chapter 4) in each concrete factory. Products are "manufactured" by two different branding factories, the SierraBrandingFactory and AcmeBrandingFactory. Each of them overrides the brandedView, brandedMainButton, and brandedToolbar factory methods declared in the abstract BrandingFactory class and returns concrete products based on the brand that the factory is designed for.

The superclass's class method factory is a factory method that returns a correct version of concrete BrandingFactory. Its subclasses are not supposed to override that method (even though subclasses are able to do that). The factory method returns an instance of a concrete branding factory based on the current build configuration. The default implementation of those factory methods (brandedView, brandedMainButton, and brandedToolbar) in the BrandingFactory returns instances of abstract products, UIView,

UIButton, and UIToolbar, without any specifics to any branding. All the specifics required for each branding will be produced by an actual, concrete branding factory in its overridden factory methods.

In this setup, a client needs to know only four entities: BrandingFactory, UIView, UIButton, and UIToolbar. So in the future, if we need to expand the branding effort in other areas of the app, we can do so by adding new products and branding factories without affecting the client code.

Listing 5–1 illustrates how we can implement our branding factories and the corresponding products.

Listing 5–1. *BrandingFactory.h*

```
@interface BrandingFactory : NSObject
{

}

+ (BrandingFactory *) factory;

- (UIView *) brandedView;
- (UIButton *) brandedMainButton;
- (UIToolbar *) brandedToolbar;

@end
```

Our no-frills, abstract BrandingFactory has a class method, + (BrandingFactory*) factory, which returns an instance of a concrete BrandingFactory subclass. It also defines three factory methods that produce instances of the actual products; brandedView returns an instance of UIView, brandedMainButton returns an instance of UIButton, and brandedToolbar returns an instance of UIToolbar. A concrete BrandingFactory will return actual products. We will get to that a little bit later. Let's take a look at the implementation of BrandingFactory in Listing 5–2.

Listing 5–2. *BrandingFactory.m*

```
#import "BrandingFactory.h"
#import "AcmeBrandingFactory.h"
#import "SierraBrandingFactory.h"


@implementation BrandingFactory

+ (BrandingFactory *) factory
{
#if defined (USE_ACME)
  return [[[AcmeBrandingFactory alloc] init] autorelease];
#elif defined (USE_SIERRA)
  return [[[SierraBrandingFactory alloc] init] autorelease];
#else
  return nil;
#endif
}

- (UIView *) brandedView
```

```
{
  return nil;
}

- (UIButton *) brandedMainButton
{
  return nil;
}

- (UIToolbar *) brandedToolbar
{
  return nil;
}

@end
```

In the factory class method shown in Listing 5–2, we use pre-processor definitions to tell the compiler which concrete factory we want the method to return. If there is a macro definition to USE_ACME brand, then a statement, return [[[AcmeBrandingFactory alloc] init] autorelease], will be used at runtime. If USE_SIERRA is defined in the macros, then a statement of return [[[SierraBrandingFactory alloc] init] autorelease] will be used instead. Otherwise, the method will just return nil.

The original implementation for those factory methods returns nil by default. We are going to see how we can implement actual product creation by overriding those methods in concrete branding factories. The first one we are going to work on is a BrandingFactory for the Acme brand, as shown in Listing 5–3.

Listing 5–3. *AcmeBrandingFactory.h*

```
#import "BrandingFactory.h"


@interface AcmeBrandingFactory : BrandingFactory
{

}

- (UIView *) brandedView;
- (UIButton *) brandedMainButton;
- (UIToolbar *) brandedToolbar;

@end
```

The AcmeBrandingFactory inherits the base class, BrandingFactory, and overrides its factory methods to produce correct UI elements for the brand. The original factory class method is not overridden, as it's meant to be used by the parent class to create an instance of concrete BrandingFactory. We cannot, though, prevent the class method getting overridden by any subclass. Let's see how we can implement AcmeBrandingFactory in Listing 5–4.

Listing 5–4. *AcmeBrandingFactory.m*

```
#import "AcmeBrandingFactory.h"
#import "AcmeView.h"
#import "AcmeMainButton.h"
```

```
#import "AcmeToolbar.h"


@implementation AcmeBrandingFactory

- (UIView *) brandedView
{
  // returns a custom view for Acme
  return [[[AcmeView alloc] init] autorelease];
}

- (UIButton *) brandedMainButton
{
  // returns a custom main button for Acme
  return [[[AcmeMainButton alloc] init] autorelease];
}

- (UIToolbar *) brandedToolbar
{
  // returns a custom toolbar for Acme
  return [[[AcmeToolbar alloc] init] autorelease];
}

@end
```

Each implementation of a factory method returns an instance of Acme* product that reflects the actual brand. Listing 5–5 shows the implementation of another brand, Sierra.

Listing 5–5. *SierraBrandingFactory.h*

```
#import "BrandingFactory.h"


@interface SierraBrandingFactory : BrandingFactory
{

}

- (UIView *) brandedView;
- (UIButton *) brandedMainButton;
- (UIToolbar  *) brandedToolbar;

@end
```

Its implementation is shown in Listing 5–6.

Listing 5–6. *SierraBrandingFactory.m*

```
#import "SierraBrandingFactory.h"
#import "SierraView.h"
#import "SierraMainButton.h"
#import "SierraToolbar.h"

@implementation SierraBrandingFactory

- (UIView *) brandedView
{
  // returns a custom view for Sierra
```

```
    return [[[SierraView alloc] init] autorelease];
}

- (UIButton *) brandedMainButton
{
    // returns a custom main button for Sierra
    return [[[SierraMainButton alloc] init] autorelease];
}

- (UIToolbar *) brandedToolbar
{
    // returns a custom toolbar for Sierra
    return [[[SierraToolbar alloc] init] autorelease];
}

@end
```

SierraBrandingFactory has almost the same implementation as the
AcmeBrandingFactory except the names of the products that each of its factory methods
returns are different. The returned UI elements are specific to the Sierra brand only. We
can subclass the BrandingFactory to create a new brand and override new and existing
factory methods to create any brand the same way as we do with Acme and Sierra.

> **NOTE:** When an existing abstract factory needs to support new products, you need to add new
> corresponding factory methods to the parent class. That means all of its subclasses also need to
> be modified to support new factory methods for the new products.

Once a factory has returned some products, a client can use them like in Listing 5–7, in
the loadView method of a view controller.

Listing 5–7. *loadView Method of a View Controller*

```
// Implement loadView to create a view hierarchy programmatically, without using a nib.
- (void)loadView
{
    // construct the view from
    // branded UI elements obtained
    // from a BrandingFactory
    BrandingFactory * factory = [BrandingFactory factory];

    //...
    UIView *view = [factory brandedView];
    //... put the view on a proper location in view

    //...
    UIButton *button = [factory brandedMainButton];
    //... put the button on a proper location in view

    //...
    UIToolbar *toolbar = [factory brandedToolbar];
    //... put the toolbar on a proper location in view
}
```

In the `loadView` method of a view controller, the controller can construct its view programmatically. In Listing 5–7, we ask the `BrandingFactory` to return an instance of an appropriate concrete `BrandingFactory` based on the current build configuration with its `factory` class method. Once we get a reference to an actual `BrandingFactory`, then we can call its factory methods to return UI elements so that we can construct any branded view elements programmatically.

A nice thing about using the class factory method to create an instance of concrete `BrandingFactory` here is that we don't need to design any complicated mechanism to determine what factory we should use at runtime. It's completely determined at compile time with some simple pre-processor definitions, and no other classes are involved in the process. Otherwise, it could be involved in more complicated changes in the app. The `BrandingFactory` is implemented as a form of class cluster in which a group of related subclasses are grouped together and created by a superclass. This kind of factory construction process is commonly found in the Foundation class library of the Cocoa Touch framework, which we are going to discuss in the next section.

Using the Abstract Factory Within the Cocoa Touch Framework

The Abstract Factory pattern is commonly seen in the Cocoa Touch framework. There are a lot of Foundation classes that have adopted the pattern. A particularly common one we use on a daily basis is `NSNumber`. The way in which we create an instance of `NSNumber` is where the picture of the Abstract Factory pattern is fitting right in.

There are two common ways to create Cocoa Touch objects: invoke the `alloc` then `init` methods (a two-step creation process) or a + className... method through a class. In the Foundation framework of the Cocoa Touch, the `NSNumber` class has numerous class methods to create different types of `NSNumber` objects, such as the following:

```
NSNumber * boolNumber = [NSNumber numberWithBool:YES];
NSNumber * charNumber = [NSNumber numberWithChar:'a'];
NSNumber * intNumber = [NSNumber numberWithInt:1];
NSNumber * floatNumber = [NSNumber numberWithFloat:1.0];
NSNumber * doubleNumber = [NSNumber numberWithDouble:1.0];
```

Each object returned belongs to a different private subclass that represents the original input value. Those class methods that create actual instances of `NSNumber` are similar to the `factory` method in the `BrandingFactory` described in the previous example. You can `NSLog` their class description as shown in the following:

```
NSLog(@"%@", [[boolNumber class] description]);
NSLog(@"%@", [[charNumber class] description]);
NSLog(@"%@", [[intNumber class] description]);
NSLog(@"%@", [[floatNumber class] description]);
NSLog(@"%@", [[doubleNumber class] description]);
```

You will see the following values in the Debugger Console output:

```
NSCFBoolean
NSCFNumber
```

```
NSCFNumber
NSCFNumber
NSCFNumber
```

Most of the actual classes are of `NSCFNumber` type, except the actual type for the `boolNumber` is `NSCFBoolean`. Although those + className class factory methods return instances of concrete subclasses of `NSNumber`, the returned instances do support the public interface of `NSNumber`.

Even though they are of different concrete subclasses of `NSNumber`, the behavior is defined by the abstract superclass `NSNumber`, and it is public. If you run the following code snippets, then you will understand what I mean.

```
NSLog(@"%d", [boolNumber intValue]);
NSLog(@"%@", [charNumber boolValue] ? @"YES" : @"NO");
```

You will see their output values in the Debugger Console as follows.

```
1
YES
```

`boolNumber` is maintaining a `BOOL` value `YES` internally, but it still implements the public `intValue` method to return a proper integer value that reflects its internal `BOOL` value. Same thing for `charNumber`—its overridden `boolValue` method returns an appropriate `BOOL` value to reflect its internal character value "a".

The class methods that take a parameter of a different type and return an instance of `NSNumber` are class factory methods (the Factory Method pattern, Chapter 4). The class factory methods in `NSNumber` produce different "number factories." `numberWithBool:` creates an instance of `NSCFBoolean` factory, while `numberWithInt:` creates an instance of `NSCFNumber`. Class factory methods in `NSNumber` define default behavior that determines what private, concrete subclasses (i.e., either `NSCFBoolean` or `NSCFNumber`) to instantiate. This version of factory method is a variant of the traditionally known Factory Method pattern, though it serves the purpose of returning abstract products, in this case, concrete `NSNumber` subclasses as factories. `NSNumber` is an example of Abstract Factory implementation. This flavor of Abstract Factory in the Foundation framework is referred to by the term "Class Clusters."

Class Clusters are a design pattern that is commonly found in the Foundation framework. They are based on the idea of the Abstract Factory pattern. They group a number of related, private, concrete factory subclasses under a public, abstract superclass. For example, "Number" contains a whole set of different numeric types, such as character, integer, floating-point number, and double. Those numeric types are a "subset" of "Number." So `NSNumber` naturally becomes a super-type of those number subtypes. `NSNumber` has a set of public APIs that defines common behavior shared by different types of numbers. Clients don't need to know the exact concrete type of an instance of `NSNumber` in order to use it.

Class Clusters are a form of Abstract Factory. As we can see, for example, `NSNumber` itself is a high-level abstract factory, while `NSCFBoolean` and `NSCFNumber` are concrete factory subclasses. The subclasses are concrete factories because they override public factory methods declared by `NSNumber` to produce products. For example, `intValue` and boolValue return values based on the internal value of an actual NSNumber object even though the data type of the value could be different. Actual values returned from those factory methods are "products" as described in the original definition of the Abstract Factory pattern.

There is a distinction between factory methods for creating abstract products and factory methods for creating abstract factories. Obviously, factory methods like intValue and boolValue should be overridden in concrete factories (NSCFNumber and NSCFBoolean) to return actual values (products). Other factory methods like numberWithBool: and numberWithInt: are not for returning products but for returning actual factories that return products. They are not intended to be overridden in concrete factory subclasses.

If you want to brew your own NSNumber, you can subclass it and override those defined class factory methods, like numberWithBool: and numberWithChar:, to return your own concrete subclasses instead of the built-in NSCFNumber and NSCFBoolean (in fact, Apple wouldn't expect us to use their private classes at all). Of course, your new NSNumber subclasses also need to implement factory methods, like intValue, boolValue, etc.

You might have already realized that the BrandingFactory is implemented as a form of class cluster. Clients don't need to know exactly what subclasses to use, but it's determined by the BrandingFactory's class factory method. The details of concrete branding subclasses are hidden from the view of clients, yet the subclasses implement the factory methods that return custom views, buttons, and toolbars declared in the public interface of BrandingFactory.

Other Foundation classes that were implemented as class clusters are NSData, NSArray, NSDictionary, and NSString.

Abstract Factory vs. Factory REDUX

What's the difference again? The first one is just what we have discussed so far, an abstract factory type shared by its multiple concrete factory types. If the word "abstract" is dropped, then it is usually referring to a "concrete" factory. At the same time, it doesn't mean a factory method (Chapter 4) as well.

So when you hear people say, "We need a factory here," it doesn't necessarily mean an abstract factory. It could just be a concrete factory that returns *abstract products* (see Flyweight pattern, Chapter 21). In the preceding example, NSNumber is an abstract factory, while NSCFBoolean and NSCFNumber are factories (concrete).

As it happens, sometimes you start off putting a concrete factory in a design, and then later you refactor it as an abstract factory with multiple concrete factories put into play.

Summary

The Abstract Factory pattern is one of the most commonly used design patterns. It is very fundamental, in that it can cover many types of object creation. A good pattern for a family of related classes should be hidden as a type of abstraction to the client. An abstract factory can provide this type of abstraction seamlessly without exposing any unnecessary details of the creation process or the exact type of object being created.

In the next chapter, we are going to look at another approach to creating abstract objects in a "Builder" way.

Chapter 6

Builder

For those people who prefer building their own houses, they would outsource the project to a contractor. A single contractor doesn't build a whole house for you; he breaks it up into several parts and subcontracts to actual builders who know how to put things together with actual components and parts. A house is composed of parts in different styles, colors, and dimensions. The client tells the contractor what he or she wants in the house. Then the contractor coordinates with house builders about *what* needs to be done. And they build it based on *how* it should be built. Building a house is a complex process. It's very difficult if not impossible to build it with only one pair of hands. The process is a lot easier and more manageable if a contractor (director) coordinates with builders who know how to build it.

Sometimes there are many different ways to build certain objects. The logic of building them can go very crazy if the logic is contained in a single method of a class that builds them (for example, a whole forest of nested if-else or switch-case statements for different building requirements). If we can break the building process down into client-director-builder relationships, then the process will be more manageable and reusable. The design pattern for these kinds of relationships is called Builder.

In this chapter, we are going to discuss the concepts of the Builder pattern. Later in other sections, we'll also discuss how to use the pattern to create different characters with complex traits in a RPG game.

What Is the Builder Pattern?

Besides a client and the product that it expects, the Builder pattern contains two key roles: Director and Builder. A Builder knows exactly *how* to build the product with some missing information that is specific to particular products (the *what*). The Director knows *what* the Builder should make by providing it some missing information as parameters in order to build specific products. The *what* and *how* are a little confusing. Even though the Director knows what the Builder should make, it doesn't mean that the Director knows exactly what the concrete Builder is. Their static relationships are illustrated in Figure 6–1 as a class diagram.

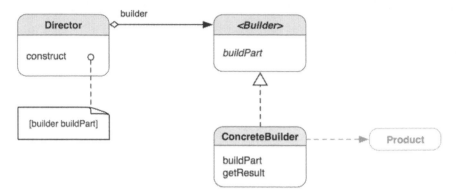

Figure 6–1. *A class diagram of the Builder pattern*

Builder is an abstract interface that declares a buildPart method, which is implemented by ConcreteBuilder to build actual Product. ConcreteBuilder has a getResult method that returns a completely built Product to a client. Director defines a construct method that tells an instance of Builder to buildPart. Director and Builder form an aggregation relationship. It means that Builder is an integral part that incorporates with Director to make the whole pattern work, but at the same time, the Director is not responsible for the lifetime of the Builder. This whole-part relationship can be made clearer with the sequence diagram in Figure 6–2.

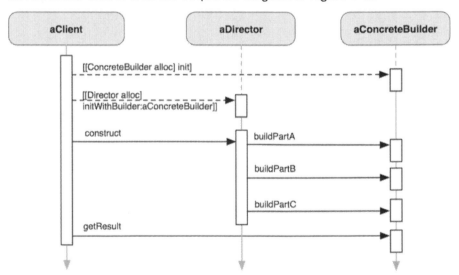

Figure 6–2. *A sequence diagram of the interactions among* aClient, aDirector, *and* aConcreteBuilder *at runtime*

aClient creates an instance of ConcreteBuilder (aConcreteBuilder) as well as an instance of Director (aDirector) with aConcreteBuilder as an initialization parameter so they can work together later on. When aClient sends a construct message to aDirector, the method sends messages to aConcreteBuilder about what to build (e.g., buildPartA, buildPartB, and buildPartC). After the construct method of aDirector returns, aClient sends a getResult to aConcreteBuilder directly to retrieve the completely built product it expected. So the "what" that aDirector knows about is what parts any Builder should be able to build.

> **THE BUILDER PATTERN:** Separates the construction of a complex object from its representation so that the same construction process can create different representations.*
>
> * The original definition appeared in *Design Patterns*, by the "Gang of Four" (Addison-Wesley, 1994).

When Would You Use the Builder Pattern?

You'd naturally think about using this pattern when

- You need to create a complex object that involves different parts. The algorithm for creating it should be independent of how the parts are assembled. A common example is building a composite object.

- You need a construction process that constructs an object in different ways (e.g., different combinations of parts or representations).

BUILDER VS. ABSTRACT FACTORY

We discussed Abstract Factory in the last chapter. You might have realized that both the Abstract Factory and Builder patterns are similar in many ways in terms of being used for abstract object creation. However, they are very different. Builder focuses on constructing a complex object step-by-step, when a lot of times the same type of object can be constructed in different ways. On the other hand, Abstract Factory's emphasis is on creating suites of products that can be either simple or complex. A builder returns a product as a final step of a multiple-step construction process, but the product gets returned immediately from an abstract factory. The following table summarizes the main differences between the Builder and Abstract Factory patterns.

Builder	Abstract Factory
Constructs complex objects	Constructs either simple or complex objects
Constructs an object in multiple steps	Constructs an object in one step
Constructs an object in many ways	Constructs an object in one way
Returns a product object as a final step of a construction process	Returns a product object immediately
Focuses on one particular product	Emphasizes a suite of products

In Figure 6–2, aClient needs to know both aDirector and aBuilder to get the product it wanted from aBuilder. You may wonder whether aBuilder can be separated from aClient's knowledge if we let aDirector return the product from its construct method or somehow the getResult method is implemented in aDirector. In that case, aDirector becomes a factory and its construct method becomes a factory method that returns an abstract product. Also, aDirector will be fixed with what products it supports, which hinders the reusability of the pattern. The whole idea is to separate "what" from "how," so aDirector can apply the same "what" (specifications) to a *different* aBuilder that knows "how" to build its own *specific* product with the provided specifications and vice versa.

In the following sections, we are going to use an example of building a chasing game that has different types of characters to illustrate how to use the Builder pattern to solve related design problems. The construction process for a game that involves different types of objects, assets, or characters can be quite complex. We can separate the algorithm that knows how to build a character from what characters to build with the Builder pattern.

Building Characters in a Chasing Game

We are going to use an imaginary chasing game as an example to show how to implement the Builder pattern. Suppose there are two types of characters, enemy and player. The enemy will be chasing after the player. You will decide where the player character should go. There might be obstacles along the path. Each of them shares some fundamental traits, such as Strength, Stamina, Intelligence, Agility, and Aggressiveness. Each of them can affect the character's ability of Protection and Power. A Protection factor reflects how much a character can protect himself from an attack, while a Power factor indicates how much he is capable of attacking his opponents. Traits are either proportionally or inversely proportionally related to both the Protection and Power factors. A matrix that shows their relationships is illustrated in Table 6–1.

Table 6–1. *Character Traits Matrix.*

	Protection	Power
Strength	↑	↑
Stamina	↑	↑
Intelligence	↑	↓
Agility	↑	↓
Aggressiveness	↓	↑

↑ denotes directly proportional, whereas ↓ denotes inversely proportional between two different character traits.

Strength and Stamina are directly proportional to Protection and Power. A character that has higher Strength and Stamina factors has a better chance of protecting himself and fighting back. Intelligence and Agility are directly proportional to the Protection factor but inversely proportional to Power. Based on our design, if a character is smarter, then he has more ability only to protect himself, not to fight back. Aggressiveness is the reverse of both Intelligence and Agility. If a character is aggressive, then he will have a higher chance of attacking but not of protecting himself during an attack. Of course, the design for the traits of characters is purely fictitious. You can have a totally different design of your own. So we are going to stick to the relationships shown in the matrix for now and use the Builder pattern to build characters for us with the different combinations for character traits.

Food For Thought

How are you going to design a class that creates a character with a combination of traits based on the matrix shown in Table 6–1 without using the Builder pattern?

We will define a class called `ChasingGame` that has two methods to create two types of characters, player and enemy. A `CharacterBuilder` builds characters based on the relationships of different traits as shown in the previous matrix. Each trait factor (value) affects the characteristics of a character being built. A class diagram that shows their static relationships is shown in Figure 6–3.

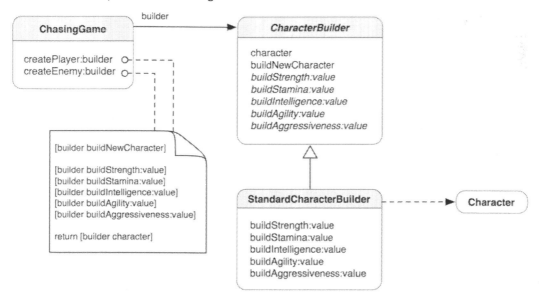

Figure 6–3. *A class diagram of* `CharacterBuilder` *as an abstract builder,* `StandardCharacterBuilder` *as a concrete builder, and* `ChasingGame` *as a director*

`ChasingGame` defines `createPlayer:builder` and `createEnemy:builder` to build player and enemy characters with an instance of `CharacterBuilder`. Each of the methods has a different set of trait factors that define the characteristics of a character. StandardCharacterBuilder is a concrete CharacterBuilder that actually builds characters based on different trait factors. When the building process is done, StandardCharacterBuilder will return an instance of Character as defined in Listing 6–1.

Listing 6–1. *Character.h*

```objc
@interface Character : NSObject
{
  @private
  float protection_;
  float power_;
  float strength_;
  float stamina_;
  float intelligence_;
  float agility_;
  float aggressiveness_;
}

@property (nonatomic, assign) float protection;
@property (nonatomic, assign) float power;
@property (nonatomic, assign) float strength;
@property (nonatomic, assign) float stamina;
@property (nonatomic, assign) float intelligence;
@property (nonatomic, assign) float agility;
@property (nonatomic, assign) float aggressiveness;

@end
```

Character defines a set of traits that are common to any type of character (either a player or an enemy), which includes protection, power, strength, stamina, intelligence, agility, and aggressiveness, just like in the matrix.

An implementation for Character is nothing more than just defining an init method and some synchronization for the properties, as in Listing 6–2.

Listing 6–2. *Character.m*

```objc
#import "Character.h"


@implementation Character

@synthesize protection=protection_;
@synthesize power=power_;
@synthesize strength=strength_;
@synthesize stamina=stamina_;
@synthesize intelligence=intelligence_;
@synthesize agility=agility_;
@synthesize aggressiveness=aggressiveness_;

- (id) init
{
  if (self = [super init])
  {
    protection_ = 1.0;
    power_ = 1.0;
```

```
    strength_ = 1.0;
    stamina_ = 1.0;
    intelligence_ = 1.0;
    agility_ = 1.0;
    aggressiveness_ = 1.0;
  }

  return self;
}

@end
```

An instance of `Character` doesn't know how to build itself to create any meaningful characters. So that's where a `CharacterBuilder` comes in the picture—to help build any meaningful characters based on the trait relationships we defined previously. In Figure 6–2, we have an abstract `CharacterBuilder` that defines an interface that any character builder is supposed to have. Its class declaration is shown in Listing 6–3.

Listing 6–3. *CharacterBuilder.h*

```
#import "Character.h"

@interface CharacterBuilder : NSObject
{
  @protected
  Character *character_;
}

@property (nonatomic, readonly) Character *character;

- (CharacterBuilder *) buildNewCharacter;
- (CharacterBuilder *) buildStrength:(float) value;
- (CharacterBuilder *) buildStamina:(float) value;
- (CharacterBuilder *) buildIntelligence:(float) value;
- (CharacterBuilder *) buildAgility:(float) value;
- (CharacterBuilder *) buildAggressiveness:(float) value;

@end
```

An instance of `CharacterBuilder` has a reference to a target `Character` that will be returned to a client after it's built. There are a few methods to build a character with specific values of Strength, Stamina, Intelligence, Agility, and Aggressiveness. Those values affect the factors for both Protection and Power. The abstract `CharacterBuilder` |defines default behaviors of setting those values to a target `Character`, as shown in Listing 6–4.

Listing 6–4. *CharacterBuilder.m*

```
#import "CharacterBuilder.h"


@implementation CharacterBuilder

@synthesize character=character_;


- (CharacterBuilder *) buildNewCharacter
```

```
{
  // autorelease the previous character
  // before creating a new one
  [character_ autorelease];
  character_ = [[Character alloc] init];

  return self;
}

- (CharacterBuilder *) buildStrength:(float) value
{
  character_.strength = value;
  return self;
}

- (CharacterBuilder *) buildStamina:(float) value
{
  character_.stamina = value;
  return self;
}

- (CharacterBuilder *) buildIntelligence:(float) value
{
  character_.intelligence = value;
  return self;
}

- (CharacterBuilder *) buildAgility:(float) value
{
  character_.agility = value;
  return self;
}

- (CharacterBuilder *) buildAggressiveness:(float) value
{
  character_.aggressiveness = value;
  return self;
}

- (void) dealloc
{
  [character_ autorelease];
  [super dealloc];
}

@end
```

The buildNewCharacter method of CharacterBuilder creates a new instance of Character to build. Every time the method is called, it will autorelease any old character before creating a new one. Using autorelease is a safer approach than just using release right away because a client may still be using the old character without realizing it's released in the builder. The rest of the methods don't do much that is meaningful to build a character until we define a concrete class for CharacterBuilder to do that. StandardCharacterBuilder is a subclass of CharacterBuilder that defines the logic of creating real characters with different correlated traits. Its class declaration is shown in Listing 6–5 and is not much different from CharacterBuilder.

Listing 6–5. *StandardCharacterBuilder.h*

```
#import "CharacterBuilder.h"

@interface StandardCharacterBuilder : CharacterBuilder
{

}

// overriden methods from the abstract CharacterBuilder
- (CharacterBuilder *) buildStrength:(float) value;
- (CharacterBuilder *) buildStamina:(float) value;
- (CharacterBuilder *) buildIntelligence:(float) value;
- (CharacterBuilder *) buildAgility:(float) value;
- (CharacterBuilder *) buildAggressiveness:(float) value;

@end
```

We are re-declaring the overridden methods for clarity. StandardCharacterBuilder doesn't override the buildNewCharacter method because the default behavior in the base class is sufficient. Let's get to the implementation of StandardCharacterBuilder in Listing 6–6 and see how the logic can be implemented to build real characters.

Listing 6–6. *StandardCharacterBuilder.m*

```
#import "StandardCharacterBuilder.h"


@implementation StandardCharacterBuilder

- (CharacterBuilder *) buildStrength:(float) value
{
  // update the protection value of the character
  character_.protection *= value;

  // update the power value of the character
  character_.power *= value;

  // finally set the strength value and return this builder
  return [super buildStrength:value];
}

- (CharacterBuilder *) buildStamina:(float) value
{
  // update the protection value of the character
  character_.protection *= value;

  // update the power value of the character
  character_.power *= value;

  // finally set the strength value and return this builder
  return [super buildStamina:value];
}

- (CharacterBuilder *) buildIntelligence:(float) value
{
  // update the protection value of the character
  character_.protection *= value;
```

```
    // update the power value of the character
    character_.power /= value;

    // finally set the strength value and return this builder
    return [super buildIntelligence:value];
}

- (CharacterBuilder *) buildAgility:(float) value
{
    // update the protection value of the character
    character_.protection *= value;

    // update the power value of the character
    character_.power /= value;

    // finally set the strength value and return this builder
    return [super buildAgility:value];
}

- (CharacterBuilder *) buildAggressiveness:(float) value
{
    // update the protection value of the character
    character_.protection /= value;

    // update the power value of the character
    character_.power *= value;

    // finally set the strength value and return this builder
    return [super buildAggressiveness:value];
}


@end
```

Each of the foregoing methods basically sets the values of Protection and Power for the character being built based on the proportionality defined in the matrix. For example, Intelligence is directly proportional to Protection, and then a new Protection value will be obtained by doing `character_.protection *= value` where `value` is an input value for Intelligence. We are using the Objective-C dot syntax here because characters' states are simple and obvious enough to justify the convenience over any possible confusion with C structs or C++ objects (beware of when you mix any C structs and Objective-C++ in your code). Likewise, Aggressiveness is inversely proportional to Protection, and then a new value for Protection is obtained with the statement `character_.protection /= value`. And finally, it sends a message to `super` to update the target character with new values, and it then returns itself.

Let's move on to `ChasingGame` and see how it can use our `StandardCharacterBuilder` to build different characters. Its class declaration is shown in Listing 6–7.

Listing 6–7. *ChasingGame.h*

```
#import "StandardCharacterBuilder.h"

@interface ChasingGame : NSObject
{

}

- (Character *) createPlayer:(CharacterBuilder *) builder;
- (Character *) createEnemy:(CharacterBuilder *) builder;

@end
```

ChasingGame has two methods, `createPlayer:` and `createEnemy:`. Each of them takes an instance of `CharacterBuilder` for building a specific type of character with a predefined set of trait factors. Its implementation is shown in Listing 6–8.

Listing 6–8. *ChasingGame.m*

```
#import "ChasingGame.h"


@implementation ChasingGame

- (Character *) createPlayer:(CharacterBuilder *) builder
{
  [builder buildNewCharacter];
  [builder buildStrength:50.0];
  [builder buildStamina:25.0];
  [builder buildIntelligence:75.0];
  [builder buildAgility:65.0];
  [builder buildAggressiveness:35.0];

  return [builder character];
}

- (Character *) createEnemy:(CharacterBuilder *) builder
{
  [builder buildNewCharacter];
  [builder buildStrength:80.0];
  [builder buildStamina:65.0];
  [builder buildIntelligence:35.0];
  [builder buildAgility:25.0];
  [builder buildAggressiveness:95.0];

  return [builder character];
}

@end
```

An instance of `ChasingGame` builds a player character with Strength 50.0, Stamina 25.0, Intelligence 75.0, Agility 65.0, and Aggressiveness 35.0 in its `createPlayer:` method. In its `createEnemy:` method, an enemy is created the same as a player but with different trait factors. Apparently, an enemy is relatively stronger and more aggressive than a player, while the player is relatively more intelligent but weaker than the enemy.

Since each build* method returns an instance of the current builder, you can group the whole building process in a single statement, like in Listing 6–9.

Listing 6–9. *An Alternative Syntactic Style for Building a Character*

```
[[[[[[builder buildNewCharacter]
            buildStrength:50.0]
            buildStamina:25.0]
            buildIntelligence:75.0]
            buildAgility:65.0]
            buildAggressiveness:35.0];
```

Which one is better? It's just a matter of preferences.

Now we have a pretty good picture of building different characters. Listing 6–10 shows what happens in client code.

Listing 6–10. *Client Code*

```
CharacterBuilder *characterBuilder = [[[StandardCharacterBuilder alloc] init]
                                                            autorelease];
ChasingGame *game = [[[ChasingGame alloc] init] autorelease];

Character *player = [game createPlayer:characterBuilder];
Character *enemy = [game createEnemy:characterBuilder];

// do something else with the
// player and enemy
```

Our client creates instances of StandardCharacterBuilder and ChasingGame. Then it sends a couple of messages to ChasingGame createPlayer: and createEnemy: with characterBuilder. After the characterBuilder has hammered out two characters for us, then we will take the game from there.

Summary

The Builder pattern can help us construct objects that involve different combinations of parts and representations. Without the pattern, the Director that knows what is needed to construct objects may end up being a monolithic "god" class, with tons of embedded algorithms for building different representations of the same class. A game that involves characters of different traits should get a good use of the pattern. Instead of defining separate Directors for building player and enemy, putting the generalized character building algorithm in a single, concrete CharacterBuilder can achieve a much better design.

In the next chapter, we are going to look at a pattern that creates and returns only a single instance of a class.

Chapter 7

Singleton

In mathematics and logic, a singleton is defined as "a set that contains exactly one element." So no matter how big a pouch is, every time you are trying to get a marble out of it you will get only the same one. Under what situations do we need a singleton in software? Think about resources that can be shared only in a system and no copies of them can be made available to others. For example, the GPS device is the sole hardware on the iPhone that provides coordinates of the device in real time. The `CLLocationManager` class of the `CoreLocation` framework provides a single access point to any services that the GPS device offers. Some people may think, if I can make a copy of `CLLocationManager`, then can I get an extra set of GPS services to my application? That sounds like a fantasy—you create two copies of software GPS for the price of one hardware GPS. But in reality, you still get only one GPS at a single time because there is only one GPS in the device that makes actual connections with satellites in the sky. So if you think you wrote a killer app that can manipulate two separate GPS connections at a time and want to brag about it to your friends, think twice!

A singleton class in an object-oriented application always returns the same instance of itself. It provides a global access point for the resources provided by the object of the class. A design pattern that is related to these kinds of designs is called the Singleton pattern.

In this chapter, we will be exploring some possibilities for implementing and using the Singleton pattern in Objective-C and the Cocoa Touch framework for the iOS.

What Is the Singleton Pattern?

The Singleton pattern is almost the simplest form of design pattern ever. The intent of the pattern is to make an object of a class be the sole instance in a system. To achieve that, we can begin with the point where clients instantiate it. So we need to "block" every access to create the object with a mechanism that allows only a single instance of the object's class to go out. We can use a factory method (Chapter 4) to bottleneck the instantiation process. That method should be a static method (class method), as it wouldn't make sense to allow an instance of the class to create another sole instance. Figure 7–1 shows a class structure of a simple singleton.

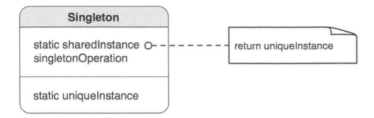

Figure 7–1. *A static structure of the Singleton pattern*

The static uniqueInstance is the only instance of Singleton as a class variable with which static sharedInstance will return it to clients. Usually, sharedInstance would check and see if uniqueInstance is instantiated. If not, it will create one before returning the uniqueInstance.

> **THE SINGLETON PATTERN:** Ensures a class has only one instance, and provide a global point of access to it.*
>
> *The original definition appeared in *Design Patterns*, by the "Gang of Four" (Addison-Wesley, 1994).

When Would You Use the Singleton Pattern?

You'd think about using the Singleton pattern when

- There must be exactly one instance of a class with which it must be accessible from a well-known access point, e.g., a factory method (Chapter 4).

- The sole instance can be extended only by subclassing, and it won't break client code with the extended object.

The Singleton pattern provides a well-known access point to client classes that want to create a unique instance of and access to a shared resource. Although a static global object reference or a class method can provide a global access point, the global object cannot prevent the class getting instantiated more than once, and the class method lacks the flexibility of decoupling.

A static global variable holds a single reference to an instance of a class. Another class or a method that can access that global variable is, in fact, sharing the same copy with other classes or methods that use the same variable. That sounds like what we are after in this chapter. Everything seems fine if we use only the same global variable throughout the whole application. So, in fact, we don't need the Singleton pattern. But hey, wait a minute; what if there is somebody in your team or a consultant who has defined the same type of static global variable as yours? Then there will be two copies of the same global object type living in the same application—so a global variable doesn't really solve the problem.

A class method provides shared services without creating an object of it. A single instance of the resource is maintained within the class method. However, this approach lacks the flexibility if the class needs to be subclassed to provide better services.

A singleton class can guarantee a single, consistent, and well-known access point to create and access a single object of the class. The pattern provides the flexibility such that any of its subclasses can override the instance method and have total control over object creation of itself without changing code in the client. Or even better, the instance implementation in the parent class can handle dynamic object creation. The actual type of a class can be determined to make sure the correct object is created at runtime. This technique will be discussed later in the chapter.

There is a flexible version of the Singleton pattern in which a factory method always returns the same instance, but you can also allocate and initialize additional instances. This less "strict" version of the pattern is discussed in "Using the NSFileManager Class" later in this chapter.

Implementing a Singleton in Objective-C

There are some things that we need to think about in order to design a singleton class properly. The first question we need to ask is, how can we make sure there is only one instance of a class that can be created? Clients in an application written in other object-oriented programming languages, like C++ and Java, cannot create an object of a class if its constructor is declared `private`. Then what about Objective-C?

Every Objective-C method is public and the language itself is dynamically typed, so every class can send each other's messages (method calling in C++ and Java) without much compile time checking (only compiler warnings if a message in question is not declared). Also the Cocoa (including Cocoa Touch) framework utilizes reference counting memory management to maintain objects' life span in memory. All of these features make implementing a singleton in Objective-C quite challenging.

In the original example of the *Design Patterns* book, the C++ example of the Singleton pattern is as shown in Listing 7–1.

Listing 7–1. *The Original C++ Singleton Class Appearing in Design Patterns*

```
class Singleton
{
public:
  static Singleton *Instance();

protected:
  Singleton();

private:
  static Singleton *_instance;
};
```

```
Singleton *Singleton::_instance = 0;

Singleton *Singleton::Instance ()
{
  if (_instance == 0)
  {
    instance = new Singleton;
  }

  return _instance;
}
```

As it is described in the book, the implementation in C++ is simple and straightforward. In the static Instance() method, the static _instance instance variable is checked to see if it is 0 (NULL). If so, a new Singleton object will be created and then an instance of it will be returned. Some of you may think an Objective-C version shouldn't be much different from its brother's version and should look like Listings 7–2 and 7–3.

Listing 7–2. *A Class Declaration of Singleton in* `Singleton.h`

```
@interface Singleton : NSObject
{

}

+ (Singleton *) sharedInstance;

@end
```

Listing 7–3. *The Implementation of the* `sharedInstance` *Method in* `Singleton.m`

```
@implementation Singleton

static Singleton *sharedSingleton_ = nil;

+ (Singleton *) sharedInstance
{
  if (sharedSingleton_ == nil)
  {
    sharedSingleton_ = [[Singleton alloc] init];
  }
  return sharedSingleton_;
}

@end
```

If that's the case, then this is a very easy chapter to write and read, and you've already learned one pattern implemented in Objective-C. In reality, there are some hurdles that we need to get over to make the implementation robust enough to live in a real application. If you need to implement a "strict" version of the Singleton pattern, then there are two major hurdles that you need to address so it can be used in the real world:

▓   A calling object cannot instantiate a singleton object through other means of allocation. Otherwise, multiple instances of the singleton class could be created.

▓   Restrictions on instantiating a singleton object should also coexist with the reference counting memory models.

Listing 7–4 shows an implementation that should be close to the one that we are looking at. The code is quite long, so we will break it up into a few parts to discuss.

Listing 7–4. *A More Appropriate Implementation of Singleton in Objective-C*

```
#import "Singleton.h"

@implementation Singleton

static Singleton * sharedSingleton = nil;

+ (Singleton*) sharedInstance
{
  if (sharedSingleton_ == nil)
  {
    sharedSingleton_ = [[super allocWithZone:NULL] init];
  }

  return sharedSingleton_;
}
```

Inside the sharedInstance method, just like in the first example, it first checks if the sole instance of the class is created, otherwise it creates a new one and returns it. But this time, it calls [[super allocWithZone:NULL] init] to create a new instance instead of using other methods such as alloc. Why super but not self? It's because we have overridden the basic object allocation methods in self, so we need to "borrow" the functionality from its parent, in this case NSObject, to help do the low-level memory allocation chores for us.

```
+ (id) allocWithZone:(NSZone *)zone
{
  return [[self sharedInstance] retain];
}

- (id) copyWithZone:(NSZone*)zone
{
  return self;
}
```

There are a few methods that are related to the memory management, which we need to take care of in the Singleton class. In allocWithZone:(NSZone *)zone, the method returns only the class instance that is returned from the sharedInstance method. In the Cocoa Touch framework, by calling a class's allocWithZone:(NSZone *)zone method, memory of an instance will be allocated, its reference count will be set to 1, and the instance will be returned. We have seen that the alloc method is used in many situations; in fact, alloc calls allocWithZone: with the zone set to NULL to allocate memory for the new instance in the default zone. The details of object creation and memory management are outside the scope of this book. You can consult the documentation for any further details.

Likewise, we also need to override the `copyWithZone:(NSZone*)zone` method to make sure it won't return a copy of the instance but the same one by returning `self`.

```objc
- (id) retain
{
  return self;
}

- (NSUInteger) retainCount
{
  return NSUIntegerMax;  // denotes an object that cannot be released
}

- (void) release
{
  // do nothing
}

- (id) autorelease
{
  return self;
}

@end
```

Other methods, like `retain`, `release`, and `autorelease`, are overridden to make sure they won't do anything (in a reference counting memory model) except just to return `self`. `retainCount` returns `NSUIntegerMax` (4,294,967,295) to keep the instance alive as long as the application lives.

WHY RETAIN A SINGLETON?

You might have noticed that we retain a singleton object returned from the `shareInstance` method in `allocWithZone:`, but `retain` is overridden and basically ignored in our implementation. With that, we will have an option to make the `Singleton` class to become less "strict" (i.e., allocating and initializing additional instances are allowed, but the `sharedInstance` factory method always returns the same instance or the `Singleton` object becomes destructible). Subclasses can override the `retain`, `release`, and `autorelease` methds again to provide appropriate memory management implementations.

A flexible version of the Singleton pattern is discussed in "Using the `NSFileManager` Class" later in this chapter.

We have pretty much covered what a singleton in Objective-C should look like. However, there is still something else that we need to think about carefully before we can use it. What if we want to subclass the original `Singleton`? We will answer that question now.

Subclassing a Singleton

The `alloc` call is forwarded to `super`, which means `NSObject` will take care of the object allocation. If we subclass `Singleton` without any modification, the returned instance is always `Singleton`. Because `Singleton` overrides all the instantiation-related methods, it is quite tricky to subclass it. But we are quite lucky; we can use some Foundation functions to instantiate whatever object based on its class type. One of them is `id NSAllocateObject (Class aClass, NSUInteger extraBytes, NSZone *zone)`. So if we want to instantiate an object of a class called "Singleton," we can do the following:

```
Singleton *singleton = [NSAllocateObject ([Singleton class], 0, NULL) init];
```

The first parameter is the type of the `Singleton` class. The second parameter is for any extra bytes for indexed instance variables, which is always 0. The third parameter is to specify an allocated zone in memory; it is `NULL` for a default zone most of the time. So you can instantiate whatever objects with this function by providing their class types. What does it have to do with subclassing `Singleton`? Let's recall that the original `sharedInstance` method looks like this:

```
+ (Singleton*) sharedInstance
{
  if (sharedSingleton_ == nil)
  {
    sharedSingleton_ = [[super allocWithZone:NULL] init];
  }

  return sharedSingleton_;
}
```

If we use the trick of `NSAllocateObject` to create an instance, then it will become like this:

```
 + (Singleton *) sharedInstance
{
  if (sharedSingleton_ == nil)
  {
    sharedSingleton_ = [NSAllocateObject([self class], 0, NULL) init];
  }

  return sharedSingleton_;
}
```

So now no matter whether we are instantiating `Singleton` or any of its subclasses, that version should take care of that nicely.

Thread Safety

If a singleton object is intended to be accessed by multiple threads, then it is crucial to make it thread-safe. The `Singleton` class in the example is good only for general use. To make it thread-safe, we can put some `@synchronized()` blocks or `NSLock` instances around the `nil` check for the `sharedSingleton_` static instance. If there are some other properties that also need to be protected, we can make them `atomic` as well.

Using Singletons in the Cocoa Touch Framework

When you wade through the Cocoa Touch Developer's documentation, you will find numerous singleton classes in the framework here and there. We will talk about a few of them in this section, UIApplication, UIAccelerometer, and NSFileManager.

Using the UIApplication Class

One of the most commonly used singleton classes in the framework is the UIApplication class. It provides a centralized point of control and coordination for iOS applications.

Every app has exactly one instance of UIApplication. It's created as a singleton object by the UIApplicationMain function when an app is launched. Thereafter, the same instance of the UIApplication can be accessed through its sharedApplication class method.

A UIApplication object does many housekeeping tasks for an application, including initial routing of incoming user events as well as dispatching action messages for UIControl objects to appropriate target objects. It also maintains a list of all the UIWindow objects being opened in the app. The application object is always assigned with a UIApplicationDelegate object, to which the application informs any significant runtime events, such as application did launch, low-memory warnings, application termination, and background process executions in an iOS application. They give an opportunity to the delegate to respond appropriately.

Using the UIAccelerometer Class

Another common singleton in the Cocoa Touch framework is the UIAccelerometer. The UIAccelerometer class allows an application to sign up to receive acceleration-related data from the built-in accelerometer in an iOS device. An application can use reported linear acceleration changes along the primary axes in three-dimensional space to detect both the current orientation of the device and any instantaneous changes to that orientation.

The UIAccelerometer is a singleton, so you cannot create its objects directly. Instead, its sharedAccelerometer singleton class method should be called to access its sole instance. Then you can set its updateInterval as well its delegate properties with your own delegate object to receive any reported acceleration data from the singleton instance.

Using the NSFileManager Class

The NSFileManager used to be a "strict" implementation of the Singleton pattern prior Mac OS X v 10.5 and in iOS 2.0. An invocation to its init method is a no-op (does nothing), and its only instance can be created and accessed only through the defaultManager class method. However, its singleton implementation is not thread-safe.

Now creating new instances of NSFileManager is recommended for thread-safety. This approach is considered a more flexible singleton implementation in which a factory method always returns the same instance, but you can allocate and initialize additional instances as well.

If you need to implement a "strict" singleton, you need to have an implementation similar to the example described in the previous sections. Otherwise, do not override allocWithZone: and the other methods following it.

Summary

The Singleton pattern is one of the most commonly used patterns in almost any type of application, not just for iOS application development.

As long as an application requires a centralized class that coordinates the services of its own, the class should generate a singleton instance rather than multiple instances.

This chapter marks the end of this part about object creation. In the next part, we will see some design patterns that focus on adapting/consolidating objects with different interfaces.

Part **III**

Interface Adaptation

Chapter 8

Adapter

Nikola Tesla invented the AC electric power system back in the 19th century. He probably couldn't imagine that we would have the annoying problem of plugging an electric device made for the United States into a wall outlet in Europe without any adapter. Picture me holding an electric razor and looking at a wall outlet in the bathroom of my hotel room in Europe but missing an adapter. "What now?" "Should I buy a new razor here?" "But then when I bring it back to the United States, I will need an adapter for it too."

In object-oriented software design, sometimes you want to reuse some useful and well-tested classes in other new areas of an application. But it's quite common that new features require new interfaces and they don't fit the existing classes that can be reused. You may ask yourself: "What now?" "Should I rewrite the same classes to fit the new interfaces?" "But then when I need to add new features again, will I need to rewrite them again?" People are smart; many years since the introduction of AC electric power, there is still a huge need for power adapters fitting US plugs in European wall outlets or the other way around. No one wants to buy a new electric razor every time they travel abroad, just like we don't want to rewrite our faithful classes for new interfaces.

Since the incompatibility issue of old classes vs. new interfaces is quite common, people came up with a solution to solve that problem. That solution was used many times until it got cataloged as a design pattern called Adapter.

What Is the Adapter Pattern?

The Adapter pattern is, so to speak, to fit two different types of objects together and make them work with each other without any problem. Sometimes it's also called "Wrapper." The idea is quite straightforward. There is an adapter that implements behavior of some sort of interface that a client is expecting. It also connects to another object that has a (totally) different interface and behavior. The adapter is standing between a target interface that a client that knows how to use and an adaptee that is (totally) foreign to it. The main role of an adapter is to bring the behavior from the adaptee to the other end of the pipe to the client.

There are basically two ways to implement the Adapter pattern. The first one is by inheritance to adapt one interface to another. It's called a class adapter. In the original *Design Patterns* book, a class adapter is achieved by multiple inheritance. C++, which is one of the main languages used in the book, doesn't have a language feature like Java's interface or Objective-C's protocol. Everything is a class. A class without actual implementation is called an abstract class. That will be a type of thing that will be used as an "Abstract" type, unlike Objective-C; it has protocol as a form of pure abstraction. In Objective-C, we can have a class that *implements* a protocol and at the same time *inherits* a superclass to achieve something similar to the multiple inheritance in C++. There are a lot of books out there that discuss language features and such. Let's not worry about them here. To implement a class adapter in Objective-C, first we need a protocol that defines a set of behaviors that a client will use, and then we need a concrete adapter class that implements the protocol. The adapter class also inherits an adaptee at the same time. Their relationships are illustrated in Figure 8–1.

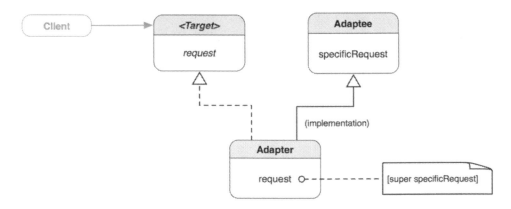

Figure 8–1. *A class diagram of a class adapter*

The Adapter is a type of Target as well as a type of Adaptee at the same time. The Adapter overrides the request method of the Target. However, the Adapter doesn't override the specificRequest method of Adaptee, but the method is used as a message call to the superclass in the Adapter's implementation of the request method. The request method sends a [super specificRequest] message to the superclass at runtime. super, being an Adaptee, executes the method with its own behavior within the scope of the request method in the Adapter. The class adapter can be implemented in Objective-C only when the Target is a protocol but not a class.

The second way to implement the Adapter pattern is called an object adapter. Unlike a class adapter, an object adapter doesn't inherit an adaptee class but composes a reference to it. Their new relationships implemented as an object adapter are illustrated in Figure 8–2.

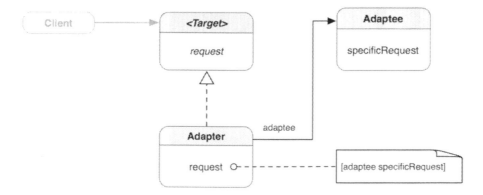

Figure 8–2. *A class diagram of an object adapter*

The relationship between the Target and Adapter is the same as in a class adapter in Figure 8–1, except that the relationship between Adapter and Adaptee has changed from a "is a" relationship to a "has a" relationship. In this relationship, Adapter needs to keep a reference to Adaptee. In the request method, it sends a [adaptee specificRequest] message to the reference, adaptee, to access its behavior indirectly and then fulfill the rest of the request by a client. Since it's a "has a" relationship between Adapter and Adaptee, Adapter can adapt subclasses of Adaptee without much problem.

> **THE ADAPTER PATTERN:** Converts the interface of a class into another interface clients expect. Adapter lets classes work together that couldn't otherwise because of incompatible interfaces.*
>
> *The original definition appeared in *Design Patterns*, by the "Gang of Four" (Addison-Wesley, 1994).

CLASS ADAPTER VS. OBJECT ADAPTER

Both class and object adapters are different ways to implement the Adapter pattern, yet they serve the same purpose. Which route should you go for before you put it in your design next time? Let's take a look at the following table to get some quick clues on their characteristics.

Characteristic Comparisons between Class Adapter and Object Adapter

Class Adapter	Object Adapter
Adapts Adaptee to Target by committing to a *single*, concrete Adaptee class only	Can adapt *many* Adaptees and all their subclasses
Easy to override Adaptee's behavior as it's done directly through subclassing	Difficult to override Adaptee's behavior; it needs to refer to the object of the subclass rather than the Adaptee itself.
One Adapter object only; no extra pointer indirection is needed to get to the Adaptee.	Requires an extra pointer to indirectly access Adaptee and adapt its behavior

Apparently, the Delegate pattern falls into the Object Adapter category.

When Would You Use the Adapter Pattern?

You'd naturally think about using the pattern when

- The interface of an existing class does not match the one you need.

- You want to have a reusable class that can cooperate with other classes with possibly incompatible interfaces.

- You need to adapt several different subclasses of a class, but it's impractical to let each of them subclass a class adapter. So you can use an object adapter (a.k.a. delegate) to adapt their parent's interface.

So You Know Delegation

In earlier chapters, we have talked a lot about delegation in the Cocoa Touch framework. A lot of iOS developers have already seen "delegate" here and there in the framework SDK. According to Apple's documentation, "delegate" is a form of the Delegation pattern that the Cocoa Touch framework has adopted. What's the Delegation pattern, by the way?

The Delegation pattern was once one of the inspirations for cataloging the Adapter pattern in the "Gang of Four" book. So what's the connection between them? Think again about what the Adapter pattern does: to convert the interface of a class into another interface clients expect. Adapter lets classes work together that couldn't otherwise because of incompatible interfaces. What could be the clients here? They will be Cocoa Touch framework classes. So what is the "Target" in this case? It is a delegation protocol. A concrete class that implements the protocol will be an adapter in that case. Then what would be the classes that wouldn't fit to the framework and need to be adapted? Other classes in our apps! So now you understand why the Delegation pattern is, in fact, the Adapter pattern.

The reason I said the Delegation pattern is mainly the Adapter pattern is that the Delegation mechanism can also fulfill the intents of some other design patterns, such as the Decorator pattern (Chapter 16). The implementation of the Delegation pattern in the Cocoa Touch framework can sometimes mix with other design patterns. For example, some framework classes that implement the Delegation pattern are also part of the Template Method pattern (Chapter 18). A template method contains a set of predefined, parameterized algorithms with some specific behavior left out for subclasses to provide, but in this case it is a delegate. During an operation of a template method, a message will be sent to a delegate (adapter) for some specific behavior when it's required. Then any specific information can be obtained from any adaptee in an application through the adapter's (delegate's) interface. It's common to see the Delegate pattern interrelated and used in a mixture of more than one design pattern.

Implementing the Adapter Pattern with Objective-C Protocol

We have seen a lot of framework classes in Cocoa Touch that are implemented with some form of delegation defined in protocols. We can implement our own delegation as an adapter.

In the discussion on designing the TouchPainter app in Chapter 2, we understood that there is a view where it allows the user to change stroke color and size for the next stroke drawn on the CanvasView. An instance of PaletteViewController presents that view when requested. On that view, there are three sliders for changing color components for the stroke color. That operation involves several components, CanvasViewController, PaletteViewController, and its sliders. You may think that we can probably do it in a few lines of code. But the catch is that everything will be tightly coupled and hard to reuse. We need a better solution so we can reuse the color changing part in other areas of the application. For example, if we change the interface for picking colors to a color wheel instead of using three sliders for different color components, we can still reuse the same object to accomplish the same thing. Likewise, if we go for implementing an iPad version of TouchPainter, we can also put the same object for changing colors in a pop-up menu that iPhone doesn't support.

When we want to reuse something, in terms of object-oriented programming, that something should be put in an object. If we want to put the color changing action into an object, a natural way to do so is to put it in a command object (see the Command pattern, Chapter 20). A command object can be queued and reused and can have undo and redo encapsulated operations. In the Command pattern chapter, we explain Cocoa implementation of the Command pattern with NSInvocation. An NSInvocation object can be generic enough to encapsulate and invoke a target-action unit for any Objective-C object as a target and any message as a selector. One of the limitations with NSInvocation, though, is that you cannot put multiple operations in its objects to invoke. Multiple operations can be as simple as checking password input by the user; if the check doesn't pass, then show an alert box to warn the user. Those operations don't need to be jammed in a particular controller, especially when they are so common that they can be reused in many places. So sometimes we still need our own command objects for that reason. You can either subclass NSInvocation or create your own from scratch. Chapter 20 has detailed explanations for the latter.

Designing and Implementing a Stroke Color Changing Mechanism

SetStrokeColorCommand is an implementation of the Command pattern. What it does is to set a stroke color value to the CanvasViewController, so the next stroke drawn on the CanvasView will be using a set color. You can go back to Chapter 2 and the other chapters for detailed discussions about CanvasViewController and CanvasView. When an instance of SetStrokeColorCommand is executed, it needs values of RGB to construct a color value as part of its operations. The SetStrokeColorCommand object doesn't care who will provide these values. The values should be obtained from any adapter that adapts a delegate protocol, SetStrokeColorCommandDelegate. Their static relationships are illustrated in Figure 8–3.

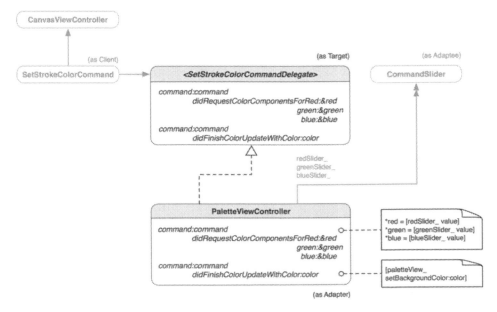

Figure 8–3. *PaletteViewController acts as an adapter for* SetStrokeColorCommandDelegate, *which is a target for* SetStrokeColorCommand *as a client by adapting values obtained from* CommandSlider *instances.*

SetStrokeColorCommand is a client here because it is the one that requests the data it needs to get its jobs done from whatever can fulfill its needs. SetStrokeColorCommand is a subclass of Command as defined in Chapter 20, as shown in Listing 8–1.

Listing 8–1. *Command.h*

```
@interface Command : NSObject
{
  @protected
  // other private member variables...
}

// other properties...

- (void) execute;

@end
```

We are not going to discuss all the methods and properties declared in the Command class but instead focus on the execute method when we get to the implementation of SetStrokeColorCommand class. SetStrokeColorCommand needs a target to tell adapters what to provide.

Defining SetStrokeColorCommandDelegate As a Target

Like other delegates you've seen in the Cocoa Touch framework, SetStrokeColorCommandDelegate is defined as a protocol. It acts as a contract between a client and an adapter, in this case, SetStrokeColorCommand and PaletteViewController objects. A protocol declaration for SetStrokeColorCommandDelegate is shown in Listing 8–2.

Listing 8–2. *SetStrokeColorCommandDelegate Protocol As a Target in the Adapter Pattern Defined in SetStrokeColorCommand.h*

```
#import <Foundation/Foundation.h>
#import "Command.h"

@class SetStrokeColorCommand;

@protocol SetStrokeColorCommandDelegate

- (void) command:(SetStrokeColorCommand *) command
          didRequestColorComponentsForRed:(CGFloat *) red
                                    green:(CGFloat *) green
                                     blue:(CGFloat *) blue;

- (void) command:(SetStrokeColorCommand *) command
          didFinishColorUpdateWithColor:(UIColor *) color;

@end
```

The command:didRequestColorComponentsForRed:green:blue: method returns separate RGB values by passing red, green, and blue parameters as reference. On the other hand, command:didFinishColorUpdateWithColor: will be invoked when the color updating process is finished. The command object will pass itself and the updated color object to the adapter, so it can take that chance to do anything else with the new color.

Implementing SetStrokeCommand As a Client

Here it comes with our client SetStrokeColorCommand. It keeps a reference of
SetStrokeColorCommandDelegate as delegate_, as shown in its class declaration in
Listing 8–3.

Listing 8–3. *A Class Declaration of* SetStrokeColorCommand *in* SetStrokeColorCommand.h

```
@interface SetStrokeColorCommand : Command
{
  @private
  id <SetStrokeColorCommandDelegate> delegate_;
}

@property (nonatomic, assign) id <SetStrokeColorCommandDelegate> delegate;

- (void) execute;

@end
```

Since this is a command object, you might wonder whether the delegate should be a
receiver that receives any action message from the command object as defined in the
Command pattern in Chapter 20. In fact, the real command's receiver is not defined
here as a property, per se, but should be obtained in the execute method, as shown in
Listing 8–4.

Listing 8–4. *An Implementation of* SetStrokeColorCommand *in* SetStrokeColorCommand.m

```
#import "SetStrokeColorCommand.h"
#import "CoordinatingController.h"
#import "CanvasViewController.h"

@implementation SetStrokeColorCommand

@synthesize delegate=delegate_;


- (void) execute
{
  CGFloat redValue = 0.0;
  CGFloat greenValue = 0.0;
  CGFloat blueValue = 0.0;

  // Retrieve RGB values from a delegate
  [delegate_ command:self didRequestColorComponentsForRed:&redValue
                                                    green:&greenValue
                                                     blue:&blueValue];

  // Create a color object based on the RGB values
  UIColor *color = [UIColor colorWithRed:redValue
                                   green:greenValue
                                    blue:blueValue
                                   alpha:1.0];

  // Assign it to the current canvasViewController
  CoordinatingController *coordinator = [CoordinatingController sharedInstance];
  CanvasViewController *controller = [coordinator canvasViewController];
```

```
    [controller setStrokeColor:color];

    // Forward a post update message
    [delegate_ command:self didFinishColorUpdateWithColor:color];
}

- (void) dealloc
{
    [super dealloc];
}

@end
```

`delegate_` is sent off a `command:didRequestColorComponentsForRed:green:blue:`
message to return individual RGB values. Then a color object is created from the
obtained values. We then obtain a sole reference to `CanvasViewController` from
`CoordinatingController`. A singleton instance of `CoordinatingController` is acting as a
mediator to coordinate different view controllers in the application (see the Mediator
pattern, Chapter 11). We assign the color that we've just put together in the previous
step to the `CanvasViewController` as its new stroke color. After that, `delegate_` is fired
again with another delegate method with a newly set color object. Whatever that
`delegate_` object is will take it from there and use the color object for other things.

Now we know about what our client and target will be. Let's see what object and its
values we should adapt for the client.

Creating CommandSlider As an Adaptee

As we've mentioned many times now, there are three sliders for adjusting color
components and whatnot. Every minute move on the slider handle kicks off an update to
a receiver with its new value. This scenario reminds us of an invoker as defined in the
Command pattern (Chapter 20). An invoker keeps a reference of a command object and
executes it when the invoker is invoked (e.g., a button click by the user). So our sliders
also need to keep a reference to a command object that can do something for them (i.e.,
color updating). However, `UISlider` didn't expect that we are going to use our command
object with it, so we need to make our own by subclassing `UISlider`. We call it
`CommandSlider`, as shown in Listing 8–5.

Listing 8–5. *CommandSlider.h*

```
#import <Foundation/Foundation.h>
#import "Command.h"

@interface CommandSlider : UISlider
{
    @protected
    Command *command_;
}

@property (nonatomic, retain) IBOutlet Command *command;

@end
```

A custom slider that takes and executes a Command object is not enough to solve our problem. We need to link it up to a SetStrokeColorCommand object. As we can see, the command property is an IBOutlet, which means we can accomplish that in the Interface Builder. Chapter 11 has a detailed explanation on linking UI elements with custom objects.

We let the sliders listen to a Value Changed event. When there is a change on the slider's handle, the runtime will fire off the event with a target-action that should be invoked. The slider will then execute the stored command object. We will get to the details of that part in the next section.

Using PaletteViewController As an Adapter

Finally, we are getting to our adapter for the design. PaletteViewController is a natural choice to adapt values from the RGB sliders because the controller owns and manipulates them. The PaletteViewController class is required to conform to the SetStrokeColorCommandDelegate in order to adapt anything for a client (i.e., a SetStrokeColorCommand object). Let's take a look at its adopted delegate methods in Listing 8–6.

Listing 8–6. *The* SetStrokeColorCommandDelegate *Methods Implemented by* PaletteViewController

```
#pragma mark -
#pragma mark SetStrokeColorCommandDelegate methods

- (void) command:(SetStrokeColorCommand *) command
            didRequestColorComponentsForRed:(CGFloat *) red
                                      green:(CGFloat *) green
                                       blue:(CGFloat *) blue
{
  *red = [redSlider_ value];
  *green = [greenSlider_ value];
  *blue = [blueSlider_ value];
}

- (void) command:(SetStrokeColorCommand *) command
            didFinishColorUpdateWithColor:(UIColor *) color
{
  [paletteView_ setBackgroundColor:color];
}
```

When the client (SetStrokeColorCommand object) asks for new RGB values and fires off command:didRequestColorComponentsForRed:green:blue: to its delegate or adapter, then PaletteViewController responds by assigning each color component value with the corresponding slider's value. Likewise, when the SetStrokeColorCommand object is done with its business updating a new stroke color, it will fire off another method for its adapter to perform any extra operations with the new color object. PaletteViewController responds to that message by updating paletteView_'s background color with the new color, where paletteView_ is the small color palette view sitting right below the color sliders.

At this point, we have a pretty good picture of how things are put together. But how are we going to use the CommandSlider instances in code? The answer is we are not going to use it directly, but we will use the help from the Interface Builder by hooking up the color sliders with PaletteViewController in a .xib file.

When there is a change to the value of any one of the color sliders, the event will be captured by invoking an onCommandSliderValueChanged: method defined in PaletteViewController, as shown in Listing 8–7.

Listing 8–7. *onCommandSliderValueChanged: Event Handler for Any Instance of CommandSlider in PaletteViewController.m*

```
#pragma mark -
#pragma mark Slider event handler

- (IBAction) onCommandSliderValueChanged:(CommandSlider *)slider
{
  [[slider command] execute];
}
```

This little event handling method in the PaletteViewController does the trick to let all types of CommandSlider objects run the same way with their own embedded Command object. Each slider returned by that method will invoke the execute method of its Command object. In this case, the execute method of the SetStrokeColorCommand will in turn try to get RGB values from the adapter (PaletteViewController). Once the delegate returns some RGB values, then the SetStrokeColorCommand will continue to update CanvasViewController's stroke color, as discussed in Listing 8–4.

Voilà! Everything is now connected in the same pipeline. Every object has its own particular duty and is highly reusable. If later we decided to change the way of adjusting the stroke size, we can still reuse the same SetStrokeColorCommand to serve the same purpose without rewriting that part again. The onCommandSliderValueChanged: event handler can also be used with other sliders that have different command objects. Do you see how they are connected but not dependent on each other?

Implementing the Adapter Pattern with Objective-C Blocks in iOS 4

We have seen that the Adapter pattern can be implemented with a protocol as a target interface that defines some standard behavior that clients expect and adapters can commit to. A protocol is a language-level feature in Objective-C that makes it possible to define interfaces that are instances of the Adapter pattern. The term "interface" is synonymous with "protocol" in other object-oriented languages like Java. Interfaces used in the Adapter pattern are essentially a series of method declarations that a client object knows how to communicate with. But with a protocol, both an adapter and a client need to know about a target as a protocol in order to make everything well defined and run correctly. A language feature called blocks is a powerful feature in Objective-C that can allow us to implement the Adapter pattern without using a protocol. Blocks are available since the introduction of iOS 4.0.

Blocks are like functions, but written inline with the rest of your code, inside other functions. Blocks have been around for some time now. They have been part of scripting and programming languages such as Ruby, Python, Smalltalk, and Lisp. Sometimes blocks can go by the names of "closures" and "lambdas." They are called "closures" because they close around variables in your scope. We will not go through any specific language details of blocks in this section, but we will briefly cover some basic syntaxes and how we can use them to implement the Adapter pattern.

Declaring a Block Reference

A block variable holds a reference to a "block" of code that can be passed around in an application. It's similar to a function pointer in C language, as follows:

```
int (^ObjectiveCblock)(int);
int (*CFunctionPointer)(float);
```

The first one is an Objective-C block variable that takes an integer as an argument and returns an integer. The syntax is very similar to the C version in the second one. The C function pointer variable takes a floating-point number as an argument and returns an integer. The main difference in terms of syntax between the two is that a C function pointer uses the * character while an Objective-C block uses the ^ character.

If you use the same block in multiple places, instead of typing the same cryptic signature every time you want to define it, it's better to create a type for it with typedef:

```
typedef int (^ObjectiveCblock)(int);
```

So you can define it later as follows:

```
ObjectiveCblock firstBlock = ...;
ObjectiveCblock secondBlock = ...;
```

Now it's much easier to read, with a simpler type name compared to a complete block signature. We're going to go over how to define a block literal in a little bit.

Creating a Block

In the previous section, we've defined a block variable, ObjectiveCblock, and declared it as a type. In order to define an actual *block literal* (the meat of a block as a function) in it, we can do the following:

```
ObjectiveCBlock aBlock = ^(int anInt) {

    return anInt++;
}
```

Then it can be used as a function in other parts of an application, like this:

```
int result = aBlock(5);
```

An amazing thing about blocks is that they are actually Objective-C objects. They are regarded as anonymous objects that live on the stack and will be destroyed once they fall out of scope. You can copy, retain, release, and autorelease them just like other regular Objective-C objects. But `retain` doesn't seem to have any real effects on a block. So if you want to "retain" a block, you need to make a "copy" of it by moving it to the heap. Like a regular Objective-C object, you need to balance `retain`/`copy` with `release`/`autorelease`. For the block just defined, we can `copy` and `release` it in this way:

```
id aBlockCopy = [ ^(int anInt) { return anInt++; } copy];
```

```
// do something with aBlockCopy...
```

```
[ aBlockCopy release];
```

Or in this way:

```
id aBlockCopy = [aBlock copy];
```

```
// do something with aBlockCopy...
```

```
[aBlockCopy release];
```

Or in this even simpler way, especially when you want to return it from another method or function:

```
id aBlockCopy = [[aBlock copy] release];
```

```
// do something with aBlockCopy...
```

Any one of the styles will achieve the same result. You get the idea.

One of the main differences between a C function pointer and an Objective-C block is that a block literal can be defined inline with the same message call:

```
[anObject doSomethingWithBlock: ^(int anInt) {

        return anInt++;
}];
```

It's something that you can't do with a C function pointer, though. Now you should be curious about how we can use a block as a "building block" for implementing the Adapter pattern.

Using a Block As an Adapter

We remember on the setting view of the `PaletteViewController` in our TouchPainter app, there are three sliders that allow the user to change the stroke color. Each slider corresponds to red, green, and blue values respectively in the RGB value of the color object that's used in iOS. One may want to, let's say, add more red to the current color, and then he or she can move the slider that corresponds to the red value to increase the red value, and the same for other sliders for other color components.

In the last part, we used a protocol to define a target for an adapter to adopt. This time, we will use a block to implement an adapter for the same purpose. A new class diagram for our new adapter is shown in Figure 8–4.

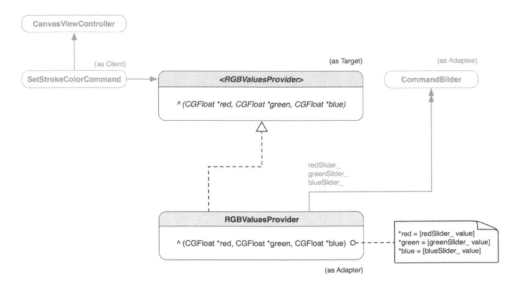

Figure 8–4. *A class diagram of a realization of an* RGBValuesProvider *block as an object adapter for* StrokeColorCommand *by adapting* UISlider *with object composition*

From the figure, we define a block called RGBValuesProvider that has a signature of CGFloat ^(CGFloat *red, CGFloat *green, CGFloat *blue). Each parameter in the signature is a pointer to a CGFloat value. It is just a type until we assign an actual block literal to it. A block literal should conform to the block signature and provide implementation that does something. In the foregoing diagram, we have a block literal RGBValuesProvider that contains the same old redSlider_, greenSlider_, and blueSlider_. When the block is called in an operation, it will retrieve values from the sliders and assign the values to the pointer values defined in the block signature to pass them back to a caller. Let's see how they could look in code (Listing 8–8).

Listing 8–8. *SetStrokeColorCommand.h*

```
#import <Foundation/Foundation.h>
#import "Command.h"

typedef void (^RGBValuesProvider)(CGFloat *red, CGFloat *green, CGFloat *blue);

@interface StrokeColorCommand : Command
{
  @private
  RGBValuesProvider RGBValuesProvider_;
}

@property (nonatomic, copy) RGBValuesProvider RGBValuesProvider;

- (void) execute;

@end
```

We typedef the RGBValuesProvider block in the header file of SetStrokeColorCommand, so we can refer the same block in other places just by its name as if it were an Objective-C object type. SetStrokeColorCommand has a private member variable of the block type we have just defined, and that variable is associated with a property that has the copy attribute turned on. We need to copy a block as it's assigned to a SetStrokeColorCommand object, as most of the time a block literal is defined and used within the scope of a method. When a method goes out of scope, so does the block literal. For more detailed discussion about memory management related to blocks, please see Apple's documentation regarding block programming.

SetStrokeColorCommand is a Command object, so it's got a definition of the execute method that it's inheriting from. We are going to see what it does in its execute method in Listing 8–9.

Listing 8–9. *StrokeColorCommand.m*

```
#import "StrokeColorCommand.h"
#import "CoordinatingController.h"
#import "CanvasViewController.h"

@implementation StrokeColorCommand

@synthesize RGBValuesProvider=RGBValuesProvider_;


- (void) execute
{
  CGFloat redValue = 0.0;
  CGFloat greenValue = 0.0;
  CGFloat blueValue - 0.0;

  // Retrieve RGB values from a block
  if (RGBValuesProvider_ != nil)
  {
    RGBValuesProvider_(&redValue, &greenValue, &blueValue);
  }

  // Create a color object based on the RGB values
  UIColor *color = [UIColor colorWithRed:redValue
                                   green:greenValue
                                    blue:blueValue
                                   alpha:1.0];

  // Assign it to the current canvasViewController
  CoordinatingController *coordinator = [CoordinatingController sharedInstance];
  CanvasViewController *controller = [coordinator canvasViewController];
  [controller setStrokeColor:color];
}

- (void) dealloc
{
  [RGBValuesProvider_ release];
  [super dealloc];
}

@end
```

When an instance of the SetStrokeColorCommand is being executed, it is trying to get values for the color components by calling its block RGBValuesProvider_(&redValue, &greenValue, &blueValue). A new UIColor object is created with the returned values, and then the SetStrokeColorCommand sets that color object to an instance of CanvasViewController.

So how are we going to use the SetStrokeColorCommand in code? Let's find out in the PaletteViewController's code in Listing 8–10.

Listing 8–10. *viewDidLoad Method in PaletteViewController.m*

```
- (void)viewDidLoad
{
  [super viewDidLoad];

  // initialize the RGB sliders with
  // a StrokeColorCommand
  StrokeColorCommand *colorCommand;

  // retrieve a reference to the command
  // being used for changing colors...

  // set each color component provider
  // to the color command
  [colorCommand setRGBValuesProvider: ^(CGFloat *red, CGFloat *green, CGFloat *blue)
    {
      *red = [redSlider_ value];
      *green = [greenSlider_ value];
      *blue = [blueSlider_ value];
    }];
}
```

We have defined a member variable for each color slider, redSlider_, greenSlider_, and blueSlider_. They are all connected and set up in the Interface Builder. Finally, we define a block literal that returns values from those sliders as color component values and assign the literal to the colorCommand object that is being referenced in those sliders.

It seems that we haven't defined any event handling method for our color sliders. But, in fact, we are going to reuse the one we have defined in the last section, as they are all the same CommandSlider type and used the same way. So we just need to simply hook up those color sliders to the same onCommandSliderValueChanged: method in the PaletteViewController in the Interface Builder. You can, of course, add another block for letting an adapter do an extra duty with the new color object, like we have in the delegation approach in the preceding section.

Done! What do you think about using a block as an adapter compared to a relatively more traditional way of using a protocol? A block allows you to define the definition of a block virtually anywhere and let a receiver (SetStrokeColorCommand) use it later. It doesn't affect any inheritance of the classes involved as well, because an adapter is defined within the viewDidLoad method. This approach offers much cleaner code and architecture compared to more formal protocol and classes involved. The adapter is more direct and casual, yet it doesn't lose the original flavor of the Adapter pattern.

Summary

This is a relatively long chapter. Now we understand how to use an Objective-C protocol to implement the Adapter pattern. Though the Delegation pattern itself can serve multiple intents other than just for the Adapter pattern, it was one of the major inspirations for the Adapter pattern in the first place! We have also explored how to take advantage of the power of Objective-C blocks to implement the Adapter pattern with a block serving as an adapter. Blocks are new to iOS development, but they are a powerful language feature. We should tap into them for more possibilities in the future.

The Adapter pattern is one of most commonly used design patterns. You can see it appear in code from time to time. The examples we used for illustrating the pattern are just a couple of them in the TouchPainter app. In real life, it's not uncommon to see design patterns used together for particular solutions, just like the examples of using an adapter with a command object. Try to check out a copy of the source code and see how many more adapters you can find in the app.

In the next chapter, we will see another pattern that helps decouple the abstraction interfaces from implementation so they can vary independently.

Chapter 9

Bridge

Let's say there is a manufacturer that produces TV sets. Each TV set has a remote control that allows the user to change channels and whatnot. A remote control is an interface to control a TV. If every TV model needs a unique remote control, then there will be an explosion of designs just for remote controls. Every remote control has some features that are common among different models of TVs, though, such as channel changing, volume, and power on/off. And each TV should be able to respond to these commands sent from a remote control with primitive command interfaces. We can separate remote control logic from actual TV models. So changes in TV models should not have any impact on the design of the remote controls. The same design of a remote control can be reused and extended without affecting other TV models either.

There is a similar situation in object-oriented software design. For example, let's say you wanted to design interfaces for displaying the same types of windows in different operating systems. Most of the time, a basic window is constructed of lines and rectangles. Operating system A draws lines and rectangles differently from operating system B. If we put each specific implementation for each type of window, the size of proliferating class hierarchy will be staggering. A solution for this problem is to separate the abstractions for different window types from each implementation for different operating systems. A design pattern that helps fix that design issue is called a Bridge pattern.

What Is the Bridge Pattern?

The goal of using the Bridge pattern is to separate an abstraction hierarchy from its implementation, so they can vary independently. An abstraction defines a high-level abstraction interface that will be used by clients. An implementation hierarchy defines a lower-level interface that will be used by the abstraction hierarchy. The bridge is formed when a reference of implementing class is encapsulated in an instance of abstraction, as illustrated in Figure 9–1.

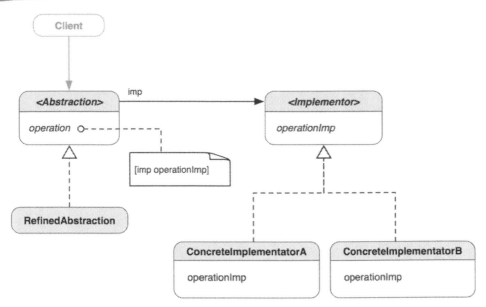

Figure 9–1. *A class diagram of the Bridge pattern*

Abstraction is the parent interface that defines the high-level abstraction interface used by clients. It has a reference to an instance of Implementor, which defines the interface for implementation classes. This interface doesn't need to correspond to Abstraction's interface; in fact, they can be quite different. The Implementor's interface provides primitive operations, and Abstraction's higher-level operations are based on these primitives. When a client sends an operation message to an instance of Abstraction, the method sends an operationImp message to imp. An actual underlying ConcreteImplementator (A or B) will respond to that and pick up the task.

So if you want to add new ConcreteImplementators to the system, all you need to do is to create a new implementing class for Implementor that responds to the operationImp message and perform any specific operations there. That won't affect anything on the Abstraction side, though. Likewise, if you want to make changes to the interface of Abstraction or create more refined Abstraction classes, you can do so without affecting the other side of the bridge as well.

THE BRIDGE PATTERN: Decouples an abstraction from its implementation so that the two can vary independently.*

* The original definition appeared in *Design Patterns*, by the "Gang of Four" (Addison-Wesley, 1994).

When Would You Use the Bridge Pattern?

You'd naturally think about using it in the following situations.

- You don't want a permanent binding between an abstraction and its implementation (so an implementation can be switched at runtime).

- Both the abstractions and their implementations should be extensible by subclassing independently.

- Changes in the implementation of an abstraction should have no impact on clients' code.

- If an extra subclass is needed for each implementation in order to refine the abstractions, then it indicates there is a need for splitting them into two parts.

- You want to share an implementation among multiple objects with different abstraction interfaces.

In the following sections, we are going to use an example of developing an emulator that can run different handheld game consoles from the 80s and 90s and illustrate how to use the Bridge pattern to solve some related design problems.

Creating a Virtual Emulator for iOS

Back in the days when Game Boy and Game Gear were so popular, it was very common to see a lot of kids holding one in their hands and playing their favorite games. Those kids have grown up, and Game Boy and Game Gear became nostalgia for them. There are a lot of people who have made different emulators that run the original Game Boy and Game Gear games on a desktop computer, as well as iOS devices with totally different hardware architectures in order to bring their long lost childhood memory back.

Without getting into details, we are going to discuss how to use the Bridge pattern to build an emulator that can support multiple portable gaming platforms like Game Boy and Game Gear (or possibly others).

There are two major components in each platform, the operating system and the control panel as a means of input from the user. Both Game Boy and Game Gear have up, down, left, and right buttons on the left-hand side of the control panel, as well as buttons A and B as action buttons on the right-hand side and a Start button in the middle. However, Game Boy has a Select button that is right next to the Start button, and Game Gear doesn't have that button at all. Despite the slight differences in the button layout and the number of buttons, the structure and the functionality of the control panel are pretty much common across different platforms.

When we design the emulator, besides the actual emulator (the OS that runs games for its platform), we also need to think about a virtual controller as the user input device for it. That virtual controller can most probably be simulated on the iOS with some sort of UI elements for the platform. If we create a specific controller for each concrete emulator, then there would be a lot of redundancy and a possible explosion of subclasses of virtual controllers. What's more, it may require different subclasses for different types of virtual input methods. For example, instead of using arrow buttons to simulate up, down, left, and right instructions, the virtual controller can get input from the accelerometer with changes in acceleration in different directions. The problem is we need to separate both a virtual controller and an emulator so they can vary independently without affecting each other's code. In other words, a group of emulators will have their own class hierarchy, while a group of virtual controllers will have their own separately. Both hierarchies have different interfaces, but they are connected with a "bridge" formed between the high-level abstract classes in both hierarchies with an object composition relationship. A static structure of the design is illustrated in Figure 9–2.

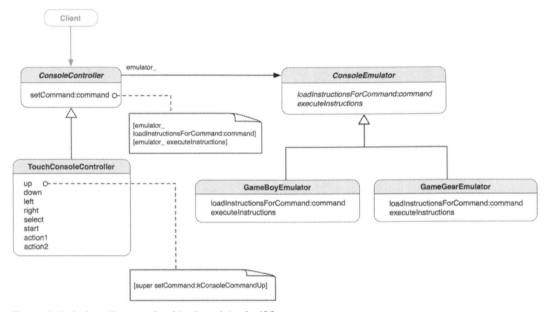

Figure 9–2. *A class diagram of a virtual emulator for iOS*

`ConsoleController` and `ConsoleEmulator` are abstract classes for virtual controllers and emulators respectively. Both classes have different interfaces. The only way to connect them is by encapsulating a reference to an instance of `ConsoleEmulator` in `ConsoleController`. So an instance of `ConsoleController` can use an instance of `ConsoleEmulator` at an abstract level. This forms a bridge between two different classes, `ConsoleController` and `ConsoleEmulator`. `ConsoleEmulator` has defined interfaces for any of its subclasses to handle low-level instructions for a particular console's OS. `ConsoleController` has a relatively low-level method to send basic command types across the bridge. The `setCommand:command` method of the `ConsoleController` takes a parameter of a predefined command type and passes it with a message, `loadInstructionsForCommand:command`, to an embedded `ConsoleEmulator` reference. And finally it sends an `executeInstructions` message to the same reference to execute any loaded instructions in the emulator. A visual representation of connecting two different class hierarchies is shown in Figure 9–3.

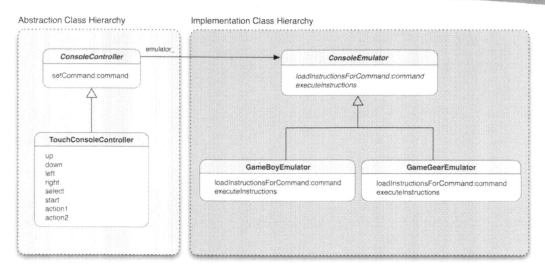

Figure 9–3. *The abstraction class hierarchy will not be affected by changes in the implementation class hierarchy or vice versa.*

The `ConsoleController` class hierarchy is representing a form of "abstraction" to any "implementation" in the `ConsoleEmulator` class hierarchy. The Abstraction class hierarchy provides a layer of abstraction to form a virtual controller layer over any compatible `ConsoleEmulator`. A concrete `ConsoleController` can talk only to an emulator on the other side of the bridge through the low-level `setCommand:` method defined in the parent `ConsoleController` class. The method is not meant to be overridden by subclasses in this configuration, as this is an interface that allows any communication between the parent and refined controllers to take place. If there are changes on the emulator side, nothing will affect any controller on the left and vice versa.

Sounds very interesting, huh? Let's see some code. First off, we need to define some commands that should be supported by any emulator, as in Listing 9–1.

Listing 9–1. *ConsoleCommands.h*

```
typedef enum
{
  kConsoleCommandUp,
  kConsoleCommandDown,
  kConsoleCommandLeft,
  kConsoleCommandRight,
  kConsoleCommandSelect,
  kConsoleCommandStart,
  kConsoleCommandAction1,
  kConsoleCommandAction2
} ConsoleCommand;
```

We have up, down, left, right, select, start, action 1, and action 2 as our generic commands defined as a group of `enum`. If we want to expand the command list in the future to support more sophisticated emulators, we can do so without breaking any design on both sides. Let's look at the definition of abstract `ConsoleEmulator` in Listing 9–2.

Listing 9–2. *ConsoleEmulator.h*

```
#import "ConsoleCommands.h"

@interface ConsoleEmulator : NSObject
{

}

- (void) loadInstructionsForCommand:(ConsoleCommand) command;
- (void) executeInstructions;

// other behaviors and properties.

@end
```

Our abstract `ConsoleEmulator` has two basic methods that we have briefly discussed previously, `loadInstructionsForCommand:` and `executeInstructions`. `loadInstructionsForCommand:` should load any specific OS instructions in an internal data structure based on the command type that we have defined in Listing 9–1. `executeInstructions` will execute any loaded instructions in the data structure. OS instructions and how to execute them are platform-specific, so concrete emulators should override these methods as in Listings 9–3 and 9–4.

Listing 9–3. *GameBoyEmulator.h*

```
#import "ConsoleEmulator.h"

@interface GameBoyEmulator : ConsoleEmulator
{

}

// overridden behaviors from the abstract class
- (void) loadInstructionsForCommand:(ConsoleCommand) command;
- (void) executeInstructions;

// other behaviors and properties.

@end
```

Both `GameBoyEmulator` and `GameGearEmulator` are subclasses of `ConsoleEmulator`. They override the abstract methods to provide specific behaviors for their platforms.

Listing 9–4. *GameGearEmulator.h*

```
#import "ConsoleEmulator.h"

@interface GameGearEmulator : ConsoleEmulator
{

}

// overridden behaviors from the abstract class
- (void) loadInstructionsForCommand:(ConsoleCommand) command;
- (void) executeInstructions;

// other behaviors and properties.

@end
```

Now we have the emulator hierarchy defined completely. On the virtual controller side of the design, ConsoleController is our starting point for the whole virtual controller class hierarchy. It keeps an internal reference to an instance of ConsoleEmulator as emulator_. It also defines a setCommand:command method that will be used by its subclasses to input a command with a predefined command type. We will get to its details in just a little bit. Its class declaration is shown in Listing 9–5.

Listing 9–5. *ConsoleController.h*

```
#import "ConsoleEmulator.h"
#import "ConsoleCommands.h"

@interface ConsoleController : NSObject
{
  @private
  ConsoleEmulator *emulator_;
}

@property (nonatomic, retain) ConsoleEmulator *emulator;

- (void) setCommand:(ConsoleCommand) command;

// other behaviors and properties

@end
```

setCommand: just simply sends loadInstructionsForCommand:command and executeInstructions messages to the emulator_ reference to finish the instruction execution process, as in Listing 9–6.

Listing 9–6. *ConsoleController.m*

```
#import "ConsoleController.h"


@implementation ConsoleController

@synthesize emulator=emulator_;

- (void) setCommand:(ConsoleCommand) command
{
  [emulator_ loadInstructionsForCommand:command];
  [emulator_ executeInstructions];
}

@end
```

The basic bridge for both the virtual controller and emulator is complete. Now we are ready to get our first virtual controller, called TouchConsoleController, to form an interface between the multi-touch screen and a concrete emulator hidden from the view. It's got some basic method declarations that reflect our predefined command types in Listing 9–1. Its class declaration is shown in Listing 9–7.

Listing 9–7. *TouchConsoleController.h*

```
#import "ConsoleController.h"

@interface TouchConsoleController : ConsoleController
{

}

- (void) up;
- (void) down;
- (void) left;
- (void) right;
- (void) select;
- (void) start;
- (void) action1;
- (void) action2;

@end
```

The methods of the TouchConsoleController are self-explanatory. Each of them simply sends a [super setCommand:ConsoleCommand] message to super with an appropriate ConsoleCommand value, as in Listing 9–8.

Listing 9–8. *TouchConsoleController.m*

```
#import "TouchConsoleController.h"
#import "ConsoleEmulator.h"


@implementation TouchConsoleController

- (void) up
{
  [super setCommand:ConsoleCommandUp];
}

- (void) down
{
  [super setCommand:kConsoleCommandDown];
}

- (void) left
{
  [super setCommand:kConsoleCommandLeft];
}

- (void) right
{
  [super setCommand:kConsoleCommandRight];
}

- (void) select
{
  [super setCommand:kConsoleCommandSelect];
}

- (void) start
```

```
{
  [super setCommand:kConsoleCommandStart];
}

- (void) action1
{
  [super setCommand:kConsoleCommandAction1];
}

- (void) action2
{
  [super setCommand:kConsoleCommandAction2];
}

@end
```

We want all the methods to use the same `setCommand:` implementation defined in the parent class by sending the message to `super` instead of `self` to avoid confusion. `self` and `super` are symbolically the same here, as the subclass doesn't override the `setCommand:` method to provide its own bridge. We still use `super` to emphasize the architecture, though. Then a forwarded `ConsoleCommand` value will be used for loading appropriate OS instructions and executing them in a concrete emulator across the bridge.

With the Bridge pattern, we can see the power of object composition. The bridge we have implemented for the `ConsoleEmulator` cannot possibly be done with straight inheritance. This is also one of the reasons we favor object composition over inheritance.

Summary

We have discussed how to use the Bridge pattern to implement an emulator app that runs on iOS. Without delving into the bells and whistles of making a truly working emulator, we focused on some design issues that the Bridge pattern can help with. So next time, when you are facing a dilemma of "how to separate abstraction from implementation yet they are still connected," you would intuitively think of the Bridge pattern. Then you can look through the sample code again and see how it can fit to yours.

The Bridge pattern is a way to adapt an interface to a different one. In the next chapter, we are going to see a different pattern that can be used not just to put different interfaces together, but also to simplify them as a single access point, like the façade of a building.

Chapter 10

Façade

You don't feel you want to drive today, so you call up a taxicab. You don't really care what the make or model of the cab is as long as it can take you to the destination you want to go to. The first thing you'd say to the cab driver is "Take me to X," where X is the place where you wanted to go. Then the cab driver begins with a sequence of actions to "execute" the "command" (releases the brakes, changes gears, presses the accelerator, etc.). The cab driver abstracts away all the bells and whistles of the underlying complexity of operating a car. He decouples you from the originally complicated interfaces to operate the vehicle by offering the driving service (a simplified interface). The interface between the cab driver and you is just a simple "Take me to X" command. And that command is not tied to any specific make/model of a vehicle, either.

In many legacy object-oriented applications, there might be a lot of classes scattered around the system with different functionalities. To use them for a particular function, you need to know all the bits and pieces in order to use them in a single group of algorithms. If some of them can be logically grouped into a simplified interface, it can make them easier to use. A way to provide a unified interface to a set of different interfaces in a subsystem is called the Façade pattern.

We are going to discuss what the Façade pattern is and how to implement the pattern in Objective-C.

What Is the Façade Pattern?

The Façade pattern helps provide a unified interface to a set of different interfaces in a subsystem. Façade defines a higher-level interface that makes the subsystem easier to use by reducing complexity and hiding the communication and dependencies among subsystems.

Let's say there is a cluster of different classes within this subsystem, as shown in Figure 10–1. Some of them are dependent on each other. It makes it difficult for clients to use the classes in the subsystem, as they need to know each one of them. Sometimes it could be unnecessarily cumbersome if the clients just need their default behavior without customizing them. Façade acts as a gateway for the whole subsystem. It provides a simplified interface for clients that need somewhat default behavior without much customizability on the subsystem classes. A façade is like the taxicab driver in the previous example. Only clients that need more customized behavior from some of the subsystem classes will look beyond the façade. A taxicab scenario can provide a driving service with "default" behavior on the road. But if you want to have a "customized" trip (e.g., taking a few pit stops or speeding on highways, etc.), then you'd be better off driving by yourself.

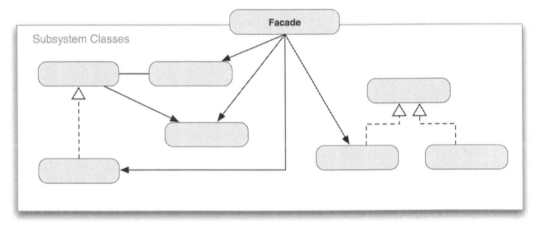

Figure 10-1. *A sample structural diagram of a Façade implementation*

FAÇADE PATTERN: Provides a unified interface to a set of interfaces in a system. Façade defines a higher-level interface that makes the subsystem easier to use.*

* The original definition appeared in *Design Patterns*, by the "Gang of Four" (Addison-Wesley, 1994).

When Would You Use the Façade Pattern?

There are three common situations in which you would consider using this pattern:

- Your subsystem is getting complex. A lot of classes are evolved from applying patterns. You can use a façade to provide a simpler interface for the subsystem classes.

- You can use façades to layer your subsystems. Each subsystem level has a façade as an entry point. You can simplify their dependencies by making them communicate through their façades.

In the coming sections, we are going to implement the Façade pattern with the taxicab driver example to illustrate the basic concepts. Also, later on, we will use the pattern to simplify the scribble saving processes of the TouchPainter app.

Providing a Simplified Interface to a Set of Interfaces in the Subsystem

Back to the taxicab example in the introduction of this chapter—we have a passenger and a taxicab that provides a simplified interface to a set of complex interfaces of driving a cab. If we put them in a class diagram, then they'd look something like Figure 10–2.

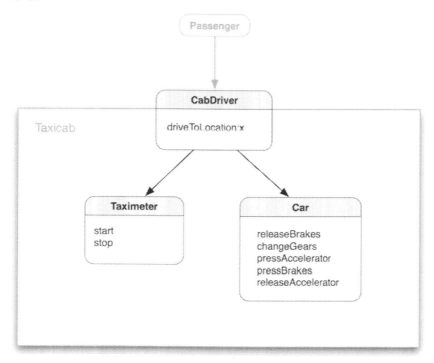

Figure 10–2. *A class diagram for the taxicab example—the* CabDriver *class is a façade of the Taxicab subsystem.*

You can see the whole taxicab service as a closed system that includes a cab driver, a car, and a taximeter. The only way you can interface with the system is to go through the interface defined in CabDriver—that's driveToLocation:x. Once you send the cab driver a message of driveToLocation:x, then CabDriver will take it from there. There are two subsystems that he or she needs to operate with, Taximeter and Car. CabDriver will first set off the Taximeter to get it ticking, and then with the Car he or she will releaseBrakes, changeGears, and pressAccelerator to start moving it. Until you've arrived at location x, the CabDriver will releaseAccelerator, pressBrakes, and stop the Taximeter to complete the trip. Everything happens within a simple driveToLocation:x command to the CabDriver. No matter how complex those two internal subsystems are, they are hidden from the view of you (or a passenger). So the CabDriver is providing a simplified interface for other complex interfaces within the subsystem of the cab. The

CabDriver is standing in between a passenger and the complex system like a façade. Let's take a look at Listing 10–1 and see what they look like in code.

Listing 10–1. *Car.h*

```
@interface Car : NSObject
{

}

// ...

- (void) releaseBrakes;
- (void) changeGears;
- (void) pressAccelerator;
- (void) pressBrakes;
- (void) releaseAccelerator;

// ...

@end
```

In Listing 10–1, Car defines several methods for operating its other internal objects, things like releaseBrakes, changeGears, pressAccelerator, pressBrakes, and releaseAccelerator. In order for a client to use Car's internal objects, it needs to know all the bells and whistles about how to use those methods to operate it properly. Besides Car, let's also take a look at the code for Taximeter in Listing 10–2.

Listing 10–2. *Taximeter.h*

```
@interface Taximeter : NSObject
{

}

- (void) start;
- (void) stop;

@end
```

Although a Taximeter is a complex system by itself, it provides two methods to let clients operate on its objects. The start and stop methods simply tell the Taximeter to either start or stop. We are not getting into the details of the Taximeter. So far, there are two complex subsystems sitting in the taxicab service system. We need a CabDriver to serve as a façade to simplify the interfaces. Its code snippets are in Listing 10–3.

Listing 10–3. *CabDriver.h*

```
#import "Car.h"
#import "Taximeter.h"

@interface CabDriver : NSObject
{

}

- (void) driveToLocation:(CGPoint) x;

@end
```

The CabDriver's façade method defines how simple clients can use the whole taxicab service system. As we have mentioned before, a client just needs to call driveToLocation:x, where x is the destination a client wants to go to, and then the rest of the operation will take place within the message call. The client doesn't need to know all the bits and pieces of what's going on under the hood. Let's see what the method actually does in Listing 10–4.

Listing 10–4. *CabDriver.m*

```objc
#import "CabDriver.h"


@implementation CabDriver

- (void) driveToLocation:(CGPoint) x
{
  // ...

  // set off the taximeter
  Taximeter *meter = [[Taximeter alloc] init];
  [meter start];

  // operate the vehicle
  // until location x is reached
  Car *car = [[Car alloc] init];
  [car releaseBrakes];
  [car changeGears];
  [car pressAccelerator];

  // ...

  // when it's reached location x
  // then stop the car and taximeter
  [car releaseAccelerator];
  [car pressBrakes];
  [meter stop];

  // ...
}

@end
```

Inside the driveToLocation: method, it will first start an object of Taximeter so it can start ticking from that moment. Then it will move to an object of Car and start operating on it. It sends a releaseBrakes message to the Car object to release the brakes, then changeGears, and finally pressAccelerator to make it start moving. When we arrive at the destination x, it will tell the Car to releaseAccelerator, then pressBrakes, and finally tell the Taximeter object to stop ticking. Then the service is completed.

It doesn't look complicated, does it? With our CabDriver in place as a façade, we can simplify the whole service system. Are you ready to see how we can put a façade in a real app, our TouchPainter app? Let's move on to the next section.

Using the Façade Pattern in the TouchPainter App

In the original design of the TouchPainter app described in Chapter 2, one of the requirements is saving what is drawn on the CanvasView as a form of Scribble and putting that data structure in the file system. An archive of a scribble can be retrieved later and resurrected to a real Scribble object back to the state right before it's saved. That operation involves different objects put together to make the process happen. Based on the original design, part of the saving process is involved with a data structure that contains the current state of the strokes onscreen as well as a screenshot of it that will be used as a thumbnail later for browsing. Another part of the process is to use an instance of NSFileManager to actually save the data structure in the file system. The data structure is created as a memento (see the Memento pattern, Chapter 23) by a Scribble object. A memento object should be saved independently from a corresponding thumbnail image. The whole process involves a lot of steps, operations, and different objects. Without simplifying the interfaces, it would easily go out of control, especially when you need to reuse the same operations later in other areas of the application. So we need a ScribbleManager to handle all the complex operations under the hood with some simplified interfaces. A class diagram illustrates their relationships in Figure 10–3.

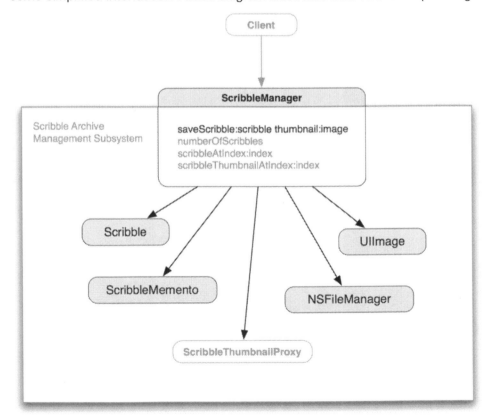

Figure 10–3. *A class diagram of* ScribbleManager *and other classes in its subsystem*

There are a few public interfaces in ScribbleManager, but we will discuss just the saveScribble:scribble thumbnail:image method. You can check out a copy of the source code on the book's web site and take a look at the actual implementation of ScribbleManager. The general idea of ScribbleManager is to simplify any operation related to saving and restoring Scribble objects. A Scribble is a model (in the sense of Model-View-Controller) that contains an internal data structure for all the current strokes drawn on the CanvasView by the user. An instance of Scribble is sitting inside in an instance of CanvasViewController (see the Observer pattern, Chapter 12) as part of its Model-View-Controller structure.

When a request is initiated to save the current Scribble (what's on the CanvasView), a reference to the current Scribble object as well as a screenshot of the scribble are passed to the saveScribble:scribble thumbnail:image method of a ScribbleManager object as part of a message. Code snippets for the ScribbleManager are shown in Listings 10–5 and 10–6.

Listing 10–5. *ScribbleManager.h*

```
#import <Foundation/Foundation.h>
#import "Scribble.h"
#import "ScribbleThumbnail.h"
#import "ScribbleThumbnailProxy.h"

@interface ScribbleManager : NSObject
{

}

- (void) saveScribble:(Scribble*)scribble thumbnail:(UIImage*)image;
- (NSInteger) numberOfScribbles;
- (Scribble*) scribbleAtIndex:(NSInteger)index;
- (ScribbleThumbnail*) scribbleThumbnailAtIndex:(NSInteger)index;

@end
```

Listing 10–6. *The Definition of the* saveScribble: *Method in* ScribbleManager.m

```
- (void) saveScribble:(Scribble*)scribble thumbnail:(UIImage*)image
{
  // get a new index for the new scribble data and its thumbnail
  NSInteger newIndex = [self numberOfScribbles] + 1;

  // use the index as part of the name for each of them
  NSString *scribbleDataName = [NSString stringWithFormat:@"data_%d", newIndex];
  NSString *scribbleThumbnailName = [NSString stringWithFormat:@"thumbnail_%d.png",
                                                             newIndex];

  // get a memento from the scribble
  // then save the memento in the file system
  ScribbleMemento *scribbleMemento = [scribble scribbleMemento];
  NSData *mementoData = [scribbleMemento data];
  NSString *mementoPath = [[self scribbleDataPath]
                                 stringByAppendingPathComponent:scribbleDataName];
  [mementoData writeToFile:mementoPath atomically:YES];

  // save the thumbnail directly in
```

```
  // the file system
  NSData *imageData = [NSData dataWithData:UIImagePNGRepresentation(image)];
  NSString *imagePath = [[self scribbleThumbnailPath]
                                stringByAppendingPathComponent:scribbleThumbnailName];
  [imageData writeToFile:imagePath atomically:YES];
}
```

In the saveScribble:scribble thumbnail:image method, it runs the whole show of saving a scribble and its screenshot as an image in the file system. It first creates paths in the file system for both the scribble data and screenshot image. Then it sends a memento message to scribble for an instance of ScribbleMemento to save the data with (see the Memento pattern, Chapter 23). The ScribbleMemento reference contains the current state of scribble. Only a Scribble object will be able to retrieve what's stored inside a ScribbleMemento object. Then it will ask the ScribbleMemento object to create an instance of NSData based on its internal structure. Once a complete path for the newly returned data is constructed, then ScribbleManager will go ahead and save that data object in the file system by sending a writeToFile:mementoPath message to the ScribbleMemento object.

Summary

When your application is getting larger and more complex, more and more small classes are evolved from the design and applying patterns to it. If there is not a simplified way to use those classes, your client code will end up getting larger and harder to understand. What's more, maintaining them will just be a chore. A façade can help provide a much cleaner way to use those classes in a subsystem. It could just be a simple method defined in a façade that handles the default behavior of the subsystem classes, instead of using them individually.

In this part of the book, we have covered design patterns that primarily focus on adapting different interfaces with simpler or different ones. Design patterns in the next part are used for dealing with decoupling many objects that work together with common or different interfaces.

Decoupling of Objects

Chapter 11

Mediator

What's going to happen if pilots are fighting for a chance to either take off or land and there is no traffic control at the airport? Without centralized air traffic control, pilots in the air or on the ground need to know each other's intent and position. It's dangerous and complicated.

Centralized traffic control makes sure every plane is under the radar with its flight information updated on the screen every now and then. So an air traffic controller can know exactly what planes are currently in the sky within the controlled airspace. Each pilot needs to ask the control center for permissions to fly, land, and take off. Even though pilots still need to have a pretty good idea about what other planes are in the traffic, it's not as critical as flying without centralized air control at all. The air traffic control center plays an important mediating role to make sure no planes will crash in mid-air due to disorganization or miscommunication.

In object-oriented software, we have seen a lot of situations like that in a design. A typical example is UI elements in an application. There could be a dialog box that contains a label, a list box, a text field, and some other input boxes. When an item in the list box is selected, then the label will be updated with the selected value from the list box. Or when the text field has a new input value from the user, the list box needs to be added with the new value to its list. Things can get wild when more UI elements are involved in that kind of crisscrossing relationship. Each element needs to know and operate each other. Eventually, it will grow to the point where they are hard reuse and maintain. They need a traffic controller to manage all the UI traffic. The centralized role that organizes interactions between different UI elements within the same context is called a mediator. A design pattern that is elaborated from this concept is called the Mediator pattern.

In this chapter, we are going discuss what the Mediator pattern is about and use the TouchPainter example to illustrate how to use the pattern to manage view transitions.

What Is the Mediator Pattern?

Object-oriented design encourages the distribution of behavior among different objects. Such distribution may result in interconnections among objects. In the worst-case scenario, each object ends up knowing and operating each other.

Even though behavior gets distributed among different objects that enhance reusability, increased interconnections reduce the benefit again. Increased interconnections make an object difficult or impossible to work without dependency of others. The overall application's behavior can be difficult to change in any significant way as the behavior is distributed among many objects. Then you may end up creating more and more subclasses to support any new behavior of the application.

The Mediator pattern is used to define a centralized place where interactions among objects can be handled in one mediator object. Other objects don't need to interact with each other directly, so it reduces dependency among them.

> **THE MEDIATOR PATTERN:** Defines an object that encapsulates how a set of objects interacts. Mediator promotes loose coupling by keeping objects from referring to each other explicitly, and it lets you vary their interaction independently.*
>
> * The original definition appeared in *Design Patterns*, by the *"Gang of Four"* (Addison-Wesley, 1994).

Figure 11–1 shows a class diagram that depicts relationships of fictitious classes involved in the pattern.

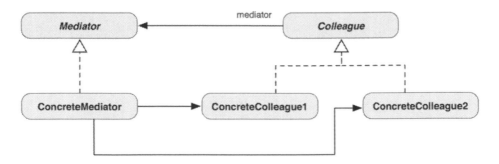

Figure 11–1. *A class diagram of the Mediator pattern*

The abstract Mediator defines generic behavior for Colleagues to interact with each other. Typical colleagues are objects that communicate with each other in well-defined ways, and also they are tightly dependent on each other. A ConcreteMediator has defined more specific behavior for ConcreteColleagues; so one can subclass the Mediator with different Colleague interaction algorithms for the same or different Colleague types. Sometimes an abstract Mediator can be omitted if only one mediator is required for an application.

An instance of `Colleague` has a reference to an instance of `Mediator`, while an instance of `Mediator` knows *every* object that is involved in the organization. The point is now every object knows only the `Mediator` but not each other. A possible object structure of the Mediator pattern at runtime is illustrated in Figure 11–2.

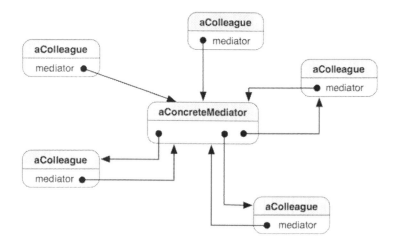

Figure 11–2. *An object diagram shows an object structure of the Mediator pattern at runtime.*

When Would You Use the Mediator Pattern?

You would naturally think about using the pattern when

- A set of objects are interdependent on each other and difficult to understand due to well-defined but complex interaction among them.

- It is difficult to reuse an object because it refers to and communicates with many other objects.

- A logic or behavior that is distributed among several classes should be customizable without a lot of subclassing.

Managing View Transition in the TouchPainter App

The Mediator pattern is not only good for centralizing crisscrossing relationships among different objects but also suitable for organizing view transition between two different views. It's quite common to see iOS applications that manage view transitions by adding one view on another. So the first view needs to know and have a reference to the second view, then the third view, and so on.

There are different ways to do view transition. We are going to discuss three of them. One of the most common ways is to add the view from the other view controller to the view of the current view controller as a subview. If you don't remove the last one that you have added before you add another one, the whole stack of subviews will be hard to manage. Eventually, the whole stack will be stuffed with many unused subviews. I wouldn't recommend it for view transitioning in general, especially if you have many views in your app. This approach is illustrated in Figure 11–3.

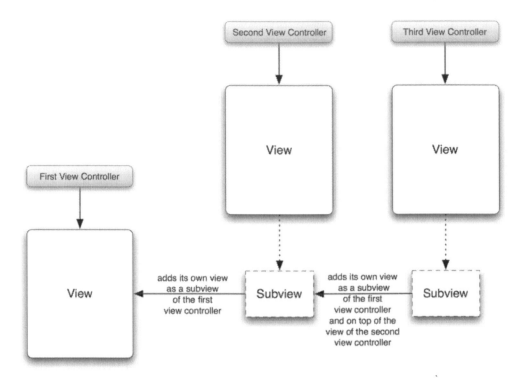

Figure 11–3. *Managing different views in an application by adding subviews of different view controllers to the view of the first view controller*

Another type of view transitioning is by using an instance of UINavigationController with a navigation bar located at the top portion of a view. This approach is more elegant than the previous approach. An instance of UINavigationController is initialized with a root controller that will provide its view to the UINavigationController as the first view. When there is another view that needs to be transitioned to, the owner of the view will push its controller to the UINavigationController. Then the UINavigationController will take care of all the bells and whistles of view changing, including transition effects and directions that the new view will move in on the screen. The UINavigationController manages an internal view controller stack. A view controller that is currently on top of the stack will be displayed on the screen. A view that "goes back" to the previous view will "pop" its controller out of the stack, and the one below will be shown instead. The idea is illustrated in Figure 11–4.

This view navigation method may be just good enough for certain apps but not the others, as it looks pretty "standard" and the framework provides very limited view transition effects. Also sometimes you need more screen real estate for your app and can't afford losing much of it for the navigation bar.

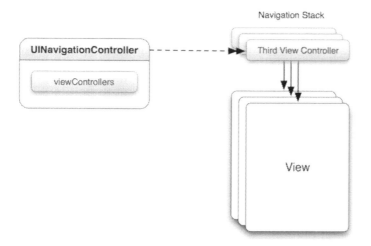

Figure 11–4. *Managing different views by pushing different view controllers to a view controller stack of a* UINavigationController

The last but not least approach is to present a modal view controller one at a time. The view transition is managed by using view controllers directly without messing with individual views from other view controllers. In my opinion, it's one of the recommended methods to do view transition if you don't need anything fancy and don't want a navigation bar to take up some screen real estate.

The flow is very clean; it presents one view controller at a time and goes from one view controller to another. The idea of this approach is illustrated in Figure 11–5.

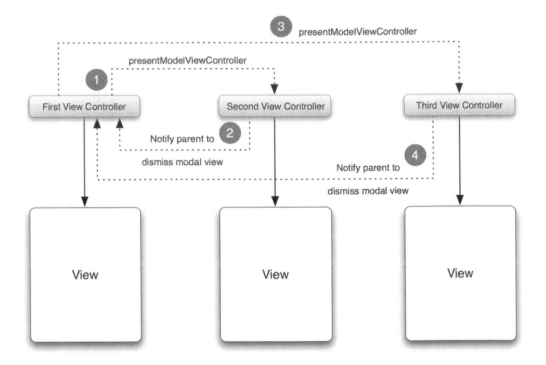

Figure 11–5. *Perform view changing by asking the first view controller to present a modal view with another view controller.*

So far we have discussed some of the view transitioning methods available in the Cocoa Touch framework. They are from something that wouldn't be easy to manage to something that has a very clean flow. No matter which approach you prefer, more or less each of the view controllers needs to know, interconnect, and interact with each other to complete the view transition process. If we need to change the method of view transition or just simply to reuse the view controllers in the future, there would be a lot of work involved to make code changes and whatnot. It's hard to maintain and error-prone.

The Troubles of Modifying the Transition Logic

A lot of times we need to add new views or modify views/view controllers to an existing UI flow. In the previous examples, the other view controllers are tightly coupled with their preceding view controllers. Let's ask one of the fundamental questions about view management: what if we need to extend the view flow *before* the first one? Since all the other view controllers need to know who the first view controller should be, they will all need to be compiled with code changes to reflect the new view controller that *owns* the flow. If your app has just a couple of view controllers, that shouldn't be that bad. It'd be a nightmare to change all that if your app has 10, 20, or even more views. Another fundamental question is: what if we need to change the navigation mechanism for the main flow? Styles of view changes depend on *how* the views are managed in a flow. If a

UINavigationController manages the flow, then the flow will be followed with the rules set by UINavigationController with a navigation bar and limited view transition effects. If the view flow is by adding other views to the first one as subviews, then there could be a few more options of transition effects from UIView than UINavigationController.

No matter which route we take and whether we change it later, we most likely need to change every view controller for *every* flow change. All the views involved the transition are tightly coupled.

An imaginary scenario of view changes among view controllers with one of the conventional approaches in the TouchPainter app is shown in Figure 11–6.

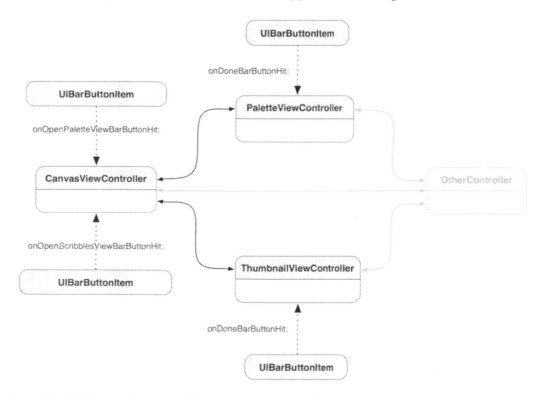

Figure 11–6. *A diagram shows a possible view change relationship among different view controllers.*

Each of the view controllers has its own buttons that trigger the flow change when the user hits one of them. The button's controller will handle any view changes right off the bat. For example, when an instance of CanvasViewController receives an event from an instance of UIBarButtonItem that has a tag that identifies it is for activating the PaletteViewController's view, CanvasViewController will put an instance of PaletteViewController in a context for a view transition. The transition could be a modal view presentation or coordinated with an instance of UINavigationController. When the user is done with the view of PaletteViewController, the user will hit its Done button (UIBarButtonItem) to "go back." In the case of modal view presentation, the instance of PaletteViewController needs to get a reference to the instance of

CanvasViewController to dismiss itself (the CanvasViewController is the parent of the modal presentation). For the user to open the ThumbnailViewController's view, it'll be pretty much the same situation.

Imagine we want to add more view controllers to the flow; it would make it look more complicated and harder to maintain. A better solution is to put the flow logic in a centralized object. A complete UI flow can be monitored in one place and can be more understandable.

Centralizing the Flow of the UI Traffic

If we have some sort of centralized role that organizes all UI flow traffic, our lives could be a lot easier as far as code reusability and maintainability go. That role should be like a traffic cop who coordinates traffic coming from different directions in a crossroad back in the day. Changing the traffic pattern of a crossroad requires new policies for only the traffic cop, not the cars on the road. A traffic cop approach provides a loosely coupled solution for managing different views.

We need some sort of application coordinator as a mediator to orchestrate the UI flow. Its role is only to coordinate the UI flow traffic and nothing else. The mediator should know all view controllers involved in the flow. It's like a director in a movie. The director should know all characters involved in the movie as well as any scene changes. If there are any last-minute changes in the movie, the director should be the first person that knows them and should organize all the resources involved for the changes. So our mediator is the boss of scene changes (view transitions).

We are going to introduce a new controller to act as the traffic cop for view transitions. We call it CoordinatingController. An instance of CoordinatingController maintains the logic of the UI flow between UI components and view controllers. A view transition will not happen without any user interaction involved. The user will hit a button to trigger a view transition request, and the CoordinatingController fulfills the request. The CoordinatingController will handle a view transition based on the button's tag. A list of valid tags defined as enum that can be used for different view activation is shown in Listing 11–1.

Listing 11–1. *An Enum That Is Defined for Various Tags That Identify Toolbar Buttons*

```
typedef enum
{
  kButtonTagDone,
  kButtonTagOpenPaletteView,
  kButtonTagOpenThumbnailView
} ButtonTag;
```

For example, when the tag of a toolbar button is set to kButtonTagOpenPaletteView (an integer value of 1), it can activate the Palette View in CoordinatingController and so on. We will get to the details in a little bit.

In our TouchPainter example, the CanvasViewController's view is the default view when the user starts the app. The controller has a toolbar button that opens the Palette View (PaletteViewController's view); the toolbar button is an instance of UIBarButtonItem with its tag set to kButtonTagOpenPaletteView (an integer value of 1). When the user hits the toolbar button, it directly sends an action message of requestViewChangeByObject: to an instance of CoordinatingController. It then first checks what object has made the request. If the object is an instance of UIBarButtonItem, then it checks its tag and sees what view it can activate. Then CoordinatingController will activate the appropriate view controller and make a transition to it. It's the same deal for opening the ThumbnailViewController's view if the button's tag is kButtonTagOpenThumbnailView. As for the Done button on the PaletteViewController, the Done button has its tag set to kButtonTagDone (an integer value of 0). When the DoneBarButton is hit, then it sends the same message to the CoordinatingController. It does the same tag check and realizes that it should dismiss the current view to go back to the main CanvasViewController's view. Their new relationships with the new CoordinatingController are illustrated in Figure 11-7.

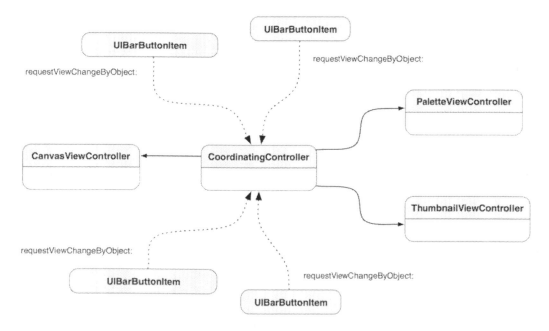

Figure 11-7. *A diagram shows* CoordinatingController *as a mediator to centralize the view transition logic.*

Now we have a pretty good idea of how things are connected. We are ready to implement them. Before we do anything, we first need to lay out a class diagram for them to make sure we know what we are doing. A class diagram for our Mediator implementation for the TouchPainter app is shown in Figure 11-8.

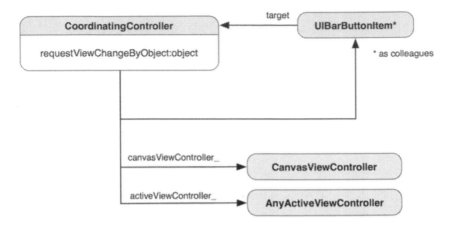

Figure 11–8. *A class diagram of* `CoordinatingController` *and other coordinated view controllers*

Our class diagram is slightly different from the original flavor of the Mediator pattern. First of all, we didn't put an abstract mediator but a concrete `CoordinatingController` as the only mediator for other participating objects to use. Secondly, we didn't use any high-level abstract Colleague type for other concrete Colleagues to perform anything. We only need the `UIBarButtonItem` type to define our Colleagues, as toolbar buttons on the views are the key elements for triggering requests for view changes. An instance of our custom `UIBarButtonItem` class will keep a reference to an instance of `CoordinatingController` as a target. When a click event occurs, it will send a message to the `CoordinatingController` as follows:

```
[target requestViewChangeByObject:self]
```

The button itself needs to know nothing more than just that, and the `CoordinatingController` will take it from there and do the view-changing magic behind the curtain.

Let's move forward to implement our `CoordinatingController` in Listing 11–2.

Listing 11–2: *CoordinatingController.h*

```
#import "CanvasViewController.h"
#import "PaletteViewController.h"
#import "ThumbnailViewController.h"


@interface CoordinatingController : NSObject
{
@private
  CanvasViewController *canvasViewController_;
  UIViewController *activeViewController_;
}

@property (nonatomic, readonly) UIViewController *activeViewController;
@property (nonatomic, readonly) CanvasViewController *canvasViewController;

+ (CoordinatingController *) sharedInstance;
```

```
- (IBAction) requestViewChangeByObject:(id)object;
```

```
@end
```

CoordinatingController needs to keep a reference only to the main view controller (CanvasViewController), so it can be returned to other requesting objects later from the canvasViewController property. Other view controllers that are used by CoordinatingController will be returned from the activeViewController property if it is actively being displayed on the screen. All the properties are readonly, as they are not supposed to be changed by some other objects at runtime. The main guts of the CoordinatingController are the (IBAction) requestViewChangeByObject:(id)object method. You may wonder why we declared IBAction as its return type. It is because we can use the CoordinatingController to link up with other UI elements in the Interface Builder. We will discuss the details in later sections.

There should be only one instance of CoordinatingController throughout the life of the application because we allow only one instance per view controller as well. Things will get messy and inconsistent if we allow multiple instances of CoordinatingController, so it's implemented as a singleton (see the Singleton pattern, Chapter 7). CoordinatingController has a sharedInstance class method that returns a singleton of it. Listing 11–3 shows how we can implement it without the singleton part for brevity.

Listing 11–3. *CoordinatingController.m*

```objectivec
#import "CoordinatingController.h"



@implementation CoordinatingController

@synthesize activeViewController=activeViewController_;
@synthesize canvasViewController=canvasViewController_;


// The singleton implementation part is snipped for brevity.


#pragma mark -
#pragma mark A method for view transitions

- (IBAction) requestViewChangeByObject:(id)object
{

  if ([object isKindOfClass:[UIBarButtonItem class]])
  {
    switch ([(UIBarButtonItem *)object tag])
    {
      case kButtonTagOpenPaletteView:
      {
        // load a PaletteViewController
        PaletteViewController *controller = [[[PaletteViewController alloc]
                                              init] autorelease];

        // transition to the PaletteViewController
```

```objc
                [canvasViewController_ presentModalViewController:controller
                                                 animated:YES];

            // set the activeViewController to
            // paletteViewController
            activeViewController_ = controller;
        }
            break;
        case kButtonTagOpenThumbnailView:
        {
            // load a ThumbnailViewController
            ThumbnailViewController *controller = [[[ThumbnailViewController alloc]
                                                    init] autorelease];


            // transition to the ThumbnailViewController
            [canvasViewController_ presentModalViewController:controller animated:YES];

            // set the activeViewController to
            // ThumbnailViewController
            activeViewController_ = controller;
        }
            break;
        default:
            // just go back to the main canvasViewController
            // for the other types
        {
            // The Done command is shared on every
            // view controller except the CanvasViewController
            // When the Done button is hit, it should
            // take the user back to the first page in
            // conjunction with the design
            // other objects will follow the same path
            [canvasViewController_ dismissModalViewControllerAnimated:YES];

            // set the activeViewController back to
            // canvasViewController
            activeViewController_ = canvasViewController_;
        }
            break;
        }
    }
    // everything else goes to the main canvasViewController
    else
    {
        [canvasViewController_ dismissModalViewControllerAnimated:YES];

        // set the activeViewController back to
        // canvasViewController
        activeViewController_ = canvasViewController_;
    }

}

@end
```

We focus mainly on the `requestViewChangeByObject:(id)object` method. The majority of the method contains a medium-sized `if-else` block (that looks medium to me, anyway) that does the magic. In the Strategy pattern chapter (Chapter 19), I mention that using a huge `switch-case/if-else` block to tell what algorithm to use could be a sign that it may need to be broken up into different strategies. For the sake of simplicity and brevity, I am using just an `if-else` block to demonstrate that part of the implementation. Of course, we should consider incorporating the Strategy pattern if the `if-else` block becomes monolithic and god-like in real applications.

> **NOTE:** The Mediator pattern trades complexity of interaction for complexity in the mediator. Because a mediator encapsulates and consolidates different collaborative logics from colleagues, it can become more complex than any of them. This can make the mediator itself a "god"-type monolith that knows everything and is hard to maintain.

The `if-else` block in the method first checks if it is an instance of `UIBarButtonItem`. If so, there is a `switch-case` block that determines the tag based on the `ButtonTag` enum defined in Listing 11–1. If the tag is `kButtonTagOpenPaletteView`, then it will ask the `canvasViewController_` to present a modal view with an instance of `paletteViewController_`. The rest of the `switch-case` block follows similar logic to present and dismiss view controllers as we have discussed in the previous sections.

Using the CoordinatingController in the Interface Builder

We can instantiate a bunch of `UIBarButtonItem` instances that we have discussed previously manually in code. But nothing can beat the convenience of using the Interface Builder, especially if we can manage all UI elements in the same place.

The following figures showcase a kind of step-by-step procedure about how to use them in the Interface Builder with the `CanvasViewController` and an instance of `UIBarButtonItem` that can activate a view transition to an instance of `PaletteViewController` as an example.

After we open the `CanvasViewController.xib` document from the project, drag an instance of Object (`NSObject`) to the main document window, as shown in Figure 11–9.

Figure 11–9. *Drag a reference of an external Object in the main* `.xib` *document window.*

Then go to the Identity Inspector window (if it's not opened, then press ⌘4 or select **Tools ➤ Identity Inspector** from the menu to open it) and set the Object's class identity to `CoordinatingController`, as shown in Figure 11–10.

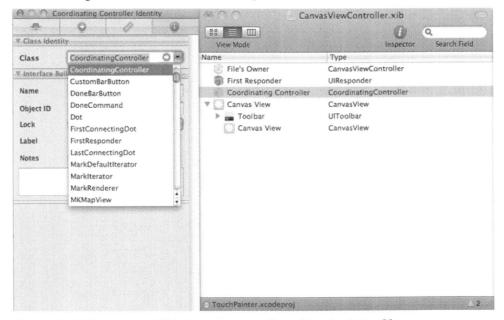

Figure 11–10. *Set the external Object to a class type of* `CoordinatingController`.

After the CoordinatingController is set, then we can go ahead and fix some attributes for one of the toolbar buttons on the view. We select the palette button and change its tag to 1 (as kButtonTagOpenPaletteView), as shown in Figure 11–11.

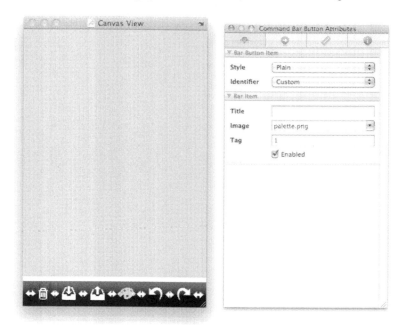

Figure 11–11. *Set the tag of the palette toolbar button to a value of 1 (kButtonTagOpenPalctteView).*

Now, by holding the Control and Option buttons, drag from the palette button to the CoordinatingController object reference in the main document window. Then select the method requestViewChangeByObject: item from a little drop-down menu there, as illustrated in Figures 11–12 and 11–13.

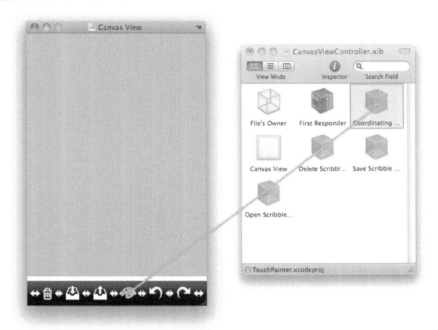

Figure 11–12. *Control+Option+Drag the palette toolbar button over the* `CoordinatingController` *item.*

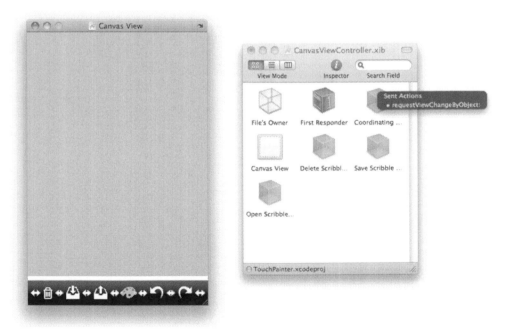

Figure 11–13. *Select the* `requestViewChangeByObject:` *method as the action selector when the palette toolbar button is clicked.*

PaletteViewController, ThumbnailViewController, and their toolbar buttons follow the same procedure to get one of them linked up—and voilà!

At this point, everything related to the view transition logic is in place. And we didn't even need to mess with a single line of code in each view controller. The whole logic is being managed by just a single method in the CoordinatingController. Since the CoordinatingController was implemented as a singleton (Chapter 17), the instances created with the .xib files at runtime are, in fact, the same instance throughout the entire life of the application with the CoordinatingController's singleton alloc and init methods.

Summary

In this chapter, we have explored quite a lot of material about the Mediator pattern as well as how to implement it in Objective-C with the Cocoa Touch framework.

Even though the Mediator pattern is very useful for situations where the application's behavior is distributed among different objects and they depend on each other, precautions should be taken to avoid making a mediator class monolithic and hard to maintain. If this becomes the case, you may consider using other design patterns to help break up the monolith. Be creative to mix and match different design patterns for the same problem. Each design pattern is like a Lego block. A whole application can be built with different "blocks" that fit each other.

In the next chapter, we are going to discuss another type of design pattern that helps decouple objects with a publish-subscribe mechanism.

Chapter 12

Observer

Like an example in the Mediator pattern chapter (Chapter 11), air traffic needs a centralized air traffic control. There are many operators sitting inside the air controller tower watching their radar screens to make sure no mid-air collision can occur. At the same time, pilots who are flying their multimillion-dollar big birds need to know what's happening around them, i.e., the traffic in the air. Pilots can tune to specific channels on their radio and listen to (observe) the surrounding traffic. If a traffic controller broadcasts certain precautions and warnings to those pilots who are observing the channel, the pilots can acknowledge the messages with certain actions. So in this model, anyone can know what traffic control they are observing but not the other way around (at least the air traffic controller doesn't know *all* observers but certain blips on the radar screen). Anyone (including real pilots) can tune in and out whenever they want without disturbing the others.

We have brought this idea to object-oriented software design to decouple objects that have different behaviors (or to extend the behavior of an object with other different ones). With this model, different objects can work together, and at the same time they could be reused in other places as well. We call it the Observer pattern.

In this chapter, we are going to discuss the concepts of the pattern as well as how it was adapted in the Cocoa Touch framework. The Observer pattern is also part of the MVC (Model-View-Controller) pattern. We will use the TouchPainter app example from Chapter 2 to discuss how to use the pattern to let a `CanvasView` reflect data changes of strokes that are stored in the Model living in `CanvasViewController`.

What Is the Observer Pattern?

The Observer pattern is also known as the Publish-Subscribe pattern. As its a.k.a. implies, it's just like a magazine subscription. When you order a subscription from a magazine publisher, you provide the publisher your name and mailing address so the new issue can find its own way to your hand. The publisher makes sure the right magazine will be delivered to the right address. You will never (supposedly) get what you have not subscribed to. This is exactly how the Observer pattern works. An observer registers (subscribes) itself for particular notifications (magazines) with a notifier (publisher). The observer only gets what it has subscribed to when it's available from the notifier. Their static relationships are illustrated in Figure 12–1.

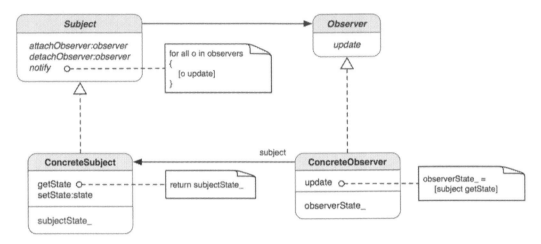

Figure 12–1. A class diagram of the Observer pattern

The Observer pattern is a publish-subscribe model. Observers subscribe to notifications from the Subject. ConcreteObservers implement an abstract Observer and override its update method. Once an instance of Subject needs to notify Observers for any new changes, the Subject will send an update message to notify any registered Observers stored in an internal list. Inside an actual implementation of the update method of a ConcreteObserver, the internal state of the Subject can be retrieved and processed later.

> **THE OBSERVER PATTERN:** Defines a one-to-many dependency between objects so that when one object changes state, all its dependents are notified and updated automatically.*
>
> * The original definition appeared in *Design Patterns*, by the *"Gang of Four"* (Addison-Wesley, 1994).

The whole idea of the publish-subscribe mechanism is pretty straightforward and quite easy to understand. The Subject provides methods to register and unregister any object that implements the Observer protocol and is interested in handling the update message call. When there is a change in an instance of Subject, it will send a notify message to itself. The notify method contains an algorithm that defines how to broadcast update messages to all registered observers. A common notify-update sequence at runtime is illustrated as a sequence diagram in Figure 12–2.

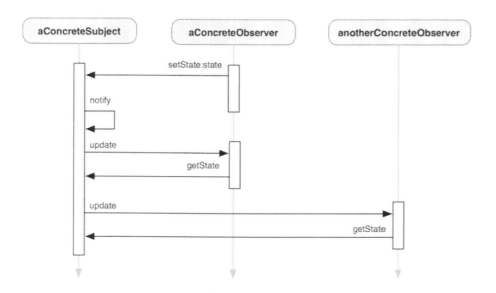

Figure 12–2. *A sequence diagram shows the interaction between* aConcreteSubject *and other concrete observers that observe updates from the* aConcreteSubject *object.*

aConcreteObserver first modifies the state of aConcreteSubject. Since there is a change in its internal state, aConcreteSubject sends itself a notify message so it broadcasts update messages to a set of aConcreteObservers. aConcreteObserver and anotherConcreteObserver receive the message and send a getState message to aConcreteSubject to retrieve its internal state for further processing.

One of the most obvious benefits of using the Observer pattern is that it can extend the behavior of the Subject with N number of Observers that have specific implementation to process the information stored in the Subject. It's also a very important pattern for decoupling among different objects. The Cocoa Touch framework has provided developers some classes to use the pattern without writing their own.

When Would You Use the Observer Pattern?

You'd naturally think about using the pattern when

- You have two types of abstraction that are dependent on each other. Encapsulating them in separate objects allows you to vary and reuse them independently.

- A change in one object requires changing others, and the number of objects that need to be changed can vary.

- An object needs to notify other objects without knowing what they are.

Using the Observer Pattern in Model-View-Controller

In earlier chapters, we discussed how the Model-View-Controller pattern (MVC) is a compound of different types of design patterns. Observer is one of them. A view will be associated with a controller for some particular events to occur that would affect the presentation of an application. For example, when the user clicks a "sort" button on the view, then it's passed to the controller to tell the model to sort its data in the back end. When the model successfully performs the operation on the data, it will notify all the associated controllers to update their views with the new data.

By using the Observer pattern in a MVC pattern, each component can be reused and extended independently without much interference with others in the relationships. The achieved high reusability and extensibility could not be achieved with all their logic put together in one class. So extra views can be added to a controller without modifying existing design and code. Likewise, different controllers can use the same model without changing other controllers that are using it. Especially for the model, multiple objects (either local or remote) can modify its internal data. So the model will broadcast specific changes to all observing controllers, and they will, in turn, tell their views to update the presentation with new information from the model. We will discuss more about this update mechanism in later sections.

Using the Observer Pattern in the Cocoa Touch Framework

The Cocoa Touch framework has adapted the Observer pattern with two technologies, Notifications and Key-Value Observing. Despite being two different Cocoa technologies, both of them implement the Observer pattern. We are going to discuss each of their characteristics and the differences between them.

Notifications

The Cocoa Touch framework implements the one-to-many, publish-subscribe model with NSNotificationCenter and NSNotification objects. They allow the subject and its observers to communicate in a loosely coupled manner. The communication can take place between them without either needing to know much about the other.

The subject that wants to notify other objects needs to create a notification object, which is identifiable by a global notification name, and post it to a notification center. The notification center determines the observers of a particular notification and sends the notification to them via a message. When the objects subscribe to a particular type of notification, they need to provide the name of a method identified by a selector. The method must conform to a certain single-parameter signature. The parameter of the method is the notification object, which contains the notification name, the observed object, and a dictionary containing any supplemental information. When a notification arrives, the method will be invoked.

A model object can post a notification to the notification center after the model's internal data is changed so the message can be broadcast to other observing objects and they can respond appropriately. The model can construct a notification and post it to the notification center as follows:

```
NSNotification *notification = [NSNotification notificationWithName:@"data changes"
                                                            object:self];
NSNotificationCenter * notificationCenter = [NSNotificationCenter defaultCenter];
[notificationCenter postNotification:notification];
```

An instance of notification can be created by a class factory method (see the Factory Method pattern, Chapter 4) of NSNotification class with a notification name and any object passed as a parameter to observers. In the foregoing example, the notification name is @"data changes". The exact name is implementation specific. If the subject wanted to pass itself as an object parameter, self can be used for that purpose during the creation process.

Once the notification is created, it will be posted to the notification center as a parameter to a [notificationCenter postNotification:notification] message call. A reference to an instance of NSNotificationCenter can be obtained by sending a defaultCenter message to the NSNotificationCenter class. There is only one default notification center per process, which makes the default NSNotificationCenter a singleton object (see the Singleton pattern, Chapter 7). defaultCenter is a factory method that returns the sole default instance of NSNotificationCenter for the application.

Any object that wants to subscribe to the notification needs to sign itself up for it in the first place. The following code snippet illustrates that:

```
[notificationCenter addObserver:self
                  selector:@selector(update:)
                      name:@"data changes"
                    object:subject];
```

The notificationCenter is obtained the same way as in the posting steps performed by the subject. To register an observer, an observing object needs to register self as an observer in an addObserver: message call. It also needs to provide a selector that identifies a method that will be invoked when the notification center notifies the observing object. The observing object can also optionally set the name of a particular notification of interest as well as any other object as a parameter for the method that will be invoked when notified. The provided information will be used by the notification center to determine what notifications should be delivered to the observing object. For the sake of our example, at least it needs to provide the same notification name in order to be able to receive the same notification.

Key-Value Observing

Cocoa (Cocoa Touch as well) provides a mechanism called key-value observing with which objects can be notified of changes to specific properties of other objects. The mechanism is particularly important in the context of the Model-View-Controller pattern, as it enables view objects to observe changes in model objects via the controller layer.

The mechanism is based on the NSKeyValueObserving informal protocol with which Cocoa provides an automatic property-observing capability to all complying objects. For automatic observing, objects that participate in key-value observing, or KVO, require compliance with the requirements of key-value coding (KVC) and complying accessor methods. KVC is based on a related informal protocol for automatic observing by accessing object properties (for detailed specifications on key-value coding compliance, please read the "Key-Value Coding Programming Guide" available on the iOS developer's website. You can also implement manual observer notifications using the methods of NSKeyValueObserving and associated categories. With the manual implementation, you can either disable the default automatic notifications or keep both of them.

Both notifications and key-value observing are Cocoa's adaptation of the Observer pattern. Despite both relying on a similar kind of publisher-subscriber relationship, they are designed for different solutions. Table 12–1 summarizes their key differences:

Table 12–1. *The Key Differences Between Notifications and Key-Value Observing*

Notifications	Key-Value Observing
A central object that provides change notifications for all observers	The observed object directly transmits notifications to observers.
Mainly concerned with program events in a broad sense	Tied to the values of specific object properties

It's not rocket science to use key-value observing to activate the true spirit of the Observer pattern, especially in the context of the Model-View-Controller pattern. However, the topic itself can be a chapter of its own. If you want to know more about that, you can go the iOS developer's web site to check out its "Key-Value Observing Programming Guide," "Key-Value Coding Programming Guide," as well as "Cocoa Bindings Programming Topics."

Let's see how to use KVO to propagate notifications of changes in a model to a view (via a controller) with our old and faithful app, TouchPainter.

Updating Strokes on the CanvasView in TouchPainter

The canvas part of the TouchPainter app that allows the user to scribble is the heart and soul of the app. We briefly cover the components involved in the previous chapters. From a bird's eye view, it is basically a Model-View-Controller structure: Scribble as Model, CanvasView as View, and CanvasViewController as Controller. The CanvasView forwards touches to the CanvasViewController through a responder chain (Chain of Responsibility pattern, Chapter 17). Then the CanvasViewController processes the information of the touches and instructs Scribble to update its internal structure with the information of the new touches. Once the Scribble has updated its internal state (Mark composite; please see the Composite pattern in Chapter 13 for more details), then it will notify any observer that is registered for an update notification. In this case, the CanvasViewController is the only observer that would like to receive any updates from the Scribble. Finally the CanvasViewController will notify the CanvasView to update its presentation. Their relationships are illustrated in a diagram in Figure 12–3.

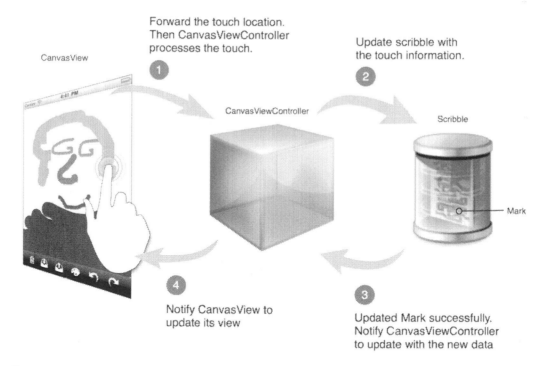

Figure 12–3. *An action-flow diagram shows how* CanvasView, CanvasViewController, *and* Scribble *interact with each other.*

We will implement the solution with the Key-Value Observing mechanism, or KVO, with NSKeyValueObserving protocol. Luckily, NSObject has implemented that for us so we don't need to create everything from scratch. A class diagram that shows a possible structure is illustrated in Figure 12–4.

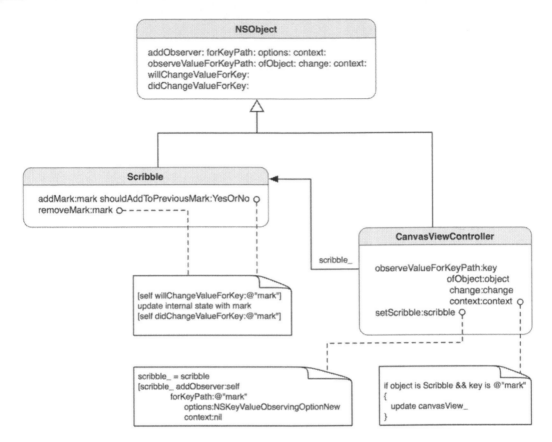

Figure 12–4. *A class diagram shows a static relationship between* `Scribble` *and* `CanvasViewController` *through the Key-Value Observing mechanism implemented by* `NSObject`.

The class diagram looks a little scary, doesn't it? For the sake of brevity, other unrelated methods are omitted in the diagram. Because we are using KVO to implement the pattern and a lot of bells and whistles are hidden from view, the class diagram in Figure 12–4 doesn't quite reconcile with the one shown in Figure 12–1. But there are two key methods in NSObject shown in the figure that will ring a bell. addObserver:forKeyPath: options:context: allows an object to be added as an observer to a receiver. The observer needs to override observeValueForKeyPath:ofObject:change:context: to receive any callback from changes in the subject and process any returned value. In the previous sections, we have mentioned that the KVO update mechanism is usually automatic whenever a key-matching property is updated through its accessor method (i.e., set<key> method). If we want to manually trigger the KVO update broadcast, then we need to use willChangeValueForKey: and didChangeValueForKey: to wrap the changes before and after they occur.

Every time a different instance of Scribble is assigned to an instance of CanvasViewController, it will add itself as an observer to the instance of Scribble with the addObserver:forKeyPath:options:context: method. If there are changes to the internal state of the instance of Scribble (adding / removing components in its Mark composite object), we need to manually trigger the universal update by a pair of wrapping calls of willChangeValueForKey:@"mark" and didChangeValueForKey:@"mark". The KVO implementation in NSObject will forward a message of observeValueForKeyPath:ofObject:change:context: to the observer CanvasViewController. In the callback method, it will update its canvasView_ with a new instance of Mark from the message and ask it to redraw itself. The class declaration of Scribble is shown in Listing 12–1.

Listing 12–1. *A Class Declaration of Scribble in* Scribble.h

```
#import "Mark.h"

@interface Scribble : NSObject
{
  @private
  id <Mark> parentMark_;
}

// methods for Mark management
- (void) addMark:(id <Mark>)aMark shouldAddToPreviousMark:(BOOL)shouldAddToPreviousMark;
- (void) removeMark:(id <Mark>)aMark;

@end
```

Scribble keeps an instance of Mark as its internal state so it won't expose to other objects. Clients can send Scribble a message of addMark:(id <Mark>)aMark shouldAddToPreviousMark:(BOOL)shouldAddToPreviousMark to insert any Mark instance to its internal composite. The BOOL parameter shouldAddToPreviousMark tells the method whether the input Mark object should be attached to the previous one as part of its aggregation (for example, a Vertex in a Stroke). removeMark:(id <Mark>)aMark allows a removal of aMark from the parent Mark.

A message of either addMark: or removeMark: for an instance of Scribble will trigger an update broadcast to its observers. Listing 12–2 shows how they are implemented.

Listing 12–2. *An Implemenation of Scribble in* Scribble.m

```
#import "Scribble.h"
#import "Stroke.h"

// A private category for Scribble
// that contains a mark property available
// only to its objects
@interface Scribble ()

@property (nonatomic, retain) id <Mark> mark;

@end


@implementation Scribble

@synthesize mark=parentMark_;

- (id) init
```

```
{
  if (self = [super init])
  {
    // the parent should be a composite
    // object (i.e. Stroke)
    parentMark_ = [[Stroke alloc] init];
  }

  return self;
}

#pragma mark -
#pragma mark Methods for Mark management

- (void) addMark:(id <Mark>)aMark shouldAddToPreviousMark:(BOOL)shouldAddToPreviousMark
{
  // manual KVO invocation
  [self willChangeValueForKey:@"mark"];

  // if the flag is set to YES
  // then add this aMark to the
  // *PREVIOUS* Mark as part of an
  // aggregate.
  // Based on our design, it's supposed
  // to be the last child of the main
  // parent
  if (shouldAddToPreviousMark)
  {
    [[parentMark_ lastChild] addMark:aMark];
  }
  // otherwise attach it to the parent
  else
  {
    [parentMark_ addMark:aMark];
  }

  // manual KVO invocation
  [self didChangeValueForKey:@"mark"];
}

- (void) removeMark:(id <Mark>)aMark
{
  // do nothing if aMark is the parent
  if (aMark == parentMark_) return;

  // manual KVO invocation
  [self willChangeValueForKey:@"mark"];

  [parentMark_ removeMark:aMark];

  // manual KVO invocation
  [self didChangeValueForKey:@"mark"];
}


- (void) dealloc
{
```

```
      [parentMark_ release];
      [super dealloc];
}

@end
```

@"mark" is the only key in the KVO in Scribble. Normally speaking, if we want to modify its internal mark, then we can use one of its accessor methods (e.g., setMark:). In that case, we don't need to do anything extra to broadcast an update once a modification is done as it's being handled by the default KVO mechanism defined in NSObject. We definitely need manual update because Scribble allows part-whole modifications to its mark but not just a complete replacement of it through its set method. In fact, we want both automatic and manual updates. So we will keep the original mechanism offered by NSObject and add a couple lines of code around where actual modifications to mark occur in the methods. In the addMark: method, there is an if block that tells whether the incoming aMark needs to be added to a parent or the last Mark. In either case, there will be a change to the internal mark, so we wrap the whole block with two statements: [self willChangeValueForKey:@"mark"] and [self didChangeValueForKey:@"mark"]. The first statement tells NSObject to keep the old value of the mark while the second one keeps the new one. Either one or both of the values will be passed to observers, depending on what they want to get from an update.

How should an observer handle an update? It's not the business of Scribble anymore once it hands off a whole bunch of update messages. Let's see how CanvasViewController can handle an update message to update its canvasView_ with code snippets shown in Listings 12–3 and 12–4.

Listing 12–3. *A Class Definition of CanvasViewController in* CanvasViewController.h

```
#import <UIKit/UIKit.h>
#import "Scribble.h"
#import "CanvasView.h"
#import "CanvasViewGenerator.h"

@interface CanvasViewController : UIViewController
{
    @private
    Scribble *scribble_;
    CanvasView *canvasView_;

    CGPoint startPoint_;
    UIColor *strokeColor_;
    CGFloat strokeSize_;
}

@property (nonatomic, retain) CanvasView *canvasView;
@property (nonatomic, retain) Scribble *scribble;
@property (nonatomic, retain) UIColor *strokeColor;
@property (nonatomic, assign) CGFloat strokeSize;
@end
```

We are reusing pretty much the same CanvasViewController that appears in other chapters. Scribble is served as a model (as in Model-View-Controller) that helps store the user's stroke and dot information. A member instance of Scribble sits squarely inside a CanvasViewController object just for the purpose.

CanvasViewController also manages an instance of CanvasView as a member variable canvasView_. It uses an instance of Mark to do that actual drawing on the screen.

The implementation code for the CanvasViewController is quite long, so I will break it into multiple parts to discuss. We are going to get the setup part of the controller, as in Listing 12–4.

Listing 12–4. *An Implementation of* CanvasViewController *Defined in* CanvasViewController.m

```
#import "CanvasViewController.h"
#import "Dot.h"
#import "Stroke.h"

@implementation CanvasViewController

@synthesize canvasView=canvasView_;
@synthesize scribble=scribble_;
@synthesize strokeColor=strokeColor_;
@synthesize strokeSize=strokeSize_;


// hook up everything with a new Scribble instance
- (void) setScribble:(Scribble *)aScribble
{
  if (scribble_ != aScribble)
  {
    [scribble_ autorelease];
    scribble_ = [aScribble retain];

    // add itself to the scribble as
    // an observer for any changes to
    // its internal state - mark
    [scribble_ addObserver:self
             forKeyPath:@"mark"
               options:NSKeyValueObservingOptionInitial |
                       NSKeyValueObservingOptionNew
               context:nil];
  }
}


// Implement viewDidLoad to do additional setup after loading the view,
// typically from a nib.
- (void)viewDidLoad
{
  [super viewDidLoad];

  // …
  // Setup a default canvas view
  // but we snip that part for brevity
  // …

  // initialize a Scribble model
  Scribble *scribble = [[[Scribble alloc] init] autorelease];
```

```
    [self setScribble:scribble];

    // other setups…
}

- (void)dealloc
{
    [canvasView_ release];
    [scribble_ release];
    [super dealloc];
}
```

Because CanvasViewController's scribble property is synthesized automatically, we normally don't need to provide any custom accessor methods for it. But here is the thing: CanvasViewController is depending on any update notifications sent from scribble_ in order to further instruct how its canvasView_ (re)draws any mark in scribble_. It needs to add itself to its private member variable scribble_ as an observer with a message call:

```
    [scribble_ addObserver:self
             forKeyPath:@"mark"
                options:NSKeyValueObservingOptionInitial |
                        NSKeyValueObservingOptionNew
                context:nil];
```

The NSKeyValueObservingOptionInitial option tells scribble_ to notify CanvasViewController right after this message call to provide the initial value for its mark property. That option is important because CanvasViewController also needs to be notified when a Scribble object is being initialized in its init* method and the mark property is being set for the first time. NSKeyValueObservingOptionNew instructs scribble_ to notifiy CanvasViewController every time when the mark property of scribble_ is set with a new value. The context parameter provides an optional object as a parameter for a notification. Ok, let's get back to the message call itself. The question is, where should we put it in? If it's only in the viewDidLoad method, then when a client assigns a different Scribble instance to the controller, the observing link will be broken. So the best place to establish a link between them is in a set accessor method for scribble_. It serves as a gateway to prevent any possibility of breaking the observing link. Also, after a different Scribble reference is assigned to the CanvasViewController, the accessor method will send a message to canvasView_ to redraw itself with the mark in a new Scribble. Details on how canvasView_ draws a complete Mark composite on the screen are discussed in Chapter 15.

So instead of putting the part where we set up an observing link between CanvasViewController and its scribble_ in the viewDidLoad method, we create the first-ever instance of Scribble there every time the controller is loaded and assign it with the accessor method.

CanvasViewController and its scribble_ are now hooked up, and we are ready to see some actions on updating scribble_ with touches on the canvasView_. We put some touch event handlers in CanvasViewController, as in Listing 12–5.

Listing 12–5. *Touch Event Handlers in* `CanvasViewController`

```objc
#pragma mark -
#pragma mark Touch Event Handlers

- (void)touchesBegan:(NSSet *)touches withEvent:(UIEvent *)event
{
  startPoint_ = [[touches anyObject] locationInView:canvasView_];
}

- (void)touchesMoved:(NSSet *)touches withEvent:(UIEvent *)event
{
  CGPoint lastPoint = [[touches anyObject] previousLocationInView:canvasView_];

  // add a new stroke to scribble
  // if this is indeed a drag from
  // a finger
  if (CGPointEqualToPoint(lastPoint, startPoint_))
  {
    id <Mark> newStroke = [[[Stroke alloc] init] autorelease];
    [newStroke setColor:strokeColor_];
    [newStroke setSize:strokeSize_];
    [scribble_ addMark:newStroke shouldAddToPreviousMark:NO];
  }

  // add the current touch as another vertex to the
  // temp stroke
  CGPoint thisPoint = [[touches anyObject] locationInView:canvasView_];
  Vertex *vertex = [[[Vertex alloc]
                     initWithLocation:thisPoint]
                    autorelease];

  [scribble_ addMark:vertex shouldAddToPreviousMark:YES];
}

- (void)touchesEnded:(NSSet *)touches withEvent:(UIEvent *)event
{
  CGPoint lastPoint = [[touches anyObject] previousLocationInView:canvasView_];
  CGPoint thisPoint = [[touches anyObject] locationInView:canvasView_];

  // if the touch never moves (stays at the same spot until lifed now)
  // just add a dot to an existing stroke composite
  // otherwise add it to the temp stroke as the last vertex
  if (CGPointEqualToPoint(lastPoint, thisPoint))
  {
    Dot *singleDot = [[[Dot alloc]
                       initWithLocation:thisPoint]
                      autorelease];
    [singleDot setColor:strokeColor_];
    [singleDot setSize:strokeSize_];

    [scribble_ addMark:singleDot shouldAddToPreviousMark:NO];
  }

  // reset the start point here
  startPoint_ = CGPointZero;

  // if this is the last point of stroke
```

```
        // don't bother to draw it as the user
        // won't tell the difference
    }

    - (void)touchesCancelled:(NSSet *)touches withEvent:(UIEvent *)event
    {
        // we don't actually need to
        // reset the start point here
        // but just in case
        startPoint_ = CGPointZero;
    }
```

Please see Chapters 2, 13, and 15 for detailed discussions on the requirements for the drawing part of the app.

We have a whole chunk of code for handling touch events. Our goal there is to create two different drawing scenarios. It'll be a single dot if the finger lifts off at the same spot where it first touched or a stroke (line) if it is a drag with the finger. The majority of the algorithm that deals with those conditions is in the touchesMoved: and touchesEnded: methods. In the touchesMoved: method, it will create a new instance of Stroke if it is the second point of the drag and assign it to the scribble_ with a message call, [scribble_ addMark:vertex shouldAddToPreviousMark:NO]. Further touches along the drag will be added as instances of Vertex to a previously added Mark (as a form of Stroke) with the same type of message call to scribble_. But this time the shouldAddToPreviousMark parameter is set to YES.

If it's a single touch from a finger, then touchesEnded: will create a new instance of Dot as singleDot and ask scribble_ to add it to its internal structure with shouldAddToPreviousMark set to NO.

scribble_ notifies its observers (maintained by NSObject) in every addMark: message call. We know that the CanvasViewController was hooked up with scribble_ with the addObserver: message a moment ago. But it also needs to define a callback method so when an update notification comes in from scribble_, it will do something meaningful. Part of the KVO deal requires observers to override at least one observing method. For this example, we need CanvasViewController to listen to an observeValueForKeyPath: message, as in Listing 12–6.

Listing 12–6. *An Implementation of* updateWithScribble: *Method in* CanvasViewController *to Handle Any Update Messages Sent from an Instance of* Scribble *in Case of Data Changes*

```
#pragma mark -
#pragma mark Scribble observer method

- (void) observeValueForKeyPath:(NSString *)keyPath
                       ofObject:(id)object
                         change:(NSDictionary *)change
                        context:(void *)context
{
    if ([object isKindOfClass:[Scribble class]] &&
        [keyPath isEqualToString:@"mark"])
    {
        id <Mark> mark = [change objectForKey:NSKeyValueChangeNewKey];
        [canvasView_ setMark:mark];
```

```
    [canvasView_ setNeedsDisplay];
  }
}
```

It first double-checks to make sure an update message is from an instance of Scribble and for its @"mark" state. If so, it will retrieve a new Mark from a change dictionary by sending it [change objectForKey:NSKeyValueChangeNewKey]. The value that is associated with NSKeyValueChangeNewKey in the dictionary will be the new value from the mark property in scribble_. After that, it tells canvasView_ to draw itself with the new Mark.

We've covered some code to show a possible way to implement the Observer pattern for the TouchPainter app. At this point, you may wonder why we needed to let the CanvasViewController update the Scribble with touch information and at the same time, expect a notification from the Scribble, and then tell the CanvasView to update itself. It seems to us there are a few extra steps for something that can be done in an easier way. If you think so, then you should go back and look at the Scribble code again. In Scribble, there are two methods that allow modifications to its internal Mark composite reference. One is to add a new Mark to a parent Mark and the other one is to remove a Mark in the parent. We already knew that the CanvasViewController would use the addMark: method to add any Dot and Stroke to the Scribble. But how about removing a Mark from it then? Who will use that one? We didn't put any code in CanvasViewController to remove a Mark in scribble_. That operation would most probably be invoked by another entity—for example, a command object (see the Command pattern, Chapter 20). An undo/redo operation can modify scribble_ without CanvasViewController's knowledge. In that case, CanvasViewController needs to know what's going on with its scribble_ behind its back. Another type of aspect that could also modify scribble_ outside the knowledge of CanvasViewController is when the model (again as in Model-View-Controller) needs to be shared with other objects just like what databases do. A database can be read and modified by objects sitting in different processes or even across the network. Changes made by one object could be vital if they are important to other objects that are supposed to be in sync but are not.

If we implemented the same thing with NSNotification and NSNotificationCenter that we have discussed in one of the previous sections instead of using KVO, then here is what's going to happen:

- We need to define a common identifier for both the subject and observers (scribble_ and CanvasViewController).

- When there is a change to scribble_'s internal state, then it will post a notification with the specified identifier and pass any necessary object as a parameter (as an instance of NSNotification) to NSNotificationCenter.

- NSNotificationCenter will in turn distribute the message to all registered observers that have subscribed to any notification tagged with the identifier.

■ Then the observers will process the notification in its selector that was provided to NSNotification as a callback function.

Besides using those two approaches provided by the framework, some of you may be tempted to homebrew your own Observer infrastructure from the ground up.

Summary

In this chapter, we have covered the background information on the Observer pattern and its uses. We have also explored how we can implement it in the TouchPainter app for its Model-View-Controller architecture as a mechanism to reflect stroke changes on the screen as the user draws with a finger.

One can also take advantage of the canned implementation of the pattern with Key-Value Observing (KVO) as well as NSNotification and NSNotificationCenter objects in the Cocoa Touch framework without implementing the whole solution from scratch.

In the next part, we are going to see some design patterns that are useful for forming structures for abstract collections and other patterns that are directly related to their behaviors.

Part **V**

Abstract Collection

Chapter 13

Composite

You can picture a composite as an entity that contains other entities of the same kind. The whole bundle is like a tree with connected entities of parents and children. It's like a family tree of the same ancestry. Every node (child) in the family tree has the same family name. For other people who want to refer to my family, they need to refer to the Chungs. So every member in my family should be covered. So if a question like "Hey, Chungs, would you please give me your $5?" was asked, then every member would shell out $5. Requests can go recursive if we ask, "Chungs, would you please give me a total number of members in the family?" We assume the great-grandfather of the family will receive the message; the operation will be passed down through the bottom of the tree. Each individual family (composite) in the tree that contains children will return a sum of total number of children with other numbers returned from the children as well. What about unmarried members (leaf nodes) in the family? They will return zero as a result. After the great-grandfather collects all numbers returned from other family members in the tree, he will sum them up and return the sum to the requester as an answer. Instead of asking each individual member (or family) in the Chungs' family tree for some particular tasks, one can send a message to the Chungs (a tree) as the operation on the whole.

We borrow a similar idea in object-oriented software design. Composite structures can be very complex, and their internal representation is not supposed to be exposed to clients. We need to refer to the whole complex structure as a whole with a unified interface, so clients don't need to figure out what a particular node is in order to use it.

In this chapter, we are going to discuss the concepts of the Composite pattern. We will also use the TouchPainter app from Chapter 2 to discuss how to implement the pattern. Later in the chapter, we will discuss how the Cocoa Touch framework adapts the pattern in the `UIView` architecture.

What Is the Composite Pattern?

The Composite pattern allows you to compose objects that have the same base type into tree-like structures in which parent nodes contain child nodes of the same type. In other words, that kind of tree-like structure forms part-whole hierarchies. What is a part-whole hierarchy? It's a hierarchical structure that contains both compositions of objects (containers) and individual objects as leaf nodes (primitives). Each composite has other nodes that could be either leaf nodes or other composites. That kind of relationship repeats itself within the hierarchy recursively. Since every composition or leaf node shares the same base type, the same operations can be applied over each of them without type-checking on the client side. A client can ignore the differences between a composition and a leaf node to operate them. An example of a composite object structure at runtime is illustrated in Figure 13–1.

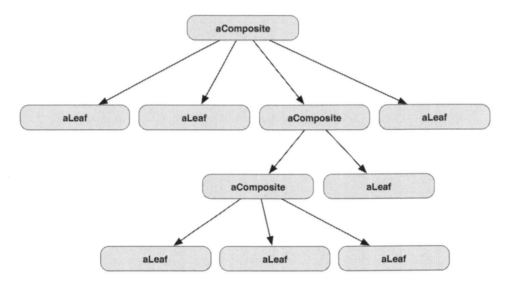

Figure 13–1. *A typical Composite object structure*

A static structure of the Composite pattern is illustrated as a class diagram in Figure 13–2.

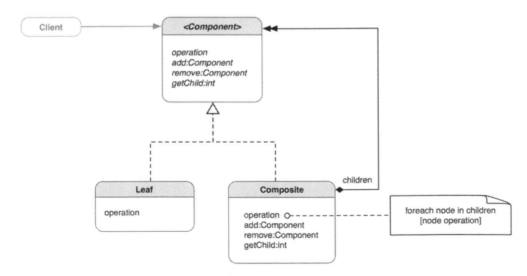

Figure 13–2. *A class diagram illustrates the conceptual structure of the Composite pattern.*

The base interface is the Component that defines operations that are shared by both the Leaf and the Composite classes.

There are some operations that are meaningful to only the Composite class, such as add:Component, remove:Component, and getChild:int. The Leaf class doesn't implement those methods for an obvious reason (in fact, it does but just an empty implementation). Why don't we put those methods in the Composite class only? We don't want clients to tell which kinds of nodes they are dealing with at runtime and to expose the internal details of the composite structure to clients as well. That's why even though operations make sense only to the Composite class; we also declare them in the base interface so every type of node share the same things. That way we can let clients treat any one of them uniformly.

CHILD MANAGEMENT IN LEAF?

We know the purpose of the Composite pattern is to allow a client to work with an object of Leaf or Composite uniformly, as if either were a single object. That means that both the Leaf and Composite classes must share a common interface (methods and properties). With that, the client doesn't need to know if an object is a Leaf or a Composite.

Composite needs methods to manage its children, such as add:component or remove:component. As both Leaf and Composite share a common interface, those methods should also be part of the interface. Confusion kicks in when Leaf is also needed to implement those methods. Some people believe that any client that manipulates the children of a Composite object must know what the client is dealing with. So sending composite manipulation messages to a Leaf object makes no sense and performs no function, and there is no logical reason they should be defined in the Leaf class.

Each node represents either a leaf node or a composite node. The main difference between the Leaf node and the Composite node is that a Leaf node doesn't contain any children of the same type but Composite does. Composite contains children of the same base type. Since both the Leaf and Composite classes share the same interfaces, any operation that is targeted for the Component type can be safely applied to each of them. Clients don't need to care about type-checking with a bunch of if- else, switch-case statements to determine the exact type of the object that is being worked on.

Let's back up to the top level of the hierarchy. The grandparent of all these nodes is treated as a reference to an instance of the Component class. If there are any changes to the internal structure, there is no client code that needs to be changed.

At the ultimate parent node, the whole aggregate structure can be referred to as their common base type, Component. Clients don't need to know any traversal strategy to use it, as a traversal or enumeration strategy is either provided by a composite structure or accessed through an external/internal iterator (see the Iterator pattern, Chapter 14).

> **THE COMPOSITE PATTERN:** Compose objects into tree structures to represent part-whole hierarchies. Composite lets clients treat individual objects and compositions of objects uniformly.*
>
> * The original definition appeared in *Design Patterns*, by the *"Gang of Four"* (Addison-Wesley, 1994).

When Would You Use the Composite Pattern?

You would naturally think about using the pattern when

- You want to have abstract tree representation of objects (part-whole hierarchies).

- You want clients to treat all objects in the composite structure and individual objects uniformly.

In Chapter 2, we briefly discussed using an abstract tree structure to maintain user-created (drawn) strokes. In the next few sections, we are going to discuss how to implement the pattern in the TouchPainter app to achieve that.

Understanding the Use of Mark in TouchPainter

Let's go back to our Mark composite structure that was defined in Chapter 2. We have a base Mark protocol that acts as a base type of both of our individual Dot, Vertex, and Stroke types. Instances of Dot are drawable on a view, while Stroke's child Vertex objects are used only for helping to connect lines together within the same stroke.

Clients that know how to construct a tree of Mark composite structures will add instances of Vertex to a Stroke instance and add the Stroke instance to the grandparent of the scribble. For adding drawable dots, the clients need to add individual instances of Dot to the grandparent. Their relationships are illustrated in Figure 13–3.

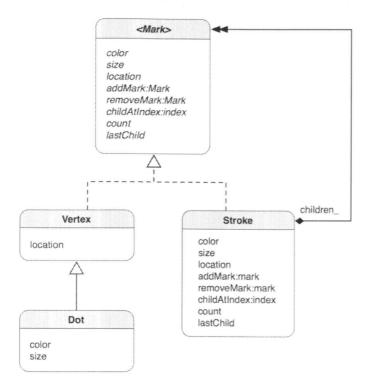

Figure 13–3. *A class diagram of a Composite structure shows the class relationships of* Dot *and* Vertex *as leaf node classes as well as* Stroke *as a container class.*

NOTE: Some people have questions like: Does the client having to know when to add a Dot vs. when to add a Vertex violate the encapsulation of the Composite pattern? Doesn't it defeat the purpose of the pattern if the client needs to know if they are working with a Stroke, a Vertex, or a Dot?

The answer for both questions is no. It's simply because there are two types of clients; one is a creator of a composite structure while the other type populates or manipulates the structure. Creators need to know *what* to put into the structure. Other clients that use the structure don't need to care about the exact types of the nodes in it.

Vertex implements only the location property. Dot subclasses Vertex and adds color and size because Vertex doesn't need color and size but Dot does. A visualized runtime structure of a Mark tree is shown in Figure 13–4.

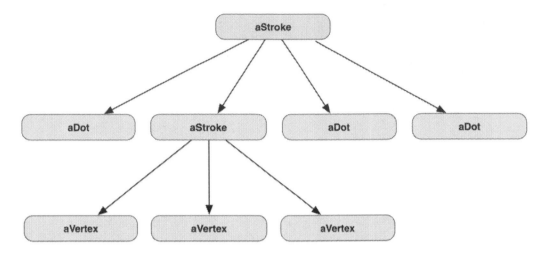

Figure 13–4. *An object structure of a Composite contains* Stroke, Dot, *and* Vertex *objects.*

aStroke can contain either Dot (aDot) or Vertex objects (aVertex) at runtime. So a Stroke object can be a parent of all kinds of Marks or a composition of a real stroke that is made out of Vertex objects and drawn on the screen as a whole group.

Let's cut some code for the Mark protocol as shown in Listing 13–1.

Listing 13–1. *Mark.h*

```
@protocol Mark <NSObject>

@property (nonatomic, retain) UIColor *color;
@property (nonatomic, assign) CGFloat size;
@property (nonatomic, assign) CGPoint location;
@property (nonatomic, readonly) NSUInteger count;
@property (nonatomic, readonly) id <Mark> lastChild;

- (void) addMark:(id <Mark>) mark;
- (void) removeMark:(id <Mark>) mark;
- (id <Mark>) childMarkAtIndex:(NSUInteger) index;

@end
```

Mark has three properties, color, size, and location. They should be common for any kinds of Marks that are drawable on the screen. In our original class diagrams, there are two methods declared in the Mark type, addMark:mark and removeMark:mark. They seem to make sense only to the Stroke class, as a Dot instance doesn't have any composition at all. The reason composite operations are declared in the top-level abstract interface is that we don't want clients to do any runtime check to know whether a Mark instance is a Stroke in order to add or remove children. Our goal is to make every node the same to clients to use. This uniformity becomes obviously important, for example, if you need to write a method that takes a parameter of Mark and adds/removes other Mark objects to/from it. The method shouldn't need to know whether the Mark of interest is a Stroke or Vertex (or Dot).

Now, here we go with our Vertex class, as shown Listing 13–2.

Listing 13–2. *Vertex.h*

```
#import "Mark.h"

@interface Vertex : NSObject <Mark>
{
  @protected
  CGPoint location_;
}

@property (nonatomic, retain) UIColor *color;
@property (nonatomic, assign) CGFloat size;
@property (nonatomic, assign) CGPoint location;
@property (nonatomic, readonly) NSUInteger count;
@property (nonatomic, readonly) id <Mark> lastChild;

- (id) initWithLocation:(CGPoint) location;
- (void) addMark:(id <Mark>) mark;
- (void) removeMark:(id <Mark>) mark;
- (id <Mark>) childMarkAtIndex:(NSUInteger) index;

@end
```

It's a good practice to re-declare properties/methods that the subclass overrides. Even though Vertex seems to implement all properties declared in the Mark protocol, only the location property is real. The location_ member variable is declared as @protected as it will be used by at least one subclass later. The rest of the properties do nothing (dummies), as shown in Listing 13–3.

Listing 13–3. *Vertex.m*

```
#import "Vertex.h"


@implementation Vertex
@synthesize location=location_;
@dynamic color, size;

- (id) initWithLocation:(CGPoint) aLocation
{
  if (self = [super init])
  {
    [self setLocation:aLocation];
  }

  return self;
}

// default properties do nothing
- (void) setColor:(UIColor *)color {}
- (UIColor *) color { return nil; }
- (void) setSize:(CGFloat)size {}
- (CGFloat) size { return 0.0; }

// Mark operations do nothing
- (void) addMark:(id <Mark>) mark {}
```

```
- (void) removeMark:(id <Mark>) mark {}
- (id <Mark>) childMarkAtIndex:(NSUInteger) index { return nil; }
- (id <Mark>) lastChild { return nil; }
- (NSUInteger) count { return 0; }


@end
```

Vertex @synthesizes only the `location` property and @dynamic `color` and `size`. @dynamic tells the compiler that we provide our own accessor methods for `color` and `size`. Although the compiler may not complain about it if we take the @dynamic directive off, it's still a good practice to keep that as it will make your life easier when you come back to the code later. The `initWithLocation:` method simply assigns the `aLocation` value to the Vertex's `location` property and returns itself. Other composite methods declared in Mark are dummies.

Dot subclasses Vertex and provides a few more implementations for the Mark protocol, as shown in Listing 13–4.

Listing 13–4. *Dot.h*

```
#import "Vertex.h"

@interface Dot : Vertex
{
  @private
  UIColor *color_;
  CGFloat size_;
}

@property (nonatomic, retain) UIColor *color;
@property (nonatomic, assign) CGFloat size;

@end
```

Dot needs to @synthesize only the `size` and `color` properties, as Vertex already covers a lot of stuff that is good enough for Dot as well. Dot's implementation is shown in Listing 13–5.

Listing 13–5. *Dot.m*

```
#import "Dot.h"


@implementation Dot
@synthesize size=size_, color=color_;

- (void) dealloc
{
  [color_ release];
  [super dealloc];
}

@end
```

We are done with Vertex and Dot. Let's move forward to Stroke, our composite class, as shown in Listing 13–6.

Listing 13–6. *Stroke.h*

```objc
#import "Mark.h"

@interface Stroke : NSObject <Mark>
{
  @private
  UIColor *color_;
  CGFloat size_;
  NSMutableArray *children_;
}


@property (nonatomic, retain) UIColor *color;
@property (nonatomic, assign) CGFloat size;
@property (nonatomic, assign) CGPoint location;
@property (nonatomic, readonly) NSUInteger count;
@property (nonatomic, readonly) id <Mark> lastChild;

- (void) addMark:(id <Mark>) mark;
- (void) removeMark:(id <Mark>) mark;
- (id <Mark>) childMarkAtIndex:(NSUInteger) index;

@end
```

As Stroke is a composite class, unlike Vertex and Dot, it does need to implement all the methods and properties declared in the Mark protocol, as shown in Listing 13–7.

Listing 13–7. *Stroke.m*

```objc
#import "Stroke.h"

@implementation Stroke

@synthesize color=color_, size=size_;
@dynamic location;

- (id) init
{
  if (self = [super init])
  {
    children_ = [[NSMutableArray alloc] initWithCapacity:5];
  }

  return self;
}

- (void) setLocation:(CGPoint)aPoint
{
  // it doesn't set any arbitrary location
}

- (CGPoint) location
{
  // return the location of the first child
  if ([children_ count] > 0)
  {
    return [[children_ objectAtIndex:0] location];
```

```objectivec
    }

    // otherwise returns the origin
    return CGPointZero;
}

- (void) addMark:(id <Mark>) mark
{
    [children_ addObject:mark];
}

- (void) removeMark:(id <Mark>) mark
{
    // if mark is at this level then
    // remove it and return
    // otherwise, let every child
    // search for it
    if ([children_ containsObject:mark])
    {
        [children_ removeObject:mark];
    }
    else
    {
        [children_ makeObjectsPerformSelector:@selector(removeMark:)
                            withObject:mark];
    }
}

// needs to be added to draft
- (id <Mark>) childMarkAtIndex:(NSUInteger) index
{
    if (index >= [children_ count]) return nil;

    return [children_ objectAtIndex:index];
}


// a convenience method to return the last child
- (id <Mark>) lastChild
{
    return [children_ lastObject];
}

// returns number of children
- (NSUInteger) count
{
    return [children_ count];
}


- (void) dealloc
{
    [color_ release];
    [children_ release];
    [super dealloc];
}

@end
```

Stroke has its own children_ as an instance of NSMutableArray to keep track of its child Mark nodes. In its init method, it initializes an instance of NSMutableArray with the arbitrary capacity of five (it doesn't hurt to make it a little bigger, though).

The location property is not @synthesized because a Stroke object doesn't provide a location value directly but from its first child. If the Stroke object doesn't have any children, the location accessor method will return CGPointZero that refers to the origin of the screen.

The addMark: (id <Mark>) mark method forwards the mark parameter to children_ with the message call addObject:mark. removeMark: (id <Mark>) mark is a little tricky. It first searches for the mark parameter at the children_ level. If there is none, then it will forward the search operation to each child node with the message makeObjectsPerformSelector:@selector(removeMark:) withObject:mark, so the search will keep going recursively until it reaches the last child of the tree. Every Mark object implements the removeMark: method, so there is no concern for us whether a particular child node is a Stroke, Vertex, or anything else before sending the message out.

childMarkAtIndex:, lastChild, and count methods simply return from similar methods in children_ (NSMutableArray).

The way a client can construct a Mark composite structure is shown in Listing 13–8.

Listing 13–8. *Client Code That Constructs a* Mark *Composite Structure with* Dot, Vertex, *and* Stroke *Objects*

```
// ...

Dot *newDot = [[[Dot alloc] init] autorelease];
Stroke *parentStroke = [[[Stroke alloc] init] autorelease];

[parentStroke addMark:newDot];

// ...

Vertex *newVertex = [[[vertex alloc] init] autorelease];
Stroke *newStroke = [[[Stroke alloc] init] autorelease];

[newStroke addMark:newVertex];

[parentStroke addMark:newStroke];

// ...
```

Individual Dot objects can be added to parentStroke as leaf nodes. parentStroke can also take composite Stroke objects that manage their own Vertex children, of which the purpose is to let the drawing algorithm draw connected lines.

In our TouchPaint app, there is a CanvasViewController that handles some basic drawing operations with touches. Touch event operations in the controller construct a main composite Mark structure that contains all individual, drawable dots as well as strokes that contain other non-drawable vertices, to form connected lines. CanvasViewController's view, called CanvasView, will present (draw) a complete Mark structure on the screen.

Figure 13–5 illustrates an actual dot and stroke drawing situation.

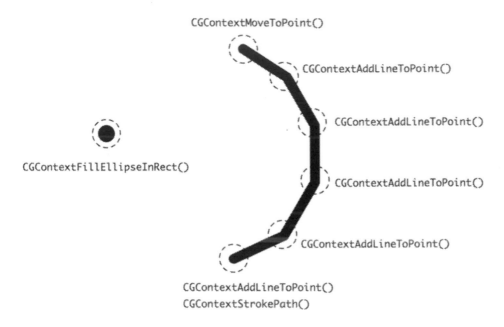

Figure 13–5. *An actual sequence of drawing a dot and a stroke with Quartz 2D*

We can add a drawing operation like drawWithContext:(CGContextRef)context to the Mark protocol so every node can draw itself according to its specific purpose. The one in Dot will go like that shown in Listing 13–9.

Listing 13–9. *drawWithContext: Implementation in Dot*

```
- (void) drawWithContext:(CGContextRef)context
{
  CGFloat x = self.location.x;
  CGFloat y = self.location.y;
  CGFloat frameSize = self.size;
  CGRect frame = CGRectMake(x, y, frameSize, frameSize);

  CGContextSetFillColorWithColor (context,[self color CGColor]);
  CGContextFillEllipseInRect(context, frame);
}
```

With an active context, an ellipse (a dot) can be drawn in the context with location, color, and size.

However, a vertex provides only a particular location in a stroke. So a Vertex object will add a point to a line only in the context (well, the Quartz 2D function in fact does add a line to a point) with its own location (coordinates), as shown in Listing 13–10.

Listing 13–10. *drawWithContext: Implementation in* Vertex

```
- (void) drawWithContext:(CGContextRef)context
{
  CGFloat x = self.location.x;
  CGFloat y = self.location.y;

  CGContextAddLineToPoint(context, x, y);
}
```

For a Stroke object, it needs to move the context to the first point of its children, and then it wraps up the whole line drawing operation with the Quartz 2D functions CGContextSetStrokeColorWithColor and CGContextStrokePath, as shown in Listing 13–11.

Listing 13–11. *drawWithContext: Implementation in* Stroke

```
- (void) drawWithContext:(CGContextRef)context
{
  CGContextMoveToPoint(context, self.location.x, self.location.y);

  for (id <Mark> mark in children_)
  {
    [mark drawWithContext:context];
  }

  CGContextSetStrokeColorWithColor(context,[self.color CGColor]);
  CGContextStrokePath(context);
}
```

The primary challenge when designing the Mark protocol is to come up with a minimal set of operations to provide open-ended functionality. Performing surgery on the Mark protocol and its subclasses for each new functionality is both invasive and error-prone. Eventually, the classes get harder to understand, extend, and reuse. So the key is to focus on a sufficient set of primitives for a simple and coherent interface.

In the chapter about the Visitor pattern (Chapter 15), we will explore how both the Composite and the Visitor patterns work together to create powerful yet flexible solutions for many problems related to tree structures.

Using Composites in the Cocoa Touch Framework

In the Cocoa Touch framework, UIViews are organized as a composite structure. Each instance of UIView can have other instances of UIViews to form a unified tree structure. It lets clients treat individual UIView objects and compositions of UIViews uniformly.

The UIViews in a window are internally structured into a view tree. At the root of the hierarchy is a UIWindow object and its content view. Other UIViews that are added to it become subviews of it. Each of them can have other views and becomes the superview of its view children. A UIView object can have only one superview and zero or more subviews. Figure 13–6 illustrates this relationship.

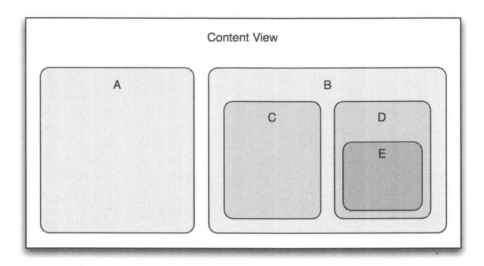

Figure 13–6. *A visual structure of the* UIView

Their relationships can be viewed from a different perspective as illustrated in a hierarchical diagram in Figure 13–7.

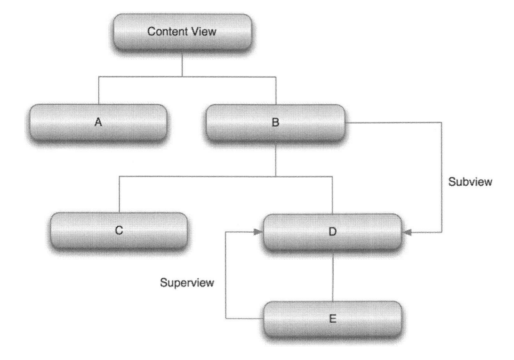

Figure 13–7. *A hierarchical structure of the* UIView

The view composite structure plays a part in both drawing and event handling. When a superview is asked to render itself for display, the message will be handled in the superview before its subviews. The message will be propagated to other subviews throughout the whole tree. Since they are all of the same type, UIView, they can be treated uniformly, and a branch of a UIView hierarchy can be treated as a unified view.

The unified view is also used as a responder chain for event handling and action messages. The drawing message is passed down the structure from superviews to their subviews, as are any event handling messages. The responder chain in the Cocoa Touch framework is the implementation of the Chain of Responsibility pattern (see Chapter 17).

Summary

The Composite pattern's main intent is for each node in a tree structure to share the same abstraction interface. So the whole structure can be used as a unified abstraction structure without exposing its internal representation. Any operation on each node (either leaf or composite) can be operated with the same interfaces that are defined in a protocol or abstraction base class.

New operations applied on the structure can be used with the Visitor pattern (Chapter 17) to have visitors "visit" each node for further processing without modifying the existing composite structure.

An internal representation of a composite structure is not supposed to be exposed to clients, so the Composite pattern is always used with the Iterator pattern to enumerate each individual item in a composite object. We will discuss the Iterator pattern and related design issues in the next chapter.

Chapter 14

Iterator

Every time you buy a soda from a soda machine, you pop some coins in it, select the type of soda you want, and then it is delivered in the delivery tray.

Obviously, there is more than one bottle stored inside the soda machine. We consumers just won't know how those bottles are organized in the big tin box and how they are dispensed unless we crack the machine open to see what's inside. Otherwise, every time we buy a bottle of soda, we can only expect the machine to dispense the *next* bottle. The dispenser software running in the machine knows all the details about which bottle should next be dispensed among the whole collection of them available.

There are at least two main parts in a soda machine that do the job:

- An internal crate that contains a collection of soda
- A dispenser that extracts the next bottle from the collection

The internal crate doesn't know about dispensing, as its sole function is to "contain" bottles. It counts on a dispenser to do all the actual dispensing and delivery chores. Unless the soda machine has a transparent casing, we will never know what's involved in the process.

The internal crate is like a model in an MVC object structure, or simply a data structure. Its sole duty is to maintain a collection of data (bottled soda), not anything else. There could be many ways to enumerate the data (dispense the bottles) in the data structure (the internal crate). If we jam multiple ways of dispensing bottles in the internal tray, the system could be very complicated and difficult to maintain. So it would be better to use a separate mechanism to dispense (enumerate) bottles, especially if a vending machine manufacturer wants to reuse the same dispensing mechanism for other models of soda machines.

A design pattern for that iterative behavior for an abstract collection in object-oriented software is called Iterator. In this chapter, we are going to discuss the idea of the pattern as well as implement various types of iterators with the Cocoa Touch Foundation framework.

What Is the Iterator Pattern?

An iterator provides a way to access the elements of an aggregate object (a collection) sequentially without exposing its underlying representation and details of the structure. The responsibility of traversing the elements of a collection is transferred from the collection itself to an iterator object. The iterator defines an interface for accessing collection elements and keeps track of the current element. Different iterators can carry out different traversal policies.

A basic relationship between a collection and an iterator can be seen in a class diagram in Figure 14–1.

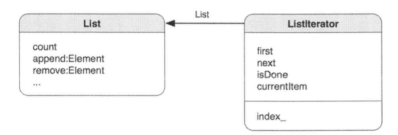

Figure 14–1. *A class diagram depicts a relationship between a* List *and a* ListIterator.

The List defines methods to modify the collection as well as a number of items in it. The ListIterator maintains a reference to a List object so the iterator can walk through the elements in the structure and return them. The ListIterator defines methods that allow clients to access the next item from the iteration process. The iterator has an internal index_ variable to keep track of the current position of the collection. A more elaborated relationship between an aggregate and an iterator is shown in a class diagram in Figure 14–2.

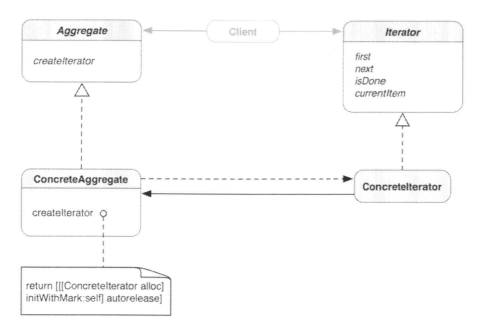

Figure 14–2. *A class diagram that shows a more in-depth relationship between abstract lists and iterators*

Abstract Aggregate defines a method, createIterator, to return an Iterator object. A ConcreteAggregate object subclasses Aggregate and overrides its createIterator method and returns an instance of ConcreteIterator. The Iterator abstract class defines the basic iterative behavior of what any Iterator should have. Clients will use the defined abstract interfaces to traverse elements in any type of Aggregate object.

ITERATOR: Provide a way to access to the elements of an aggregate object sequentially without exposing its underlying representation.*

* The original definition appeared in *Design Patterns*, by the "Gang of Four" (Addison-Wesley, 1994).

EXTERNAL ITERATOR VS. INTERNAL ITERATOR

There are basically two types of iterators: external and internal. An external iterator allows clients to directly manipulate the iteration process, so the clients need to know the external iterator in order to use it. On the other hand, a collection object (a target object that is being iterated) maintains and operates an external iterator *internally*. A typical collection object that provides an internal iterator defines an interface for clients to either access one item at a time from its underlying collection or send messages to each of the items. The differences between external and internal iterators are summarized in this table.

Table 14–1. *A Summary of Differences Between External and Internal Iterators*

External Iterator	Internal Iterator
Clients need to know the external iterator in order to use it, but it provides more control to the clients.	Clients don't need to know any external iterator; instead they can use special interfaces of a collection object to either retrieve one item at a time or send messages to each of the items in the collection.
Clients create and maintain an external iterator.	The collection object itself creates and maintains its external iterator.
Clients can use different external iterators for multiple types of traversals.	The collection object can select different external iterators without any modifications to clients' code.

When Would You Use the Iterator Pattern?

You'd naturally think of using the Iterator pattern when

- You need to access contents of a composite object without exposing its internal representation.

- You need to traverse composite objects in multiple ways.

- You need to provide a uniform interface for traversing different types of composite objects.

In the following sections, we are going to implement the pattern with iterators that traverse scribbles in the TouchPainter example app that we saw in Chapter 2.

Using Iterators in the Cocoa Touch Framework

Apple has adapted the Iterator pattern with its naming convention of "enumerator/enumerate" for various methods in related Foundation classes. From now on, I will use enumerat* as Apple's version of iterat*. They mean the same thing as far as the pattern goes. The NSEnumerator class in the Foundation framework implements the Iterator pattern. The private, concrete subclass of the abstract NSEnumerator class returns enumerator objects that sequentially traverse collections of various types— arrays, sets, dictionaries (values and keys)—returning objects in the collection to clients.

NSDirectoryEnumerator is a distantly related class. Instances of this class recursively enumerate the contents of a directory in the file system.

The collection classes such as NSArray, NSSet, and NSDictionary define methods that return an instance of the NSEnumerator subclass appropriate to the type of collection. All enumerators work in the same manner. You can retrieve an object from an enumerator by sending it a nextObject message in a loop until it returns nil to signal the end of traversal.

NSEnumerator

Since iOS 2.0, NSEnumerator has been available for enumerating elements in NSArray, NSDictionary, and NSSet objects. The NSEnumerator itself is an abstract class. It relies on some factory methods, (see the Factory Method pattern, Chapter 4) like objectEnumerator or keyEnumerator, to create and return a corresponding concrete enumerator object. Clients use a returned enumerator object to traverse elements in a collection, as illustrated in the following code snippet.

```
NSArray *anArray = ... ;
NSEnumerator *itemEnumerator = [anArray objectEnumerator];

NSString *item;
while (item = [itemEnumerator nextObject])
{
   // do something with the item
}
```

We assume the anArray is storing a collection of NSString objects. We process each item in the while loop with operations in NSString.

When the array's content is exhausted, the message call [itemEnumerator nextObject] will return nil and the enumeration process is complete.

With the introduction of iOS 4.0, there is another method to enumerate collection objects of the Cocoa Touch framework. It's called Block-Based Enumeration.

Block-Based Enumeration

The Block-Based Enumeration was introduced in the iOS 4 for collection objects in the Cocoa Touch framework. Block is part is the language features of Objective-C (as of this writing, Apple is still trying to standardize block as an extension to the C language). A block is a typed function, which means a block is a function yet it's also a type. A defined block is a variable that can be passed around between method calls just like other variables in an object. At the same time, a block variable can be used as a function within a method. When a method is passed with a block as a parameter, the block can be used as a callback function just like a function pointer in a C program. So the idea of block is perfect for implementing internal iterators (enumerators). Clients do not need to create iterators manually anymore but just provide a defined block that fits the required signature of the target collection object. Then the block will be called upon in each traversal step. An algorithm defining the block can process a returned element each time when the block is called by the target collection object.

Block is a really cool feature in the Objective-C language. It allows us to define callback algorithms in line within the same message call. Without using Block, the traditional way to do "callback" in the Cocoa Touch framework is to use delegation (see the Adapter pattern, Chapter 8). You need to define a separate protocol (a target) for any object (an adapter) that will respond to a callback from a client. If that part of an application is complex enough to justify another adapter mechanism, then that's fine. Sometimes a block can provide a more elegant solution than enumerators.

Apple has introduced new methods for the Block-Based Enumeration in NSArray, NSDictionary, and NSSet objects in iOS 4. One of them is called enumerateObjectsUsingBlock:(void (^)(id obj, NSUInteger idx, BOOL *stop))block. You can define your own algorithm for the block in line with the message call, or predefine a block elsewhere, then pass it as a parameter in the message call. The following code snippet illustrates how it can be accomplished in code with an NSArray object.

```
NSArray *anArray=[NSArray arrayWithObjects:@"This", @"is", @"a", @"test", nil];
NSString *string=@"test";

[anArray enumerateObjectsUsingBlock:^(id obj, NSUInteger index, BOOL *stop)
{
  if([obj localizedCaseInsensitiveCompare:string] == NSOrderedSame)
  {
    // do something else with the returned obj
    *stop=YES;
  }
}
];
```

When one of the words in the anArray object is @"test", then set the pointer *stop=YES to tell the anArray object to stop the enumeration early. Except id obj and BOOL *stop parameters for the block, there is also the NSUInteger index parameter. The index parameter lets an algorithm in the block know the position of the current element, and it's very useful for concurrent enumeration like this. Without the parameter, the only way to access the index would be to use the indexOfObject: method, which is inefficient.

The Block-Based Enumeration in an NSSet object is very similar to the one in an NSArray object, except the block signature doesn't have the index parameter as part of the callback process. An NSSet object is a data structure that simulates a set data structure; each element in a set doesn't have an index to refer the element's position in the structure.

A big benefit of using an internal iterator of NSArray, NSDictionary, and NSSet is that an algorithm that processes their contents can be defined elsewhere by different developers. Unlike algorithms defined in a traditional for loop, well-defined blocks can be reusable. When blocks are getting very large, we can put them in separate implementation files without crowding other code. Even though block is a convenient way to put inline algorithms without defining separate delegation protocols to complicate things, you should consider using the Strategy pattern (Chapter 19) for blocks that are too big to maintain.

Fast Enumeration

Objective-C 2.0 offers a type of enumeration called Fast Enumeration. It's the preferred method to do enumeration by Apple. It allows an enumeration of a collection object to be used as part of a for loop directly without using other enumerator objects, and it's more efficient than traditional index-based for loops. The syntax of Fast Enumeration is as follows.

```
NSArray * anArray = ... ;

for (NSString * item in anArray)
{
  // do something with the item
}
```

The enumeration loop now uses pointer arithmetic, which makes it more efficient than the standard methods of using NSEnumerator to achieve the same thing.

In order to utilize Fast Enumeration, a collection class needs to implement NSFastEnumeration protocol to provide necessary information regarding the underlying collection to the runtime. All collection classes as well as NSEnumerator in the Foundation framework support Fast Enumeration. So instead of enumerating each item from an NSEnumerator in a while loop until nextObject returns nil, you can use its Fast Enumeration version, like the following code snippet.

```
NSArray * anArray = ... ;
NSEnumerator * itemEnumerator = [anArray objectEnumerator];

for (NSString * item in itemEnumerator)
{
  // do something with the item
}
```

Even though you can use Fast Enumeration with a collection object as well as its enumerators, it would make more sense to fast enumerate a collection object directly if you need only a default traversal (mostly just by ascending order). NSEnumerator uses its nextObject method to implement the NSFastEnumeration protocol. Performance-wise, it might not be a whole lot better than just calling that method manually in a while loop. The for loop in Fast Enumeration seems cleaner than the traditional while loop with nextObject, though.

Implementing NSFastEnumeration is outside the scope of this book, so we will not discuss it here.

Internal Enumeration

NSArray has an instance method called (void)makeObjectsPerformSelector:(SEL)aSelector, which allows clients to send a message to each item in the array so each of them executes a provided aSelector (given an item supports it). You can achieve the same thing with one of those enumeration methods mentioned previously to let each of them execute the same selector. The method enumerates the underlying collection internally and sends a performSelector: message to each item. The downside of this approach is if any one of the items in the collection doesn't respond to the selector, an exception will be thrown. So it's mostly good for some simple operations without much runtime checking.

Enumerating Vertices of a Scribble

In the TouchPainter app that we discussed in Chapter 2, there is a composite data structure that contains all touched points that are used for drawing strokes on the screen. The structure has an abstract type called Mark. Its implementer is Stroke. A detailed discussion on Mark and the Composite pattern is in Chapter 13. Mark defines the behaviors of a part-whole composite structure (a tree) that contains individual dots and strokes with vertices. The part-whole structure doesn't have any logic as to how it's supposed to be traversed. Because it's a tree, it can be traversed in different orders. If we hard-coded any traversal behaviors in the tree, there'd be a lot of brute-force changes to the interfaces and implementations of Mark as well client code. A better solution than mixing traversal strategies in a tree structure is to add a factory method to Mark (see the Factory Method pattern, Chapter 4), so its implementers will create and return an appropriate enumerator to traverse the tree in a specific order. We are going to implement an iterator (enumerator) for Stroke by subclassing NSEnumerator. And we'll call it MarkEnumerator, which traverses a Mark composite tree post-orderly. NSEnumerator has two abstract methods, allObjects and nextObject. allObjects returns an array of un-traversed Mark instances in the composite, while nextObject returns the next item in the roll. A class diagram that illustrates the idea is shown in Figure 14–3.

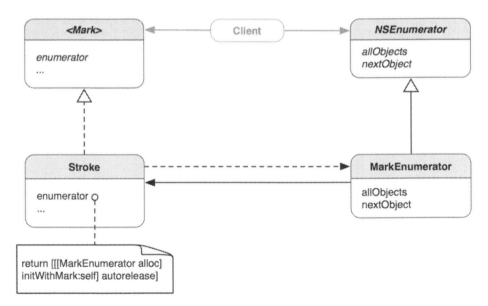

Figure 14–3. *A class diagram shows the relationships among* Client, Mark, Stroke, NSEnumerator, *and* MarkEnumerator.

Before we get to MarkEnumerator, let's first take a quick look at Mark so we'll have a better idea about how MarkEnumerator can traverse its children. We need to add a factory method called enumerator to Mark so its implementers can use that method to return an instance of an NSEnumerator's subclass (i.e., MarkEnumerator), as shown in Listing 14–1.

Listing 14–1. *Mark.h*

```
@protocol Mark <NSObject>

@property (nonatomic, retain) UIColor *color;
@property (nonatomic, assign) CGFloat size;
@property (nonatomic, assign) CGPoint location;
@property (nonatomic, readonly) NSUInteger count;
@property (nonatomic, readonly) id <Mark> lastChild;

- (void) addMark:(id <Mark>) mark;
- (void) removeMark:(id <Mark>) mark;
- (id <Mark>) childMarkAtIndex:(NSUInteger) index;

- (NSEnumerator *) enumerator;

@end
```

MarkEnumerator will perform post-order traversal on a Mark tree structure and enumerate each item at a time. So we are going to use a stack to do that. However, there is no ready-to-use stack class available from the Foundation framework. We will need to DIY it ourselves. But before we get to that, let's continue with the class definition of MarkEnumerator. Even though we are not required to re-declare overridden methods in subclasses in Objective-C because of its dynamic binding runtime, it's still a good practice to do so. The class definition of MarkEnumerator with overridden NSEnumerator methods is shown in Listing 14–2.

Listing 14–2. *MarkEnumerator.h*

```
#import "NSMutableArray+Stack.h"
#import "Mark.h"

@interface MarkEnumerator : NSEnumerator
{
  @private
  NSMutableArray *stack_;
}

- (NSArray *)allObjects;
- (id)nextObject;

@end
```

Based on our class design, a MarkEnumerator object is supposed to be created and initialized by one of the Mark's implementing classes. At the same time, a MarkEnumerator needs to know what Mark it needs to work on at the time of creation, so we need to define a private initWithMark: method in its anonymous category, as in Listing 14–3.

Listing 14–3. *An Anonymous Category That Declares Private Methods in* MarkEnumerator+Private.h

```
@interface MarkEnumerator ()

- (id) initWithMark:(id <Mark>)mark;
- (void) traverseAndBuildStackWithMark:(id <Mark>)mark;

@end
```

The reason we put the private methods in an anonymous category is that we wanted the implementation for them in the main @implementation block as well. In that private category, we also define another private method for traversing a Mark composite object. Although there are both public and private methods defined in two different places, their implementations are living in the same .m file, as in Listing 14–4.

Listing 14–4. *MarkEnumerator.m*

```objc
#import "MarkEnumerator.h"
#import "MarkEnumerator+Internal.h"

@implementation MarkEnumerator

- (NSArray *)allObjects
{
  // returns an array of yet-visited Mark nodes
  // i.e. the remaining elements in the stack
  return [[stack_ reverseObjectEnumerator] allObjects];
}

- (id)nextObject
{
  return [stack_ pop];;
}

- (void) dealloc
{
  [stack_ release];
  [super dealloc];
}

#pragma mark -
#pragma mark Private Methods

- (id) initWithMark:(id <Mark>)aMark
{
  if (self = [super init])
  {
    stack_ = [[NSMutableArray alloc] initWithCapacity:[aMark count]];

    // post-orderly traverse the whole Mark aggregate
    // and add individual Marks in a private stack
    [self traverseAndBuildStackWithMark:aMark];
  }

  return self;
}

- (void) traverseAndBuildStackWithMark:(id <Mark>)mark
{
  // push post-order traversal
  // into the stack
  if (mark == nil) return;

  [stack_ push:mark];

  NSUInteger index = [mark count];
```

```
    id <Mark> childMark;
    while (childMark = [mark childMarkAtIndex:--index])
    {
      [self traverseAndBuildStackWithMark:childMark];
    }
  }
}

@end
```

In its private initWithMark: method, it uses a reference to an incoming Mark reference and then fires up its own traverseAndBuildStackWithMark:(id <Mark>)mark method to traverse mark. The method calls itself recursively and pushes mark as well as any of its children in the stack (post-order traversal construction in stack). Notice that the children are pushed in reverse order (right-to-left). When we visit the elements in the stack, the children will be retrieved in their original order (left-to-right). Now the stack has all elements in the Mark aggregate, and it's ready to be used when a client sends the nextObject message to a MarkEnumerator object to retrieve the next Mark in the collection.

You might have noticed that the nextObject method has only one statement: return [stack_ pop];. After a traversal with Mark aggregate, elements that were pushed in a stack first will be popped out last. So the first child will be the first element returned by the nextObject method. Their parent will be returned after all of its children. allObjects is supposed to return an instance of NSArray that contains a collection of unvisited elements. As the stack pops forward in the collection and any popped element will be removed from it, returning what's left in the stack in the ascending direction will be just right.

We are using a stack to help traverse a Mark tree, but there is no such thing called NSStack packed in the Foundation framework for us to use. So we need to hack one of the closest Foundation classes, NSMutableArray, to make our own stack, as shown in Listing 14–5.

Listing 14–5. *NSMutableArray+Stack.h*

```
@interface NSMutableArray (Stack)

- (void) push:(id)object;
- (id) pop;

@end
```

We've added two methods to NSMutableArray as a category to push and pop objects like what a real stack does. Its push method pushes an object to the first position of itself, and pop always returns the first item and removes it, as shown in Listing 14–6.

Listing 14–6. *NSMutableArray+Stack.m*

```
#import "NSMutableArray+Stack.h"


@implementation NSMutableArray (Stack)

- (void) push:(id)object
{
  [self addObject:object];
```

```
}

- (id) pop
{
  if ([self count] == 0) return nil;

  id object = [[[self lastObject] retain] autorelease];
  [self removeLastObject];

  return object;
}

@end
```

Now let's get back to the Mark's family where we left off a little earlier. Stroke is the only member in the family whose objects will contain children; so it implements the enumerator method, while other family members don't. We omit them here for brevity. Its enumerator method simply creates and initializes an instance of MarkEnumerator with self as a parameter, and then it returns the instance, as shown in Listing 14–7.

Listing 14–7. *Stroke.m*

```
#import "Stroke.h"
#import "MarkEnumerator+Internal.h"

@implementation Stroke

@synthesize color=color_, size=size_;

- (id) init
{
  if (self = [super init])
  {
    children_ = [[NSMutableArray alloc] initWithCapacity:5];
  }

  return self;
}

- (void) setLocation:(CGPoint)aPoint
{
  // it doesn't set any arbitrary location
}

- (CGPoint) location
{
  // return the location of the first child
  if ([children_ count] > 0)
  {
    return [[children_ objectAtIndex:0] location];
  }

  // otherwise returns the origin
  return CGPointZero;
}

- (void) addMark:(id <Mark>) mark
```

```objectivec
{
  [children_ addObject:mark];
}

- (void) removeMark:(id <Mark>) mark
{
  // if mark is at this level then
  // remove it and return
  // otherwise, let every child
  // search for it
  if ([children_ containsObject:mark])
  {
    [children_ removeObject:mark];
  }
  else
  {
    [children_ makeObjectsPerformSelector:@selector(removeMark:)
                             withObject:mark];
  }
}

// needs to be added to draft
- (id <Mark>) childMarkAtIndex:(NSUInteger) index
{
  if (index >= [children_ count]) return nil;

  return [children_ objectAtIndex:index];
}

// a convenience method to return the last child
- (id <Mark>) lastChild
{
  return [children_ lastObject];
}

// returns number of children
- (NSUInteger) count
{
  return [children_ count];
}

- (void) dealloc
{
  [color_ release];
  [children_ release];
  [super dealloc];
}

#pragma mark -
#pragma mark enumerator method

- (NSEnumerator *) enumerator
{
  return [[[MarkEnumerator alloc] initWithMark:self] autorelease];
}

@end
```

Since enumerator is a factory method, it can return an object of a different MarkEnumerator subclass without modifications to client code. If we want the factory method to support different traversal methods, we can have the method accept a parameter that specifies the type of traversal so it can select a different MarkEnumerator at runtime.

> **NOTE:** It can be dangerous to modify an aggregate object while you're traversing it. If elements are added or deleted from the aggregate, you might end up accessing an element twice or missing it completely. A simple solution is to make a deep copy of the aggregate and traverse the copy, but it might be expensive if making and storing another copy of the aggregate can cause performance implications.
>
> There are many ways to implement iterators that wouldn't be interfered with by element insertions and removals. Most rely on registering the iterator with the aggregate. One way to achieve that is on insertion or removal; the aggregate either adjusts the internal state of iterators it has produced, or it maintains information internally to ensure proper traversal.

Enumerating Vertices of a Scribble (Internally)

The iterator (enumerator) that we have discussed so far is an external iterator that we have seen in the original description of the Iterator pattern. It needs a client to ask the collection object to return its iterator, and then loop through the iterator to visit each of its elements. The client each time sends a nextObject message to the iterator to retrieve an element in a loop until the collection is exhausted.

Without letting the client use any iterator (enumerator) directly, we can implement an internal iterator as another approach. The internal or passive iterator (usually the collection object itself) controls the iteration. You can implement an internal iterator by letting clients provide some sort of callback mechanism to the internal iterator so it can return the next element in a collection when it's ready.

Since the introduction of iOS SDK 4.0, we can use Objective-C blocks for application development. A block is a form of function type. Once it is defined, it can be reused anywhere in the application. Blocks are much more powerful than C function pointers in many ways. They are a natural choice for implementing internal iterators in Objective-C.

The class diagram in Figure 14–4 illustrates a possible way to implement an internal iterator for the Mark family.

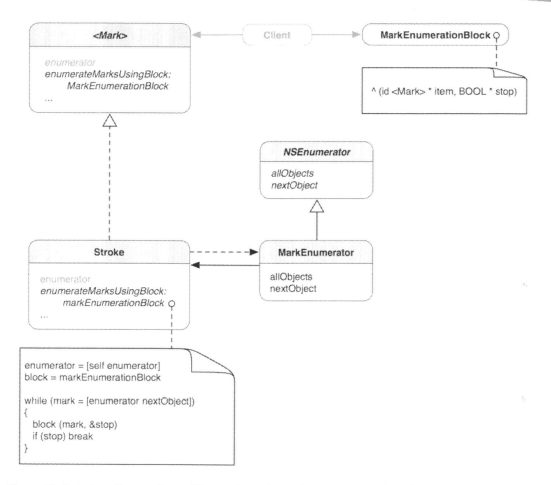

Figure 14–4. *A class diagram of a modified version of the* MarkEnumerator *and* Stroke *that implements an internal iterator with an introduction of* MarkEnumerationBlock

We have added a new method to the Mark, enumerateMarksUsingBlock:markEnumerationBlock. A client will provide a defined block with a signature of ^(id <Mark> item, BOOL *stop) as a parameter. The block defines an algorithm that processes each Mark element returned from the internal iterator. If the algorithm wants to stop the enumeration at the current position, it can set the *stop variable to YES to do so. As discussed in the sidebar table, a composite object itself, instead of clients, maintains an internal iterator. The enumerateMarksUsingBlock: method monitors the enumeration process with a loop that runs through an instance of MarkEnumerator. Every element obtained from the enumerator will be passed to a provided block, so the algorithm in it will be able to process the element.

If you want to let clients use the internal iterator exclusively, then you can put the enumerator factory method that returns an instance of MarkEnumerator in an anonymous category, just like we did for the MarkEnumerator class in Listing 14–3. It totally depends on the design.

Code snippets in Listings 14–8 and 14–9 show changes in both the Mark protocol and the Stroke class.

Listing 14–8. *Mark.h*

```
@protocol Mark <NSObject>

@property (nonatomic, retain) UIColor *color;
@property (nonatomic, assign) CGFloat size;
@property (nonatomic, assign) CGPoint location;
@property (nonatomic, readonly) NSUInteger count;
@property (nonatomic, readonly) id <Mark> lastChild;

- (void) addMark:(id <Mark>) mark;
- (void) removeMark:(id <Mark>) mark;
- (id <Mark>) childMarkAtIndex:(NSUInteger) index;

- (NSEnumerator *) enumerator;

// for internal iterator implementation
- (void) enumerateMarksUsingBlock:(void (^)(id <Mark> item, BOOL *stop)) block;

@end
```

The implementation of the enumerateMarksUsingBlock:(void (^)(id <Mark> item, BOOL * stop)) block in Stroke is as follows.

Listing 14–9. *The* enumerateMarksUsingBlock: *Method Implementation in* Stroke.m

```
- (void) enumerateMarksUsingBlock:(void (^)(id <Mark> item, BOOL *stop)) block
{
  BOOL stop = NO;

  NSEnumerator *enumerator = [self enumerator];

  for (id <Mark> mark in enumerator)
  {
    block (mark, &stop);
    if (stop)
      break;
  }
}
```

Summary

The Iterator pattern is somewhat similar to the Visitor pattern (Chapter 15), especially if you push the traversal algorithms into the Visitor pattern or let an internal iterator execute operations on elements while traversing an aggregate.

Other related patterns are the Composite (Chapter 13), Factory Method (Chapter 4), and Memento (Chapter 23). The Composite often relies on iterators to traverse its recursive structure. Polymorphic iterators rely on factory methods to instantiate the appropriate iterator concrete subclasses. Sometimes, mementos are used in conjunction with the

Iterator pattern. An iterator can use a memento to capture the state of iteration. The iterator stores the memento internally and restores its internal state later from it.

We have discussed some design patterns that are primarily related to abstract collection and its traversal. Next, we are going to talk about some other patterns that extend the behavior of abstract collection or other types of objects with minimal impact to the existing design.

Part VI

Behavioral Extension

Chapter 15

Visitor

Imagine you have some plumbing problems in your house but you don't know how to fix them. Even though you are the owner of the house, that doesn't mean you know all the ins and outs of it. Therefore, the most efficient way to solve this problem is to call in an expert to get it fixed as soon as possible.

In software design, a class can become extremely complex if the architect stuffs too many methods into it to extend its functionality. A better approach is to have an external class that knows how to extend it without changing the original code much.

The Visitor pattern can be easily described by using examples from your everyday life. In the case of the household plumbing problem, you don't want to learn how to fix plumbing (add more methods to a class). So you call in a plumber (visitor). When he arrives and rings your doorbell, you open the door and let him in (accept). Then he enters the house and fixes the plumbing (visits).

This chapter will cover the concepts of the Visitor pattern and how the plumber example relates to the pattern. We will design and implement a visitor that renders user strokes for the TouchPainter app that first appeared in Chapter 2.

What is the Visitor Pattern?

There are two key roles/components involved in the Visitor pattern, a visitor and an element that it visits. An element can be any object, but it is usually a node in a part-whole structure (see the Composite pattern in Chapter 13). A *part-whole structure* contains composite and leaf nodes or any other complex object structure. The element itself is not only limited to these kinds of structures. A visitor that knows every element in a complex structure can visit each of the element's nodes and perform any operations based on the element's attributes, properties, or operations. The class diagram in Figure 15–1 illustrates their static relationships.

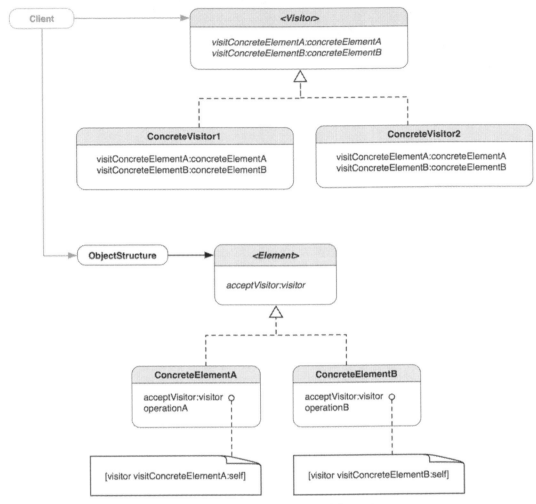

Figure 15–1. *A class diagram illustrating the static structure of the Visitor pattern*

The Visitor protocol declares a couple of similar-looking visit* methods that are used for visiting and processing objects of different Element types. ConcreteVisitor (1 or 2) implements the protocol and its abstract methods. A visit* operation defines appropriate operations that target a particular Element type. The Client creates a ConcreteVisitor (1 or 2) object and passes it to an Element object structure in which there is a method that accepts a generic Visitor type. The operation in each accept* method in the Element classes is almost the same. There is only a single statement that allows a Visitor object to visit the calling concrete Element object. The only difference between concrete Element classes is that the type of visit* message actually used is defined in each concrete Element class. Each time an acceptVisitor: message is passed to an Element structure, each node will be forwarded with the same message. The correct version of visit* method will be used, based on the actual type of the Element object determined at runtime.

> **NOTE:** The Visitor pattern represents an operation to be performed on the elements of an object structure. Visitor lets you define a new operation without changing the classes of the elements on which it operates. *
>
> * The original definition appeared in *Design Patterns*, by the "Gang of Four" (Addison-Wesley, 1994).

The class diagram in Figure 15–2 shows how the house contractor scenario can fit in the previous visitor-element relationships.

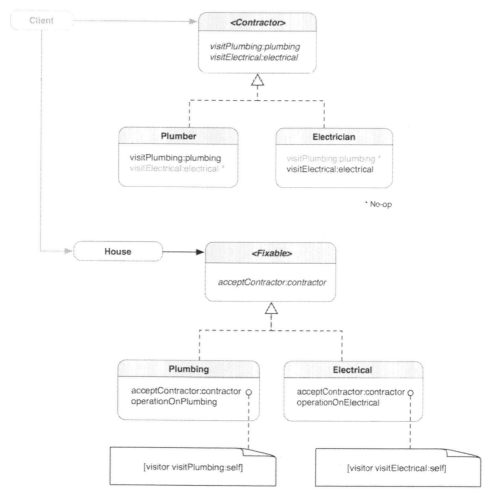

Figure 15–2. *A class diagram of the contractor examples as visitors*

This contractor version of the Visitor pattern reflects an implementation of the pattern in terms of the house contractor examples. Plumber and Electrician are visitors. House is a complex structure that contains Fixable abstraction items that a Contractor can visit and fix. A Plumber can visit the Plumbing structure of the House to fix it with its proprietary visitPlumbing: operation. Likewise, an Electrician can visit the Electrical components of the same House for the same reason with his own visitElectrical: operation. A general Contractor seems to know how to fix both Plumbing and Electrical, but in fact, it sub-contracts those jobs to a real person who knows how to get the job done, just like in the real world. You don't even need to care about the details; you just open the door to let him in and you pay for it after the job is done. Contractors (visitors) can perform certain technical jobs without the house owners needing to learn new skills (modifying existing code).

When Would You Use the Visitor Pattern

You can use the Visitor pattern in the following scenarios:

- A complex object structure contains many other objects with differing interfaces (e.g. a composite), and you want to perform operations based on their concrete types.

- You need to perform many unrelated operations on objects in a composite structure without polluting their classes with these operations. You can keep related operations together in one visitor class and use it when the operations defined in the visitor are needed.

- You often need to add new operations to a complex structure and the classes that define the structure rarely change.

Rendering Marks in TouchPainter with Visitors

One of the key features of the TouchPainter app discussed in Chapter 2 is that the user can draw anything on the screen with touches. In Chapter 13, you defined a composite data structure that contains user-created strokes and dots. The main purpose of the composite structure is to maintain the abstraction for clients that manipulate it without exposing its internal representation and the complexity. The high-level abstract interface for all types of leaf and composite nodes declares some primitive operations with which each of them can perform. If you need to add operations to a composite, you need to make changes to all of the interfaces for each node classes. If it happens often, the impact could be huge, especially for large projects. Class designers can try to predict possible feature extensions on a composite and add them to the class design, but this is not really a solution for an open-ended problem like this one.

A better solution is to apply the Visitor pattern to a composite. A visitor can be a consolidation of related operations that can be performed through a composite object based on the type of each node. It's like the plumber example where a plumber is a visitor who visits a house to fix plumbing related problems. Each node in a composite "accepts" a visitor to "visit" the node to fix problems or perform operations.

You can apply the same idea to extend the behavior of a Mark composite. In the code in Chapter 13, you added a drawing operation for each node to perform some basic drawing with an active graphics context on the CanvasView. You can also refactor the drawing algorithm out into a separate visitor called MarkRenderer. A MarkRenderer object can visit each node of a Mark composite and perform any Quartz 2D operations to render dots, vertices, and strokes on the screen. A visual diagram that illustrates how a MarkRenderer walks through a Mark composite to draw lines and dots is shown in Figure 15–3.

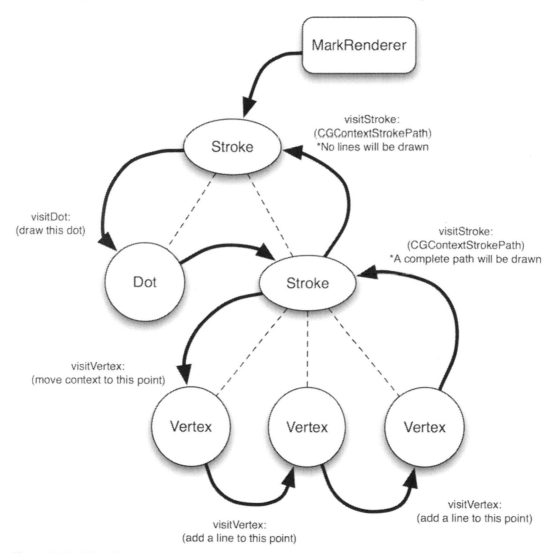

Figure 15–3. *A flow diagram of an actual rendering process with visitor MarkRenderer*

When a MarkRenderer object is visiting through the Mark composite structure, it invokes corresponding Quartz 2D operations based on the type of each node visited. Their static relationships are shown in the class diagram in Figure 15–4.

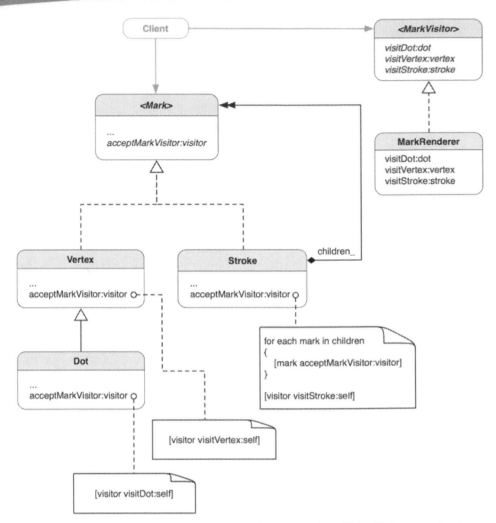

Figure 15–4. *A class diagram of MarkRenderer and its relationships with the Mark composite classes*

`MarkRenderer` implements the `MarkVisitor` protocol for various visiting operations on a `Mark` composite. Each `visit*` method should be only good for visiting one particular type of node and a parameter of a node is provided by the node itself at runtime.

On the side of the `Mark` family, each node has added a new method, `acceptMarkVisitor:`. When a client passes a `MarkVisitor` object to a `Mark` composite through the `acceptMarkVisitor:` method, the `MarkVisitor` object will be passed along the whole structure. The client has no idea how the visitor object gets passed down the pipeline. But every time the visitor object visits a particular node, an `acceptMarkVisitor:` method of the node will send a corresponding `visit*` message to the visitor. Based on the `visit*` method, appropriate operations will be carried out accordingly.

Let's look at how to put the whole thing in code. First, let's look at the `MarkVisitor` protocol, as shown in Listing 15–1.

Listing 15–1. *A Protocol Declaration of MarkVisitor in MarkVisitor.h*

```
@protocol Mark;
@class Dot, Vertex, Stroke;

@protocol MarkVisitor <NSObject>

- (void) visitMark:(id <Mark>)mark;
- (void) visitDot:(Dot *)dot;
- (void) visitVertex:(Vertex *)vertex;
- (void) visitStroke:(Stroke *)stroke;

@end
```

One of the reasons you define the top-level abstract type for `MarkVisitor` as a protocol is because you are not sure whether future `MarkVisitor` implementing classes need to subclass other classes for their services.

For now, your `MarkRenderer` is a subclass of `NSObject`, as shown in Listing 15–2.

Listing 15–2. *A Class Declaration of MarkRenderer in MarkRenderer.h*

```
#import "MarkVisitor.h"
#import "Dot.h"
#import "Vertex.h"
#import "Stroke.h"

@interface MarkRenderer : NSObject <MarkVisitor>
{
  @private
  BOOL shouldMoveContextToDot_;

  @protected
  CGContextRef context_;
}

- (id) initWithCGContext:(CGContextRef)context;

- (void) visitMark:(id <Mark>)mark;
- (void) visitDot:(Dot *)dot;
- (void) visitVertex:(Vertex *)vertex;
- (void) visitStroke:(Stroke *)stroke;

@end
```

`MarkRenderer` has some private and protected member variables. I'll get to them in a bit. `MarkRenderer` implements `MarkVisitor` and its `visit*` operations. It also declares an initialization method that takes a `CGContextRef` for drawing things later with all the nodes in a Mark composite. Now let's look at the implementation of `MarkRenderer` in Listing 15–3. I'll walk you through several major areas of the code.

Listing 15–3. *The Implementation of MarkRenderer in MarkRenderer.m*

```
#import "MarkRenderer.h"

@implementation MarkRenderer

- (id) initWithCGContext:(CGContextRef)context
```

```
{
  if (self = [super init])
  {
    context_ = context;
    shouldMoveContextToDot_ = YES;
  }
  return self;
}

- (void) visitMark:(id <Mark>)mark
{
  // default behavior
}
```

The visitMark: method should define any default behavior for any unknown Mark type or be used as a "catch-all" visitor method for any new node classes in the future (see the Note later in the chapter for a discussion on related issues). Your MarkRenderer doesn't implement any default behavior for Mark and leaves that method empty. Let's move forward to the next method, shown in Listing 15–4.

Listing 15–4. *Obtaining the Location, Size, and Color Information from the Node*

```
- (void) visitDot:(Dot *)dot
{
  CGFloat x = [dot location].x;
  CGFloat y = [dot location].y;
  CGFloat frameSize = [dot size];
  CGRect frame = CGRectMake(x - frameSize / 2.0,
                            y - frameSize / 2.0,
                            frameSize,
                            frameSize);

  CGContextSetFillColorWithColor (context_,[[dot color] CGColor]);
  CGContextFillEllipseInRect(context_, frame);
}
```

When it visits a Dot node, it obtains the location, size, and color information from the node. Then it draws a filled circle in context at a particular location on the screen, as shown in Listing 15–5.

Listing 15–5. *Drawing a Filled Circle at a Particular Location*

```
- (void) visitVertex:(Vertex *)vertex
{
  CGFloat x = [vertex location].x;
  CGFloat y = [vertex location].y;

  if (shouldMoveContextToDot_)
  {
    CGContextMoveToPoint(context_, x, y);
    shouldMoveContextToDot_ = NO;
  }
  else
  {
    CGContextAddLineToPoint(context_, x, y);
  }
}
```

When it comes to drawing a Vertex, things are done differently. There are three basic parts for drawing a line in Quartz 2D: move the context to a point, add a line to a point, and stroke the whole path. The first two steps should be determined when visiting vertices. Use a BOOL value shouldMoveContextToDot to determine whether it is visiting the Vertex node in a Stroke composite. The path-stroking step is the final step to realize the stroke when the visitor is finished visiting all the vertices in it, as shown in Listing 15–6.

Listing 15–6. *Drawing a Vertex*

```
- (void) visitStroke:(Stroke *)stroke
{
  CGContextSetStrokeColorWithColor (context_,[[stroke color] CGColor]);
  CGContextSetLineWidth(context_, [stroke size]);
  CGContextSetLineCap(context_, kCGLineCapRound);
  CGContextStrokePath(context_);
  shouldMoveContextToDot_ = YES;
}

@end
```

Then the visitStroke: method wraps up the stroke plotting process. The Stroke object determines attributes of a whole stroke, like color and line width. You also want to have the line ends appear rounded. The final function call of CGContextStrokePath() concludes the stroke drawing process.

> **NOTE:** A notable drawback of the Visitor pattern is that a visitor is coupled with target classes. So if a visitor needs to support new classes (such as adding a new node type to the Mark family), the parent visitors as well as other subclasses need to be changed to reflect the new functionality. If you don't add new classes to your target class family often, you should be fine.
>
> Because of unpredictable changes to the visitors in the future, it's a good idea to have a "catch-all" visit method for each visitor to support future target types. You have defined a visitMark: method in the MarkVisitor protocol (in Listing 15–1). The method should be able to cover any future new Mark types. However, it's just a stopgap solution. Should you need to add new nodes often, you may need to bite the bullet and change the visitor interfaces for supporting the new node types.

So far, you're done implementing your visitors for the Mark composite family. If no Mark family member accepts the visit from the visitors, your scheme won't work.

As mentioned previously, every node needs to have the acceptMarkVisitor: method that allows a visitor from any MarkVisitor. Each node type implements the same interface but allows a MarkVisitor to visit it differently. Let's take a look at the implementation of the acceptMarkVisitor: method in Dot in Listing 15–7.

Listing 15–7. *The Implementation of the acceptMarkVisitor: Method in Dot*

```
- (void) acceptMarkVisitor:(id <MarkVisitor>)visitor
{
  [visitor visitDot:self];
}
```

The method tells the `visitor` to visit a Dot (self). Now look at the same method in `Vertex` in Listing 15–8.

Listing 15–8. *The Implementation of the acceptMarkVisitor: Method in Vertex*

```
- (void) acceptMarkVisitor:(id <MarkVisitor>)visitor
{
  [visitor visitVertex:self];
}
```

The `visit*` message is almost the same as the one in `Dot` but this time it tells the visitor to visit a `Vertex`, which is referred as `self`.

Things look a bit different in `Stroke` because it is a composite class and its objects need to take care of their children. Its implementation for the same method is shown in Listing 15–9.

Listing 15–9. *The Implementation of the acceptMarkVisitor: Method in Stroke*

```
- (void) acceptMarkVisitor:(id <MarkVisitor>)visitor
{
  for (id <Mark> dot in children_)
  {
    [dot acceptMarkVisitor:visitor];
  }

  [visitor visitStroke:self];
}
```

It loops through all of its children and sends each of them a message of `acceptMarkVisitor:`. The type of node at runtime will determine what kind of `visit*` method the `visitor` should use, as discussed Listings 15–7 and 15–8. Then it finally tells the visitor to visit itself with a `visitStroke:` message. In a tree traversal term, this is called *post-ordered traversal*. It means that all the child nodes in a tree will be visited before their parents. Why do children go first? You need to make sure all the `Dots` are processed before any finalized steps performed in the `Stroke`. Of course, you can define your own traversal strategy for the composite; it all depends on the problem. A composite should be the only entity that knows its own internal structure and traversal strategies. With an iterator (see the Iterator pattern in Chapter 4), clients can enumerate every node in a composite structure without knowing any of its internal representation. There are also pre-order and in-order traversals, but post-ordered traversals are more common in composite objects. It's because operations in composite objects are mostly related to consolidating results from child nodes before finalizing and returning a result from the composite node.

So now you have set up all the pipelines for your plumbers to come in. Let's put the rest together in `CanvasView` and roll everything out in Listing 15–10.

Listing 15–10. *The drawRect: Method of CanvasView*

```
- (void)drawRect:(CGRect)rect
{
  // Drawing code
  CGContextRef context = UIGraphicsGetCurrentContext();

  // create a renderer visitor
  MarkRenderer *markRenderer = [[[MarkRenderer alloc] initWithCGContext:context]
                                                            autorelease];
  // pass this renderer along the mark composite structure
  [mark_ acceptMarkVisitor:markRenderer];
}
```

CanvasView has been mentioned in the previous chapters. It is responsible for presenting the user-drawn strokes and dots. Any custom drawing algorithm is put in the drawRect: method of UIView. When the view needs to redraw or refresh its content, it will call this method to execute any custom drawing code in it. As usual, before you can draw anything, you need to get a current graphics context. Then you use that context to instantiate a MarkRenderer object. A CanvasView object has a private member variable mark_, which represents the whole abstract composite structure of user's strokes at runtime. CanvasView will render mark_ on the screen by passing the MarkRenderer as a visitor to it with a message of acceptMarkVisitor:. Then the rendering process will be propagated along the structure as the MarkRenderer object pays a visit to each node. No matter how complex a Mark object is, it only takes three lines of code to draw the whole thing on the screen. Isn't it amazing?

What Else Can A Visitor Do?

In this example, you extended the Mark family classes with a visitor that renders their node objects so they can be displayed on the screen. You could also add another visitor that, for example, applies an *affine transformation* (rotation, scaling, shear, and translation) to a Mark composite by visiting each node. Other possible operations include changing the style of the strokes by applying different styling visitors to a Mark composite object or creating a visitor that debugs the structure. Note that if you put these operations in the Mark interface, you need to change every node class as well. So implementing the Visitor pattern to the composite structure should usually be your last task due to the interface changes in the composite classes.

Can't I Just Use Categories Instead?

Sure, you can use categories to extend the behavior of any Mark family members. In Chapter 13, you learned that you could define a drawWithContext: method in each node to render it on the screen. But instead of defining the method in each node, you can factor it out in individual categories. Each category for each node type implements the same drawWithContext: method. For your example, you need three different categories for your Mark composite and leaf nodes versus just one visitor that can consolidate related algorithms for all nodes in a single place. Also, should you extend the nodes again, you will either need to modify the existing categories or create new ones for them. In terms of the efforts you put in extending the existing Mark interfaces and its node classes, using categories is not a whole lot different from modifying them directly. In many cases, it's not much better than using visitors.

Summary

The Visitor pattern is a very powerful approach to extend functionality of a composite structure. If a composite structure has well thought-out primitive operations and the structure won't be changed in the future, different visitors can access the composite structure the same way but for different purposes. The Visitor pattern lets you separate a composite structure from other related algorithms in other visitor classes with minimal modification possible.

In the next chapter, you are going to see a pattern that can also help extend the object's behavior by "decorating" it from outside.

Chapter 16

Decorator

Most of the time, when you take pictures, you wouldn't think of how you would decorate them later. You take them just because you want to capture the moment. Let's say you have one of them printed later, and then you decide to put it in a nice frame with a type of special glass, so on and so forth. But you can put the same picture in a different frame later if you change your mind. Even though you have changed the frame for the picture, the picture is still the same one without being affected, because you were just adding something to the picture but not *changing* it.

In object-oriented software, we borrowed a similar idea to add "something" (behavior) to other objects without losing their original flavor—so an augmented object would be an enhanced version of the same class (a framed picture). Any "enhancement" (a frame) can be put on and taken off dynamically. We call this design pattern Decorator, as a decorator object can add to another decorator or the original object to extend its features, leaving the original behaviors intact.

In this chapter, we will first discuss the concepts of the pattern and when to use it. Then we will move forward to discuss how to take advantage of the pattern to design a series of image filtering classes for UIImage objects.

What Is the Decorator Pattern?

A classic Decorator pattern contains a parent, abstract Component class that declares some common operation for other concrete components. An abstract Component class can be refined into another abstract class called Decorator. A Decorator contains another Component reference. A ConcreteDecorator defines some extended behavior for other Components or Decorators alike and will execute the embedded Component's operation with its own. Their relationships are illustrated in Figure 16–1.

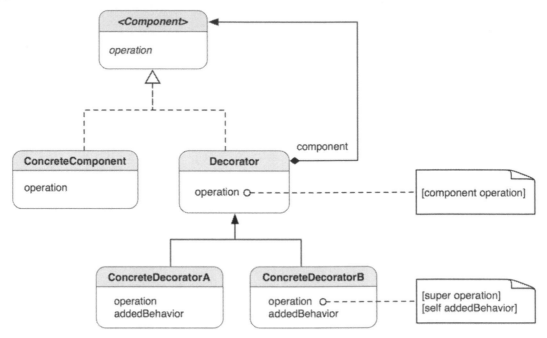

Figure 16–1. *A class diagram of the Decorator pattern*

Component defines some abstract operation that its concrete classes will override to
have their own specific operations. Decorator is an abstract class that defines a
"decorative" behavior to extend other instances of Component (or Decorator) by
embedding it in a Decorator object. Its default operation method is just simply to send a
message to its embedded component. ConcreteDecoratorA and ConcreteDecoratorB
override the parent's operation to augment its own added behavior to the component's
operation through super. If you need to add just one responsibility to the component,
then you can omit the abstract Decorator class and let the ConcreteDecorators forward
any requests to the component directly. If there are objects linked up this way, then it's
like forming a chain of operations with adding one behavior over another, as illustrated in
an object diagram in Figure 16–2.

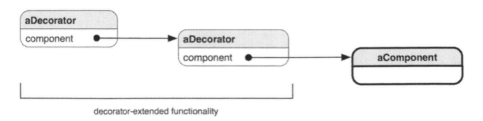

Figure 16–2. *An implementation of the Decorator pattern with decorator-extended functionality*

THE DECORATOR PATTERN: Attaches additional responsibilities to an object dynamically. Decorators provide a flexible alternative to subclassing for extending functionality.*

* The original definition appeared in *Design Patterns*, by the *"Gang of Four"* (Addison-Wesley, 1994).

When Would You Use the Decorator Pattern?

There are three common situations where you would consider using it:

- You want to add responsibility to individual objects dynamically and transparently without affecting other objects.

- You want to extend the behavior of a class that is impractical to do so. A class definition may be hidden and unavailable for subclassing—or each behavioral extension to a class would require a tremendous amount of subclasses to support each combination of features.

- Extended responsibilities of a class can be optional.

Changing the "Skin" vs. "Guts" of an Object

In the previous section, we discussed how different decorators can be connected at runtime with an internal component embedded in each decorator node, as shown in Figure 16–2. It also illustrates that each decorator is changing an embedded component from outside, or simply changing the skin of an object. The key is each node has no idea what's changing it.

However, when each node is aware of other different nodes internally, the link will instead grow in a different direction, i.e., inside the guts. That pattern is called Strategy (see Chapter 19). Each node needs to accommodate a set of different APIs internally to hook up another strategy node. A visual representation of the concept is shown in Figure 16–3.

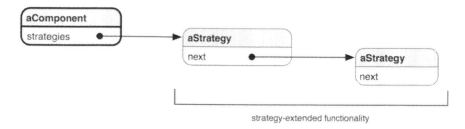

Figure 16–3. *Changing the "guts" of objects with the Strategy pattern*

The bottom-line differences between changing the "skin" (decorators) and "guts" (strategies) of an object are summarized in Table 16–1.

Table 16–1. *A Table of Summarized Differences Between Decorators and Strategies*

"Skin" Changing (Decorators)	"Guts" Changing (Strategies)
Change from outside	Change from inside
Each node is not aware of the changes.	Each node is aware of a set of predefined ways of changes.

Creating Image Filters for UIImage

Image filtering is a process with which we can modify images' attributes, like colors and geometry. We can have a filter that can change the hue of an image, or a Gaussian filter for blurring it so it looks like it is out of focus. We can even apply some sort of 2D warping transformation to it, so it doesn't look flat on a surface. There are many different possible filters out there we can use to put some "special effects" on images. A lot of photo editing software packages, like Photoshop and GIMP, come with a variety of filters. What does the image filtering do with the Decorator pattern in the first place?

The Decorator pattern is a way to add new behavior and responsibility to an object without altering any existing behaviors and interfaces. So let's say an image object contains only interfaces that allow clients to manage its attributes but nothing else. We want to add some fancy stuff to it, like a transformation filter, but we don't want to modify the existing interfaces that the image object already has. What we can do is to define another class that is the *same* as the image object but contains a reference to another image object to augment any behavior to. The new class has a method to draw itself to a drawing context. In its draw method, it applies its transformation algorithm to its embedded image reference, draws the whole thing, and returns a resulting image. We can picture the process as laying an extra layer of glass on top of a picture. The picture doesn't need to care about the glass, and when we look at it we still call it a picture. The glass itself can have some sort of tint, a wavy texture on the surface, or anything else to make the picture look different. Later if we want to apply another layer of filter to the image, then we can define another filter class, just like the one for transformation with which we can apply the same mechanism to augment its own operations to an image. Filters other than the transformation filter can pick up the resulting image and continue the process. One thing, though—the image being passed along the line of decorating filters doesn't need to be always the original one but should be the same *type*. So the image returned from a transformation filter is a transformed image. Then when it's passed through to a color filter, the returned image will be a tinted-transformed image, so on and so forth.

UIImage in the UIKit of the Cocoa Touch framework can be instantiated as image objects. The UIImage class itself has quite limited interfaces to manipulate an image. There is nothing more than just a few properties about an image, such as the image size, color space, etc. We are going to extend an ordinary image object with some image manipulation tools available from the Quartz 2D framework. There are two approaches to implement the pattern, true subclasses and categories.

Implementing Decorators with True Subclasses

In the true subclass approach, we will have a structure similar to the original flavor of the pattern, as shown in Figure 16–1. The only difference is that the terminal component type is a category of UIImage, not a subclass of it. There is a little structural problem that prevents us from sharing with the same "interface" that UIImage implements. UIImage is a direct subclass of NSObject but nothing else. It's a sort of terminal class on its own. In order to use a kind of "Component" interface (like the parent interface in the class diagram in Figure 16–1) to bring both UIImage and our filter classes together, we need to have a creative solution. At this point, we are facing two problems:

- We need to make our image filter classes the same as UIImage, but UIImage doesn't have any high-level interface to share with (subclassing is not a kind of solution that this pattern suggests).

- UIImage has multiple methods related to drawing its content to a current drawing context, such as drawAsPatternInRect:, drawAtPoint:, drawAtPoint:blendMode:alpha:, drawInRect:, and drawInRect:blendMode:alpha:. Allowing image filter classes to implement the same methods is complicated and may not achieve the kind of result we want due to the way Quartz 2D works. We will get to that a little later.

What are we going to do? First of all, it's for sure that we need an interface to share UIImage with a bunch of filter classes to make this pattern work, so both types of classes can share the same base type. And we don't like the idea of using UIImage as a high-level type for that purpose (i.e., subclassing it) because it will make every filter heavy to use. We create an interface called ImageComponent as a protocol as the ultimate base type for everyone. But wait a minute; did we just mention UIImage doesn't inherit any interface but just a direct subclass of NSObject? That's correct—so that's where we need a creative solution. We will create a category of UIImage that implements ImageComponent. Then the compiler will know UIImage and ImageComponent are related and won't complain about it. UIImage doesn't even know it has a new base type. Only the people who use the filters will need to know about that.

Also, we are not going to mess with the original draw* methods defined in UIImage, but how can we augment any drawing behavior to another ImageComponent? We will get to that in just a little bit.

The class diagram that shows their static relationships is shown in Figure 16–4.

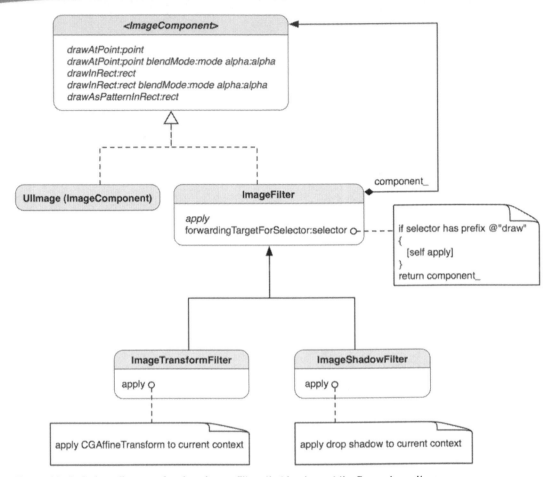

Figure 16–4. *A class diagram of various image filters that implement the Decorator pattern*

ImageComponent protocol declares an abstract interface with all draw* methods from UIImage. Any concrete ImageComponent and decorators alike should be able to handle those calls. A draw* message for an instance of UIImage will let it draw its own content in the current graphics context. Each of the methods also respects any transforms and other effects applied to the context. So we can inject our own filtering before any draw* operations.

Our concrete component here is a type of UIImage, but we don't want to make a subclass of it just for making it part of the game, so we define a category for it. The UIImage (ImageComponent) category adopts ImageComponent protocol. Since all methods declared in the protocol are already in UIImage, we don't need to implement them in the category. The category basically does nothing more than to tell the compiler that it's also a kind of ImageComponent.

ImageFilter is like the abstract Decorator class in Figure 16–1. ImageFilter's apply method allows concrete filter subclasses to augment extra behavior to the base component_'s behaviors. Instead of overriding all draw* methods to inject any filtering behavior, we use a single method, (id) forwardingTargetForSelector:(SEL) aSelector, to handle all that. forwardingTargetForSelector: is defined in NSObject, which allows subclasses to return an alternate receiver to handle aSelector. An instance of ImageFilter will first test to see if aSelector is a draw* message. If so, it will send itself an apply message to augment any behavior before returning the base component_ to respond with default behavior. The default implementation of apply does nothing. That missing information should be provided by subclasses. This approach can keep the architecture simple rather than letting each concrete filter class implements the same mechanism to augment behaviors.

Both ImageTransformFilter and ImageShadowFilter focus on providing their own filter algorithms by overriding the apply method. They inherit the abstract ImageFilter base class that has a reference to another ImageComponent with a private member variable component_. Different objects of ImageComponent can be connected at runtime, like in Figure 16–5.

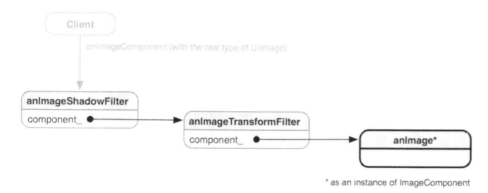

Figure 16–5. *An object diagram showing each* ImageComponent *is referenced in another instance of* ImageComponent *at each level.*

The right end of the chain is the original image as shown on the left side in Figure 16–6. After we first add it to anImageTransformFilter and then add anImageTransformFilter to anImageShadowFilter, the client will get something like the right-hand image in Figure 16–6. Each node is encapsulated as component_ of another instance of ImageComponent. An analogy of it is a bigger fish swallowing another smaller fish and so on. Obviously, the client doesn't realize any details about the decorators and whatnot but just a reference to an instance of the same old UIImage (as a form of ImageComponent because UIImage is implementing ImageComponent through its category).

Figure 16–6. *An original image vs. the same image after applying a series of image filters*

It's getting exciting. Let's see how we can knock it off in code. The first one we are going to look at is the abstract ImageComponent that is declared as a protocol in Listing 16–1.

Listing 16–1. *ImageComponent.h*

```
@protocol ImageComponent <NSObject>

// We will intercept these
// UIImage methods and add
// additional behavior
@optional
- (void) drawAsPatternInRect:(CGRect)rect;
- (void) drawAtPoint:(CGPoint)point;
- (void) drawAtPoint:(CGPoint)point
        blendMode:(CGBlendMode)blendMode
            alpha:(CGFloat)alpha;
- (void) drawInRect:(CGRect)rect;
- (void) drawInRect:(CGRect)rect
        blendMode:(CGBlendMode)blendMode
            alpha:(CGFloat)alpha;

@end
```

The entire draw* methods are declared as @optional, as we want any ImageComponent to be able to support the operations but we don't actually override them in implementing classes. The keyword @optional tells the compiler not to complain when it can't find the corresponding implementations for the methods.

Listing 16–2 shows the declaration of a category for UIImage so we can use it with other decorators later.

Listng 16–2. *UIImage+ImageComponent.h*

```
#import "ImageComponent.h"

@interface UIImage (ImageComponent) <ImageComponent>

@end
```

It conforms to the ImageComponent protocol without any actual implementation at all. Now we move forward to our core decorator class, ImageFilter. Its class declaration is shown in Listing 16–3.

Listing 16–3. *ImageFilter.h*

```
#import "ImageComponent.h"
#import "UIImage+ImageComponent.h"

@interface ImageFilter : NSObject <ImageComponent>
{
  @private
  id <ImageComponent> component_;
}

@property (nonatomic, retain) id <ImageComponent> component;

- (void) apply;
- (id) initWithImageComponent:(id <ImageComponent>) component;
- (id) forwardingTargetForSelector:(SEL)aSelector;

@end
```

It's keeping a reference to ImageComponent as component_ , which would be decorated by any other concrete decorators. ImageFilter overrides forwardingTargetForSelector: and declares apply. Its implementation is shown in Listing 16–4.

Listing 16–4. *ImageFilter.m*

```
#import "ImageFilter.h"

@implementation ImageFilter

@synthesize component=component_;


- (id) initWithImageComponent:(id <ImageComponent>) component
{
  if (self = [super init])
  {
    // save an ImageComponent
    [self setComponent:component];
```

```
    }

    return self;
}

- (void) apply
{
  // should be overridden by subclasses
  // to apply real filters
}

- (id) forwardingTargetForSelector:(SEL)aSelector
{
  NSString *selectorName = NSStringFromSelector(aSelector);
  if ([selectorName hasPrefix:@"draw"])
  {
    [self apply];
  }

  return component_;
}

@end
```

There is not much going on in the initWithImageComponent: method. It just simply assigns an ImageComponent reference from the parameter to itself. Also, its apply method does nothing for now until we see it again in concrete filter classes later.

What's interesting here is that we are using forwardingTargetForSelector: to intercept message calls that an instance of ImageFilter doesn't know how to respond to. The method allows subclasses to forward an alternative receiver to the runtime so the original message will be forwarded. But we are interested only in anything with a prefix of @"draw", and then we forward anything else straight to component_ by returning it to the runtime. For example, when the message drawAtRect: is sent to an instance of ImageFilter, it will be caught in the forwardingTargetForSelector: method pending for an alternative receiver because ImageFilter doesn't have any implementation for it. Since the message contains a prefix of "draw", it forwards itself an apply message to do anything before component_ picks up the message later.

Next, we are ready to get some real filters. The first one we are going to create is ImageTransformFilter, as shown in Listing 16–5.

Listing 16–5. *ImageTransformFilter.h*

```
#import "ImageFilter.h"

@interface ImageTransformFilter : ImageFilter
{
  @private
  CGAffineTransform transform_;
}

@property (nonatomic, assign) CGAffineTransform transform;

- (id) initWithImageComponent:(id <ImageComponent>)component
                    transform:(CGAffineTransform)transform;
```

```
- (void) apply;
```

`@end`

ImageTransformFilter is a subclass of ImageFilter and overrides the apply method. It also declares a private member transform_ as CGAffineTransform with an associated property that can access it. Since CGAffineTransform is a C struct, the property should be an assign type because a value of it cannot be retained like other Objective-C objects. The filter has its own method for initialization. The initWithImageComponent: (id <ImageComponent>)component transform: (CGAffineTransform)tranform method takes an instance of ImageComponent and a value of CGAffineTransform during initialization. component will be forwarded to the initWithComponent: method of super, and transform will be assigned to the private member variable, as shown in Listing 16–6.

Listing 16–6. *ImageTransformFilter.m*

```
@implementation ImageTransformFilter

@synthesize transform=transform_;


- (id) initWithImageComponent:(id <ImageComponent>)component
                    transform:(CGAffineTransform)transform
{
  if (self = [super initWithImageComponent:component])
  {
    [self setTransform:transform];
  }

  return self;
}

- (void) apply
{
  CGContextRef context = UIGraphicsGetCurrentContext();

  // setup transformation
  CGContextConcatCTM(context, transform_);
}

@end
```

In the apply method, we get a reference of CGContextRef from a Quartz 2D function UIGraphicsGetCurrentContext(). We are not going into the details of Quartz 2D drawing here. Once we have a valid current context reference, we pass the transform_ value to CGContextConcatCTM() to add it to the context. Whatever is drawn on the context later will be transformed with the passed-in CGAffineTransform value. The affine transform filtering is now complete.

Like ImageTransformFilter, ImageShadowFilter is also a direct subclass of ImageFilter and overrides only the apply method. In the method shown in Listing 16–7, we obtain a current graphics context to draw stuff in, then we set up a Quartz 2D function call, CGContextSetShadow(), to add a drop shadow in the context. Then the rest of the process is pretty much the same as the ImageTransformFilter's. Whatever is drawn in the context afterward will have a drop shadow effect, as shown in the right-hand image in Figure 16–6.

Listing 16–7. *ImageShadowFilter.m*

```
#import "ImageShadowFilter.h"

@implementation ImageShadowFilter

- (void) apply
{
  CGContextRef context = UIGraphicsGetCurrentContext();

  // set up shadow
  CGSize offset = CGSizeMake (-25,  15);
  CGContextSetShadow(context, offset, 20.0);
}

@end
```

Now we have fleshed out all the filters and are ready to keep the ball rolling in client code. In the sample project for this chapter, there is a class called DecoratorViewController that will run all the filters just defined in its viewDidLoad method, as shown in Listing 16–8.

Listing 16–8. *viewDidLoad Method in DecoratorViewController.m*

```
- (void)viewDidLoad
{
  [super viewDidLoad];

  // load the original image
  UIImage *image = [UIImage imageNamed:@"Image.png"];


  // create a transformation
  CGAffineTransform rotateTransform = CGAffineTransformMakeRotation(-M_PI / 4.0);
  CGAffineTransform translateTransform = CGAffineTransformMakeTranslation(
                                            -image.size.width / 2.0,
                                             image.size.height / 8.0);
  CGAffineTransform finalTransform = CGAffineTransformConcat(rotateTransform,
                                                translateTransform);


  // a true subclass approach
  id <ImageComponent> transformedImage = [[[ImageTransformFilter alloc]
                                            initWithImageComponent:image
                                            transform:finalTransform]
                                            autorelease];
  id <ImageComponent> finalImage = [[[ImageShadowFilter alloc]
                                        initWithImageComponent:transformedImage]
                                        autorelease];

  // create a new DecoratorView
  // with a filtered image
  DecoratorView *decoratorView = [[[DecoratorView alloc]
                                      initWithFrame:[self.view bounds]]
                                      autorelease];
```

```
    [decoratorView setImage:finalImage];
    [self.view addSubview:decoratorView];
}
```

We first create an image reference to the original butterfly image shown on the left side in Figure 16–6. Then we construct a `CGAffineTransform` to rotate and translate the image accordingly. Both the image and the transform are used to initialize an instance of `ImageTransformFilter` as the first filter for the image. Then we use the whole component to construct an instance of `ImageShadowFilter` to add a drop shadow obtained from the `ImageTransformFilter` step. At this point, `finalImage` is the head of the link that contains `ImageTransformFilter`, `ImageShadowFilter`, and the original image. Then we assign the whole component to an instance of `DecoratorView` before we add it to the controller as a subview. What `DecoratorView` does is to draw an image in its `drawRect:rect` method, as shown in Listing 16–9.

Listing 16–9. *drawRect:rect Method in DecoratorView.m*

```
- (void)drawRect:(CGRect)rect
{
    // Drawing code.
    [image_ drawInRect:rect];
}
```

`DecoratorView` keeps a target reference of `UIImage` as `image_`. The `drawRect:rect` method forwards a message of `drawInRect:rect` to `image_` with its `rect` parameter. Then the whole chain of decorative operations will go from there. `ImageShadowFilter` will pick up the message first. After it sets up a drop shadow in a current graphics context and returns the embedded `component_` from the `forwardingTargetForSelector:` method, the same message will be forwarded to the returned `component_` as the next step. At this time, `component_` is, in fact, the instance of `ImageTransformFilter` when we constructed the chain in the previous steps. It also gets caught with the same `forwardingTargetFor Selector:` method and sets a current context up with a predefined `CGAffineTransform` value. Then it returns the embedded `component_` again like what `ImageShadowFilter` does. But this time, it's the original butterfly image—so when it's returned from `ImageTransformFilter` and picks up the message as the last step, it will draw in the current context with respect to all the drop shadows and affine transform. That's the whole sequence of operations in which we get a transformed and drop-shadowed image, as shown in Figure 16–6.

> **NOTE:** Filters can be connected in different orders.

We can use categories to create the same thing with a little twist. The next section will show you how.

Implementing Decorators with Categories

In the category approach, we only need to add the filters to the `UIImage` class as categories, and they will work just like separate `UIImage` classes—but they are not. This is the beauty of categories in Objective-C. We are going to add two filters, one for applying a 2D transformation to an image and the other one for dropping a shadow on it. A class diagram that illustrates their relationships is shown in Figure 16–7.

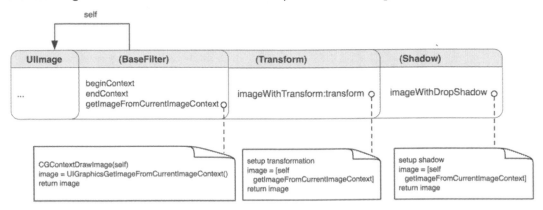

Figure 16–7. *A class diagram of different image filters as private categories of* UIImage

Like in the previous section, we will implement transformation and shadow filters. We have three categories for this approach, UIImage (BaseFilter), UIImage (Transform), and UIImage (Shadow). From now on, I will refer to them as BaseFilter, Transform, and Shadow respectively. BaseFilter defines some basic 2D drawing chores that draw itself in the current drawing context similar to the abstract class ImageFilter in the last section. Other filter categories can use the same method to draw whatever image reference is being held by it. Both Transform and Shadow are not inheriting the BaseFilter, but they are in the same lineage, as they are all categories of the UIImage. Methods defined in the BaseFilter can be used in both Transform and Shadow categories without any inheritance like subclassing does. The Transform category defines an imageWithTransform:transform method that takes a transform reference (we will get to the details a bit later), applies it to an internal image reference, and lets it draw itself and then return the transformed image. The Shadow category defines an imageWithDropShadow method that drops a shadow to an internal image reference and returns a final image that has the effect applied. You have probably already noticed that they can also be linked up like the ones in the true subclass approach described in the previous section. An object diagram that illustrates that is shown in Figure 16–8.

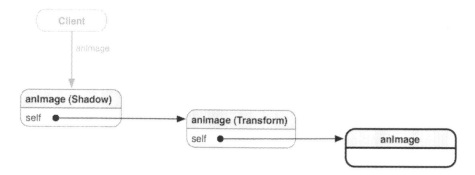

Figure 16–8. *An object diagram shows how different filter categories refer to other instances of* `UIImage` *at runtime.*

The right end of the link is the original image, like the left-hand image in Figure 16–6. After adding the original image to a `Shadow` filter and then a `Transform` filter, the client that is referencing an image object will get something that looks like the right-hand image in Figure 16–6. The structure of the link is very similar to the true subclass version except that each category is using `self` as a reference to the underlying image reference instead of a separate reference like `component_`.

Let's cut some code. We will first define `BaseFilter` that has some default behaviors for other concrete filters, as illustrated in Listing 16–10.

Listing 16–10. *UIImage+BaseFilter.h*

```
@interface UIImage (BaseFilter)

- (CGContextRef) beginContext;
- (UIImage *) getImageFromCurrentImageContext;
- (void) endContext;

@end
```

`BaseFilter` has three methods that help draw itself in the current context, as in Listing 16–11.

Listing 16–11. *UIImage+BaseFilter.m*

```
#import "UIImage+BaseFilter.h"


@implementation UIImage (BaseFilter)

- (CGContextRef) beginContext
{
  // Create a graphics context with the target size
  // On iOS 4 and later, use UIGraphicsBeginImageContextWithOptions
  // to take the scale into consideration
  // On iOS prior to 4, fall back to use UIGraphicsBeginImageContext
  CGSize size = [self size];
  if (NULL != UIGraphicsBeginImageContextWithOptions)
    UIGraphicsBeginImageContextWithOptions(size, NO, 0);
  else
```

```
    UIGraphicsBeginImageContext(size);

  CGContextRef context = UIGraphicsGetCurrentContext();

  return context;
}

- (UIImage *) getImageFromCurrentImageContext
{
  [self drawAtPoint:CGPointZero];

  // Retrieve the UIImage from the current context
  UIImage *imageOut = UIGraphicsGetImageFromCurrentImageContext();

  return imageOut;
}

- (void) endContext
{
  UIGraphicsEndImageContext();
}

@end
```

beginContext is almost the same as the one in the true subclass version. All necessary scaffolding for drawing itself in the current context is taking place in there. Once a context is ready to be drawn on, the method will return it to whoever asked for it.

getImageFromCurrentImageContext draws itself with the context and returns an image out of it by calling UIGraphicsGetImageFromCurrentImageContext().

Then a message of endContext wraps up the process with a Quartz 2D function call, UIGraphicsEndImageContext(), to clean up context-related resources.

Now we are ready for our real filter categories. The first one we are going to look at is the Transform category. Transform has only one method that takes a CGAffineTransform structure and applies it to an image. Its declaration is in Listing 16–12.

Listing 16–12. *UIImage+Transform.h*

```
@interface UIImage (Transform)

- (UIImage *) imageWithTransform:(CGAffineTransform)transform;

@end
```

Its implementation is very straightforward, as shown in Listing 16–13.

Listing 16–13. *UIImage+Transform.m*

```
#import "UIImage+Transform.h"
#import "UIImage+BaseFilter.h"

@implementation UIImage (Transform)

- (UIImage *) imageWithTransform:(CGAffineTransform)transform
{
  CGContextRef context = [self beginContext];
```

```
    // setup transformation
    CGContextConcatCTM(context, transform);

    // Draw the original image to the context
    UIImage *imageOut = [self getImageFromCurrentImageContext];

    [self endContext];

    return imageOut;
}

@end
```

It takes a CGAffineTransform structure that has information to an affine transform matrix. The method passes transform and a context to a Quartz 2D function, CGContextConcatCTM(context, transform). Then transform is added to the current drawing context. Now it sends the getImageFromCurrentImageContext message self that was defined in the BaseFilter category to draw itself on the screen. After an instance of UIImage is returned from the message call, it sends an endContext message to itself to close the current drawing context and finally returns the image.

We've got our Transform filter done. It's easy, isn't it? Now we can define our Shadow filter just as easily as that one, as in Listing 16–14.

Listing 16–14. *UIImage+Shadow.h*

```
@interface UIImage (Shadow)

- (UIImage *) imageWithDropShadow;

@end
```

Just like the Transform filter, Shadow is a category of UIImage and has a single method. The method doesn't take any parameters, but it has a couple more steps in an implementation than the Transform filter does. We can see how to drop a shadow on an image in Listing 16–15.

Listing 16–15. *UIImage+Shadow.m*

```
#import "UIImage+Shadow.h"
#import "UIImage+BaseFilter.h"

@implementation UIImage (Shadow)

- (UIImage *) imageWithDropShadow
{
    CGContextRef context = [self beginContext];

    // set up shadow
    CGSize offset = CGSizeMake (-25,  15);
    CGContextSetShadow(context, offset, 20.0);

    // Draw the original image to the context
    UIImage * imageOut = [self getImageFromCurrentImageContext];

    [self endContext];
```

```
    return imageOut;
}


@end
```

We first construct some attributes for a shadow we want with a Quartz 2D function call, `CGSizeMake (-25, 15)`, where the two parameters represent offsets in both X and Y directions. Then we pass a graphics context in `CGContextSetShadow(context, offset, 20.0)`, which is another Quartz 2D function, with a floating-point parameter 20.0 that indicates a blurring factor. Finally, like in the `addTranform:` method of the `Transform` category, it draws itself out onscreen, grabs a returned `UIImage` from it, and then returns it.

So far, we've got everything we needed to do image filtering for an instance of `UIImage`. How are we going to use them? We are going to throw them in the same `viewDidLoad` method of `DecoratorViewController`, as shown in Listing 16–16.

Listing 16–16. *viewDidLoad Method in DecoratorViewController.m*

```
- (void)viewDidLoad
{
    [super viewDidLoad];

    // load the original image
    UIImage *image = [UIImage imageNamed:@"Image.png"];


    // create a transformation
    CGAffineTransform rotateTransform = CGAffineTransformMakeRotation(-M_PI / 4.0);
    CGAffineTransform translateTransform = CGAffineTransformMakeTranslation(
                                              -image.size.width / 2.0,
                                               image.size.height / 8.0);
    CGAffineTransform finalTransform = CGAffineTransformConcat(rotateTransform,
                                                      translateTransform);


    // a category approach
    // add transformation
    UIImage *transformedImage = [image imageWithTransform:finalTransform];

    // add shadow
    id <ImageComponent> finalImage = [transformedImage imageWithDropShadow];

    // create a new image view
    // with a filtered image
    DecoratorView *decoratorView = [[[DecoratorView alloc]
                                        initWithFrame:[self.view bounds]]
                                        autorelease];
    [decoratorView setImage:finalImage];
    [self.view addSubview:decoratorView];
}
```

The original image reference and the transformation setup, etc., are the same as in Listing 16–8 of the true subclass version. The only differences are that `imageWithTransform:` that applies a transformation to an image is executed by the image itself, and it returns a transformed image (the original is intact). Then the transformed image executes imageWithDropShadow to drop a shadow on itself, and then returns a dropped-shadow version of itself as a new image called finalImage. Then finalImage will be added to imageView and displayed on the screen just like in the true subclass approach. A one-line version of putting all the filters together with the original image can go like this:

```
finalImage = [[image imageWithTransform:finalTransform] imageWithDropShadow];
```

At this point, can you tell any differences between the category and true subclass approaches? That's correct—the filters of UIImage in categories are instance methods vs. real subclasses in the true subclass approach. There is no inheritance in the category approach as all of the filters are still part of UIImage! We use ImageComponent as an abstract type in the true subclass approach, while we can use UIImage all the way throughout the category approach. However, like using true subclasses, any filter can be applied in different orders in the category approach.

The design for the category version seems simpler for implementing the same image filtering on a UIImage object. It's simpler because we were using categories and no actual subclassing and encapsulating of another UIImage object in order to extend a decorator link. In the next section, we will talk about some pros and cons of using categories to adopt the pattern.

OBJECTIVE-C CATEGORIES AND THE DECORATOR PATTERN

A category is an Objective-C language feature that enables you to add behavior (method interface and implementation) to a class without subclassing it. There is no adverse effect on the original methods of the class with methods added by the category. The methods in the category become part of the class and can be inherited by its subclasses.

Like we have seen in the previous example, we can use categories to implement the Decorator pattern. However, it's not a strict adaptation of it; it is fulfilling the intent but being done as a variant. The behavior added by Decorator categories is a compile-time artifact even though Objective-C supports dynamic binding (what implementation of a method should be used) by nature. Also Decorator categories don't actually encapsulate an instance of the class being extended.

Despite the fact that using categories to implement the pattern is slightly deviated from the original flavor of it, they are lightweight and easier to implement for small amounts of decorators than the true subclass approach. Although the UIImage categories in the previous example don't have strict encapsulation of another component, the instance being extended is indirectly referenced as self in UIImage.

Summary

We have introduced the Decorator pattern with its concepts and different approaches to implement it in Objective-C. A true subclass implementation uses a more structured approach to connect different decorators. A categories approach is simpler and more lightweight than its counterpart. It's suitable for applications that require only a small amount of decorators for existing classes. Although categories are different from actual subclassing and cannot strictly adapt the original flavor of the pattern, They fulfill the intent to solve the same kind of problems. The Decorator pattern is a natural choice for designing applications like the image filtering example. Any combination of image filters can be applied or removed dynamically without affecting the integrity of the original behaviors of `UIImage`.

In the next chapter, we will see a design pattern that is similar to the Decorator pattern but serves different purposes. It's called Chain of Responsibility.

Chapter 17

Chain of Responsibility

No one can know everything, so there is a saying that "two brains are better than one." If it's true, then more brains chained together will be even better. Everybody knows a little bit of something and can unite together to form a powerful entity. It's pretty much like families helping each other in the same neighborhood or collaborations among team members on projects in an organization. Every unit in a chain of brains can contribute to tackling problems. If a unit of the chain doesn't know how to handle a problem, then it will pass the problem along the chain and somebody may be able to handle it. Or sometimes, the problem may still be passed along even though there is a unit that knows how to handle it. So a particular process to solve a problem can be complete. It's analogous to an assembly line; every worker knows how to put particular parts to every unfinished product on the conveyer belt. But the product needs to be passed along the chain of workers on the assembly line until the last one to complete it before it can be shipped. Each worker has his own specialties and responsibility on a production line. So the chain of responsibility can be formed like, "I don't know this problem, maybe you would" or "I am done with my part, now it's your turn." This kind of chain of "brains" or "responsibility" allows further upgrades or expansion without modifying what existing units can do. New units are just simply added to the chain, and then the chain will be more capable. Extra workers are added to the end of the line for adding some more parts to the product. The process of adding workers to the production line shouldn't affect other existing workers.

This kind of concept can benefit object-oriented software design when you want to have some objects in the same group handle particular requests and adding or removing handlers in the group should not affect the integrity of the group.

In this chapter, we are going to discuss the concepts of the Chain of Responsibility pattern and how to implement it for the design of a protection mechanism for avatars in a role-playing game (RPG).

What Is the Chain of Responsibility Pattern?

The main idea of the Chain of Responsibility pattern is that an object has a reference to another object of the same type to form a chain. Each object in the chain implements the same method to handle the same request that is initiated on the first object in the chain. If any one of the objects doesn't know how to handle the request, then it will pass the request to the next responder (successor). The relationship between the object that can handle a request and its successor is illustrated in Figure 17–1.

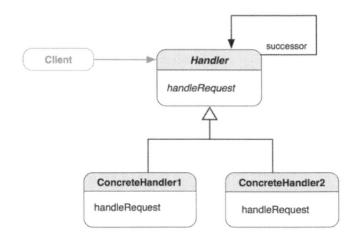

Figure 17–1. *A class diagram of the Chain of Responsibility pattern*

Handler is a high-level abstract class that defines a single method, handleRequest, to handle any request object that any instance of Handler would know how to handle. ConcreteHandler1 and ConcreteHandler2 implement the handleRequest method to handle any request object that they can recognize. Handler also has a reference to another instance of the same type as successor. When a message of handleRequest is invoked on an instance of Handle and the instance doesn't know how to handle the request, it will forward the request to the successor with the same message. If the successor can handle that, then it's fine; otherwise it will pass the request to the next successor if it has any. The process can go on until the request hits the last Handler in the chain. The way that instances of Handler form a chain with their successors is illustrated in an object diagram in Figure 17–2.

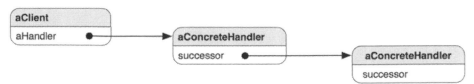

Figure 17–2. *A typical object structure of a chain of request handlers at runtime*

aClient has a reference to an instance of Handler as aHandler. aHandler is the first object in the handler chain as aConcreteHandler. aConcreteHandler is connected with another instance of Handler (as aConcreteHandler) with its internal reference as successor. The bottom line of this strategy to handle requests is if you don't know this request, pass it to the next handler (some implementations may still require a handler to pass a request along regardless of whether the handler can handle the request).

> **CHAIN OF RESPONSIBILITY PATTERN:** To avoid coupling the sender of a request to its receiver by giving more than one object a chance to handle the request. It chains the receiving objects and passes the request along the chain until an object handles it.*
>
> * The original definition appeared in Design Patterns, by the "Gang of Four" (Addison-Wesley, 1994).

When Would You Use the Chain of Responsibility Pattern?

You'd naturally think about using the pattern when

- There is more than one object that may handle a request and the handler is known only at runtime.

- You want to issue a request to a group of objects without specifying a particular receiver that will handle the request explicitly.

In the next sections, we are going to see how to use the Chain of Responsibility pattern to implement different protection gear for avatars in an RPG.

Using the Chain of Responsibility Pattern in an RPG

Assume that you are building an RPG in which each avatar can earn credits to upgrade its protection gear. Protection gear can be a shield or armor. Each form of protection can handle only a particular type of attack. If the protection gear doesn't recognize a form of attack, then it will pass the effect from the attack to the next "entity" that would respond to that. A visual diagram that illustrates this idea is shown in Figure 17–3.

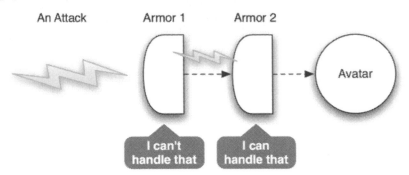

Figure 17–3. *A visual representation of chained protection layers for an avatar; even though Armor 1 cannot handle an attack, Armor 2 can absorb the attack, and the avatar is intact.*

In Figure 17–3, Armor 1 doesn't know how to handle an attack issued by an opponent, so it passes it on to the next armor, Armor 2. Armor 2 happens to know how to respond to that attack and dissipate the damage that it might have caused to the avatar. For some reason, if none of the armors can respond to an attack, then any effects that come from the attack will eventually be passed to the avatar. When the avatar responds to an attack, it will appear to be a form of damage. This scenario is illustrated in Figure 17–4.

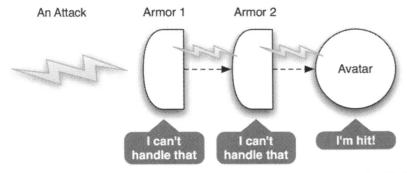

Figure 17–4. *The same visual representation as in Figure 17–3 above, except for this time both armors cannot handle the attack and the avatar absorbs the damage*

The mechanism of letting each individual protection gear respond to a particular type of attack and nothing else simplifies the complexity of using different types of protection gear for an avatar. Every type of armor and shield has its own responsibility for a very specific function. This is where the Chain of Responsibility comes into the picture.

We are going to see how to implement this design with the pattern. Let's say we want to have two forms of protection: a metal armor and a crystal shield. They cannot handle any forms of attacks other than the ones that they are designed for. A metal armor can protect an avatar from sword attacks, while a crystal shield can handle any magic fire attacks. As illustrated in previous diagrams, the avatar is also part of the response chain, so it should share the same behavior as other protection gear to respond an attack. Their static relationships are illustrated in a class diagram in Figure 17–5.

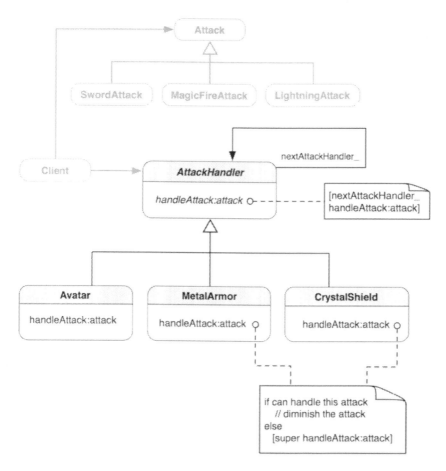

Figure 17–5. *A class diagram of a set of* `AttackHandler` *that will be formed by a chain of attack handlers*

`Avatar`, `MetalArmor`, and `CrystalShield` are subclasses of `AttackHandler`. `AttackHandler` defines a single method, `handleAttack:attack`, which passes an attack to another `AttackHandler` being referenced as a member variable, `nextAttackHandler_`, as a default behavior. Subclasses override that method to provide actual responses to an attack. If an `AttackHandler` doesn't know how to respond to an attack, then it will forward it to super with a `[super handleAttack:attack]` message so the default implementation in super will pass the attack down the chain.

There are three types of attacks defined in the class diagram: `SwordAttack`, `MagicFireAttack`, and `LightningAttack`. We will discuss which `AttackHandler` can respond to what type of attack in a little bit. But first, let's take a look at the code for the `AttackHandler` parent class in Listing 17–1.

Listing 17–1. *AttackHandler.h*

```
#import "Attack.h"

@interface AttackHandler : NSObject
{
  @private
  AttackHandler *nextAttackHandler_;
}

@property (nonatomic, retain) AttackHandler *nextAttackHandler;

- (void) handleAttack:(Attack *)attack;

@end
```

AttackHandler defines a private variable of the same type as nextAttackHandler_, which is supposed to be the next responder for an attack. Subclasses of AttackHandler should override the handleAttack: method to respond to a type of attack that it can recognize. The abstract AttackHandler defines a default behavior for that method in Listing 17–2.

Listing 17–2. *AttackHandler.m*

```
#import "AttackHandler.h"


@implementation AttackHandler

@synthesize nextAttackHandler=nextAttackHandler_;

- (void) handleAttack:(Attack *)attack
{
  [nextAttackHandler_ handleAttack:attack];
}

@end
```

If a subclass doesn't override that method, then the default implementation of handleAttack: will be called. The method just simply passes an attack to nextAttackHandler_ to handle it.

Let's take a look at the first protection gear for an Avatar, MetalArmor. MetalArmor subclasses AttackHandler and overrides its handleAttack: method, as shown in Listing 17–3.

Listing 17–3. *MetalArmor.h*

```
#import "AttackHandler.h"

@interface MetalArmor : AttackHandler
{

}

// overridden method
- (void) handleAttack:(Attack *)attack;

@end
```

As we have seen in other chapters, overridden methods are not necessary to be re-declared in a subclass's header file but are there just for clarity. MetalArmor can recognize only instances of SwordAttack. If an attack is indeed a type of SwordAttack, then handleAttack: will print out a message of @"No damage from a sword attack!" with NSLog. Otherwise, it will print out a different message and forward the attack to super with a [super handleAttack:attack] message, as shown in Listing 17–4.

Listing 17–4. *MetalArmor.m*

```
#import "MetalArmor.h"
#import "SwordAttack.h"

@implementation MetalArmor

- (void) handleAttack:(Attack *)attack
{
  if ([attack isKindOfClass:[SwordAttack class]])
  {
    // no damage beyond this armor
    NSLog(@"%@", @"No damage from a sword attack!");
  }
  else
  {
    NSLog(@"I don't know this attack: %@", [attack class]);
    [super handleAttack:attack];
  }
}

@end
```

Likewise, CrystalShield is also a type of AttackHandler. Its class declaration is almost the same as MetalArmor except for the class name, so we are not going to repeat ourselves here. The implementation of CrystalShield is similar to MetalArmor's as well, which recognizes only one type of attack. In this case, it needs to be MagicFireAttack. Otherwise, it will just forward the attack that it doesn't know about to super with the same [super handleAttack:attack] message to let the next AttackHandler take care of it, as shown in Listing 17–5.

Listing 17–5. *CrystalShield.m*

```
#import "CrystalShield.h"
#import "MagicFireAttack.h"

@implementation CrystalShield

- (void) handleAttack:(Attack *)attack
{
  if ([attack isKindOfClass:[MagicFireAttack class]])
  {
    // no damage beyond this shield
    NSLog(@"%@", @"No damage from a magic fire attack!");
  }
  else
  {
    NSLog(@"I don't know this attack: %@", [attack class]);
    [super handleAttack:attack];
```

```
  }
}

@end
```

If none of the protection gear can handle an attack, the attack will eventually get passed to an `Avatar`. `Avatar` is also a subclass of `AttackHandler` and has the same mechanism to respond to any `Attack` that `MetalArmor` and `CrystalShield` do. However, when an attack comes to this point, an `Avatar` will take it as damage not any protection. Its overridden `handleAttack:` method prints out the name of an attack being used with `NSLog(@"Oh! I'm hit with a %@!", [attack class])`, as shown in Listing 17–6.

Listing 17–6. *Avatar.m*

```
#import "Avatar.h"


@implementation Avatar

- (void) handleAttack:(Attack *)attack
{
  // when an attack reaches this point,
  // I'm hit.
  // actual points taken off depends on
  // the type of attack.
  NSLog(@"Oh! I'm hit with a %@!", [attack class]);
}

@end
```

Now we have all of our `AttackHandlers` defined. Let's take a look at client code and see how they can be connected to form a response chain of protection, as in Listing 17–7.

Listing 17–7. *Client Code That Manages an Avatar and Various Attacks*

```
// create a new avatar
AttackHandler *avatar = [[[Avatar alloc] init] autorelease];

// put it in metal armor
AttackHandler *metalArmoredAvatar = [[[MetalArmor alloc] init] autorelease];
[metalArmoredAvatar setAttackHandler:avatar];

// then add a crytal shield
// to the avatar who's in
// a metal armor
AttackHandler *superAvatar = [[[CrystalShield alloc] init] autorelease];
[superAvatar setAttackHandler:metalArmor];

// ... some other actions

// attack the avatar with
// a sword
Attack *swordAttack = [[[SwordAttack alloc] init] autorelease];
[superAvatar handleAttack:swordAttack];

// then attack the avatar with
// magic fire
Attack *magicFireAttack = [[[MagicFireAttack alloc] init] autorelease];
```

```
[superAvatar handleAttack:magicFireAttack];

// now there is a new attack
// with lightning...
Attack *lightningAttack = [[[LightningAttack alloc] init] autorelease];
[superAvatar handleAttack:lightningAttack];

// ... further actions
```

Our chain of attack handlers is formed like a stack (i.e., first in, last out). We need an Avatar to be the last stop for an attack, so it needs to be created first. Then we create an instance of MetalArmor with the instance of Avatar as its next AttackHandler. They are treated as an "enhanced" Avatar with MetalArmor being the first gate towards the real Avatar instance. Just MetalArmor is not enough; we also need to create an instance of CrystalShield as another form of protection for the Avatar. We use the instance of AttackHandler as a form of MetalArmor (connected with the Avatar) to be the next attack handler for the instance of CrystalShield. At this point, the Avatar is now a "super avatar" with two forms of protection.

At some point in the game, we create three types of attack, swordAttack, magicFireAttack, and lightningAttack for the "super avatar" to handle with its handleAttack: method. We collect some outputs generated from various AttackHandlers in the chain so we can understand what's going on, as shown in Listing 17–8.

Listing 17–8. *An Output from the Client Code*

```
I don't know this attack: SwordAttack
No damage from a sword attack!
No damage from a magic fire attack!
I don't know this attack: LightningAttack
I don't know this attack: LightningAttack
Oh! I'm hit with a LightningAttack!
```

The metal armor protected the avatar from the first sword attack and then a magic fire attack, as the second attack didn't do any damage to the avatar either because of the crystal shield. When there was a third attack with lightning, both the armor and shield didn't know how to handle it but spit out a message: "I don't know this attack: LightningAttack". Eventually, the attack was handled by the avatar itself, and it printed out the message "Oh! I'm hit with a LightningAttack!" to indicate the damage caused by the lightning attack.

The simple RPG example illustrates how to use the Chain of Responsibility pattern to simplify the coding and the logic for handling different attacks on avatars. Without using the pattern, the protection logic would most probably be cramped in a single class (e.g., Avatar) and the code for it would be spaghetti-looking.

Summary

We have used the example of implementing different protection mechanism for avatars in an RPG (role-playing game) as the Chain of Responsibility pattern. Each type of protection mechanism can handle only one particular type of attack. A chain of attack handlers can determine what attacks an avatar can be protected from. Any attack handler can be added or removed at any given time during the game without affecting other behaviors of the avatar. The Chain of Responsibility pattern is a natural choice for this kind of design. Otherwise, complex combinations of attack handlers would bloat the avatar and make it difficult to change handlers.

We have discussed a few patterns that focus on extending the object's behaviors with zero or minimal modifications to it. Next, we are going to see how to change the object's behavior by encapsulating and extending its algorithms.

Part VII

Algorithm Encapsulation

Chapter 18

Template Method

As in cooking, there are certain steps that can be generalized in common procedures, such as preparing ingredients, cooking the ingredients, and serving the dish. An actual recipe can vary within the scope of each of the steps. For a particular type of food, steps to take can be even further generalized. For example, there are common steps to make a sandwich, no matter what type it is. Each type of sandwich can vary by the type of bread that will be used, the type of meat that will be put in the bread, as well as condiments. Some sandwiches might be a little bit different from a generic sandwich, with some extra steps, but still basically follow the common steps to prepare.

A group of generalized steps (a recipe) to prepare a sandwich is a template method. It's a template because it's still missing some specific pieces in the steps to complete the procedure. Those missing pieces will be filled up when a particular type of sandwich needs to be made. When we prepare a Reuben sandwich, we need to prepare a couple slices of rye bread in a "prepare bread" step. A hamburger requires hamburger buns in the same step. No matter what type of sandwich it is, it still needs "bread" to complete the process. So we can group those generalized steps into a single operation called "make a sandwich." A specific type of sandwich recipe fills in some empty steps with unique procedures and ingredients.

In this chapter, we will look at the concepts of the Template Method pattern. We will also implement the pattern with an example of preparing different kinds of sandwiches with a template "recipe."

What Is the Template Method Pattern?

The Template Method pattern is one of the simplest forms of design patterns in object-oriented software design. The basic idea is to define a "standard" algorithm in a method of an abstract class. Within the method, it will call other primitive operations that are supposed to be overridden by subclasses. The method is called "template" because the method defines the algorithm in which some unique operations are missing. The relationship between an abstract class that defines a template method and a concrete subclass that overrides primitive operations to provide unique operations when those methods are called in the template method is illustrated in Figure 18–1.

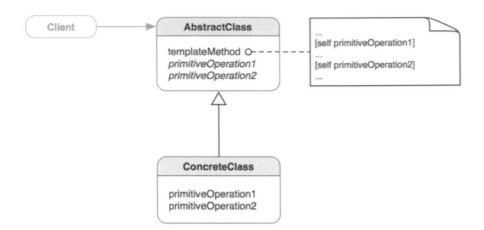

Figure 18–1. *A class diagram of the Template Method pattern that shows* ConcreteClass *overrides* AbstractClass's primitiveOperation1 *and* primitiveOperation2 *to provide unique operations when Client invokes* templateMethod *in* AbstractClass

AbstractClass partially defines some methods and algorithms with some operations left out. When ConcreteClass overrides primitiveOperation1 (and/or 2), it fills up the "gaps" of templateMethod in AbstractClass when clients invoke the method.

> **THE TEMPLATE METHOD PATTERN:** Define the skeleton of an algorithm in an operation, deferring some steps to subclasses. Template Method lets subclasses redefine certain steps of an algorithm without changing the algorithm's structure. *
>
> * The original definition appeared in *Design Patterns*, by the *"Gang of Four"* (Addison-Wesley, 1994).

When Would You Use the Template Method?

You should consider using the Template Method pattern when

- You need to implement the invariant parts of an algorithm once and leave it up to subclasses to implement any specific behavior that can vary.

- Common behavior of subclasses should be factored in a common class to avoid code duplication. Differences in existing code should be separated into new operations. Then you replace the differing code with a template method that calls each of these new operations.

- Controlled subclass extensions are required. You can define a template method that calls "hook" operations at specific points. Subclasses can extend the functionality at those points with the hook implementation.

A hook operation provides default behavior that subclasses can extend. It often does nothing by default. Subclasses can override that method to provide extra operations for the template algorithm.

The flow of control structure in the Template Method pattern is inverted, as a template method of a parent class calls operations of its subclass and not the other way around. It's analogous to "the Hollywood principle": don't call us, we'll call you.

There are five types of operations that template methods would call:

- Concrete operations either on concrete classes or client classes
- Concrete operations on abstract classes
- Abstract operations
- Factory methods (see Chapter 4)
- Hook operations (optional abstract operations)

Using the Template Method to Make a Sandwich

Let's take a look at making a sandwich and see how it can be related to the Template Method pattern.

I think anyone can make a simple sandwich. What should a (non-vegetarian) sandwich have to be considered a sandwich?

- Bread
- Meat
- Condiments

So we have all the ingredients to make a simple sandwich. Then a basic procedure to make a simple sandwich should be somewhat like the following:

1. Prepare the bread.
2. Put the bread on a plate.
3. Add meat on the bread.
4. Add condiments.
5. Serve.

We can define a template method called make in which other specific steps like the foregoing ones are called to make a real sandwich. The default algorithm to make real sandwiches has some unique operations left out, so the template method defines only a generic way to make any sandwich. When there are concrete sandwich subclasses overriding some of the sandwich's behaviors, clients can use only the same make message to make real sandwiches. The static relationship between AnySandwich and ConcreteSandwich is illustrated in a class diagram in Figure 18–2.

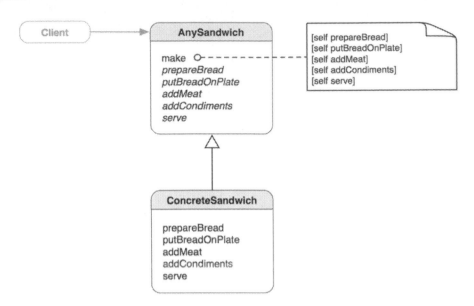

Figure 18–2. *A class diagram of* AnySandwich *class with a* ConcreteSandwich *that overrides abstract operations that are called by a template method,* make

If we make an Objective-C class for AnySandwich, here we go in Listing 18–1.

Listing 18–1. *AnySandwich.h*

```objc
@interface AnySandwich : NSObject
{
}

- (void) make;

// Steps to make a sandwich
- (void) prepareBread;
- (void) putBreadOnPlate;
- (void) addMeat;
- (void) addCondiments;
- (void) serve;

@end
```

Just like what we have seen in the class diagram in Figure 18–2, make will call the generic steps when it is invoked to make a sandwich, as shown in Listing 18–2.

Listing 18–2. *AnySandwich.m*

```objc
#import "AnySandwich.h"

@implementation AnySandwich

- (void) make
{
  [self prepareBread];
  [self putBreadOnPlate];
```

```
    [self addMeat];
    [self addCondiments];
    [self serve];
}

- (void) putBreadOnPlate
{
    // We need first to put bread on a plate for any sandwich.
}

- (void) serve
{
    // Any sandwich will be served eventually.
}

#pragma mark -
#pragma Details will be handled by subclasses

- (void) prepareBread
{
    // we need to make sure subclasses override this
}

- (void) addMeat
{
    // we need to make sure subclasses override this
}

- (void) addCondiments
{
    // we need to make sure subclasses override this
}

@end
```

The prepareBread, addMeat, and addCondiments methods are stubbed out because they need to be overridden by subclasses later to provide any specifics to real sandwiches. We need to provide some mechanism to make sure subclasses override those methods that make sense to a real sandwich-making process. We will discuss related issues in "Ensuring That the Template Method Is Working" section later in this chapter.

Now we want to make a real sandwich, a Reuben sandwich. Since a Reuben sandwich is a type of sandwich, steps to make it should be the same as any other sandwich, though it has its own ingredients and some little operations that are specific to it. An Objective-C class for a Reuben sandwich should look like Listing 18–3.

Listing 18–3. *ReubenSandwich.h*

```
#import "AnySandwich.h"

@interface ReubenSandwich : AnySandwich
{
}

- (void) prepareBread;
- (void) addMeat;
- (void) addCondiments;
```

```
// ReubenSandwich's specific operations
- (void) cutRyeBread;
- (void) addCornBeef;
- (void) addSauerkraut;
- (void) addThousandIslandDressing;
- (void) addSwissCheese;

@end
```

ReubenSandwich is a subclass of AnySandwich. There are specific steps and ingredients to make a Reuben sandwich. A Reuben sandwich needs rye bread as bread, corn beef as meat, sauerkraut, Thousand Island dressing, and Swiss cheese as condiments. Even though cheese is not a type of condiment, we put it in there to simplify the generic steps to make any sandwich because not all sandwiches have cheese. We put the Reuben sandwich operations in the generic sandwich methods, as shown in Listing 18–4.

Listing 18–4. *ReubenSandwich.m*

```
#import "ReubenSandwich.h"

@implementation ReubenSandwich

- (void) prepareBread
{
  [self cutRyeBread];
}

- (void) addMeat
{
  [self addCornBeef];
}

- (void) addCondiments
{
  [self addSauerkraut];
  [self addThousandIslandDressing];
  [self addSwissCheese];
}

#pragma mark -
#pragma mark ReubenSandwich Specific Methods

- (void) cutRyeBread
{
  // A Reuben sandwich requires two slices of rye bread
}

- (void) addCornBeef
{
  // ... add tons of corn beef
}

- (void) addSauerkraut
{
  // ... and sauerkraut.
}
```

```
- (void) addThousandIslandDressing
{
  // ... don't forget to put Thousand Island dressing
}

- (void) addSwissCheese
{
  // ... as well as some good Swiss cheese.
}

@end
```

Our ReubenSandwich doesn't need to care about putBreadOnPlate and serve. Our common AnySandwich has defined those behaviors, and other concrete sandwiches share them. What ReubenSandwich needs to care about are the bread, the meat, and any condiments.

The prepareBread method calls ReubenSandwich's specific method cutRyeBread to prepare slices of rye bread for the sandwich. If the sandwich class is ReubenSandwich, then the prepareBread method is actually preparing slices of rye bread, not anything else.

Almost any Reuben sandwich has corn beef in it. So our Reuben class has an addCornBeef method, which is, in fact, our actual addMeat step in our original AnySandwich abstract class. Of course, if you have your own version of a Reuben sandwich, then you can put a different type of meat in the sandwich or add your other meat with corn beef together.

OK, so the last step that a Reuben sandwich needs to care about is to addCondiments. We know there are a lot of variations, but let's stick with something common. For the condiments, we will addSauerkraut, addThousandIslandDressing, and addSwissCheese. So when addCondiments is invoked, ReubenSandwich will add sauerkraut, Thousand Island dressing, and Swiss cheese on the meat.

When the last step, serve, is done, then our Reuben sandwich will be ready to be enjoyed. What about other types of sandwiches? Can we use the same procedure to make ourselves a different sandwich? The answer is, yes, absolutely! How about a hamburger? Let's see how it looks in Listing 18–5.

Listing 18–5. *Hamburger.h*

```
#import "AnySandwich.h"

@interface Hamburger : AnySandwich
{
}

- (void) prepareBread;
- (void) addMeat;
- (void) addCondiments;

// Hamburger specific methods
- (void) getBurgerBun;
- (void) addKetchup;
```

```objc
- (void) addMustard;
- (void) addBeefPatty;
- (void) addCheese;
- (void) addPickles;

@end
```

Hamburger is also a subclass of AnySandwich, it also has its own specifics to prepare. A hamburger needs a bun as bread, a beef patty (unless you want a double cheeseburger) as meat, ketchup, mustard, pickles, and cheese as condiments. Like ReubenSandwich, we are treating cheese as a type of condiment here for the same reason. When we put the specific hamburger operations in the slots of generic sandwich-making operations, the code should look like Listing 18–6.

Listing 18–6. *Hamburger.m*

```objc
#import "Hamburger.h"

@implementation Hamburger

- (void) prepareBread;
{
  [self getBurgerBun];
}

- (void) addMeat
{
  [self addBeefPatty];
}

- (void) addCondiments
{
  [self addKetchup];
  [self addMustard];
  [self addCheese];
  [self addPickles];
}

#pragma mark -
#pragma mark Hamburger Specific Methods

- (void) getBurgerBun
{
  // A hamburger needs a bun.
}

- (void) addKetchup
{
  // Before adding anything to a bun, we need to put ketchup.
}

- (void) addMustard
{
  // Then add some mustard.
}

- (void) addBeefPatty
```

```
{
    // A piece of beef patty is the main character in a burger.
}

- (void) addCheese
{
    // Let's just assume every burger has cheese.
}

- (void) addPickles
{
    // Then finally add some pickles to it.
}

@end
```

There are so many combinations you can use to make your own sandwiches. All you need to do is to create your own sandwich class that provides specific implementation of prepareBread, addMeat, and addCondiments. Then by invoking the make method of an instance of AnySandwich (the parent class), the standard procedure will be carried out until the sandwich is ready to be served.

The "standard procedure" in our AnySandwich parent class represents our algorithm to make a sandwich. The algorithm is implemented in the make method with some stubbed-out operations; subclasses implement the details. So a subclass actually doesn't need to know any of the details of an algorithm, and at the same time the parent class doesn't need to know any details of any concrete operations that a subclass provides.

TEMPLATE METHOD VS. DELEGATION

Both the Template Method and Delegation patterns (a.k.a. Adapter pattern, see Chapter 8) are commonly found in the Cocoa Touch framework. They are a very natural choice for framework class designs. Why? User applications can reuse (or extend) framework classes, and the framework classes won't be able to know what other classes are going to use them at the time they were designed. But which one should we use for particular software design problems? The following are brief guidelines:

Template Method	Delegation (Adapter)
A parent class defines a common algorithm that is missing some specific/optional information or algorithm with which it is served as an algorithm "recipe."	A delegate (adapter) defines a specific algorithm in conjunction with a predefined delegation interface.
The missing information is provided by subclasses through inheritance.	The specific algorithm is provided by any object through object composition.

Ensuring That the Template Method Is Working

Objective-C doesn't provide any attributes to methods, so subclasses must override them. So how can we make sure the stubbed-out, generic sandwich-making methods are overridden by ReubenSandwich and Hamburger?

As we know, if a sandwich doesn't prepareBread, addMeat, or addCondiments, it's not a sandwich anymore (based on our original assumption about a sandwich). It means our application wouldn't make sense if any one of those steps were missing. That sounds like an exception in some sense (e.g., Oops! There is no meat in the addMeat method). There are many ways to do that. A simple one is to have the methods return a BOOL value with a default value set to NO. So the make method will check each operation's returned value to make sure no one is left open. But there is a catch—if for some reason the methods were reused and the new invoking method didn't have the same check to make sure the flow of the algorithm is correct, then the algorithm would be screwed. Why don't we throw an exception if the required primitive methods are not overridden? Throwing an instance of NSException guarantees the trouble will get caught as early as during development. The exception doesn't mean to be caught when the user is using your app though. When an exception is thrown, it can print an error message that includes the method and class names as well as the reason of the problem. Such information is invaluable to debug later if you did forget to override the abstract methods in a concrete AnySandwich subclass. After we put some exception throwing statements in those methods, they would look something like Listing 18–7.

Listing 18–7. *A Statement That Raises an Instance of* NSException *Is Added in Each of the Original Stubbed-Out, Generic Sandwich-Making Methods*

```
- (void) prepareBread
{
  [NSException raise:NSInternalInconsistencyException
          format:@"You must override %@ in a subclass", NSStringFromSelector(_cmd)];
}

- (void) addMeat
{
  [NSException raise:NSInternalInconsistencyException
          format:@"You must override %@ in a subclass", NSStringFromSelector(_cmd)];
}

- (void) addCondiments
{
  [NSException raise:NSInternalInconsistencyException
          format:@"You must override %@ in a subclass", NSStringFromSelector(_cmd)];
}
```

The prepareBread, addMeat, and addCondiments methods were no-op in the original version, and now each of them gets fleshed out with raising an instance of NSException. When a client invokes the make method in AnySandwich and it hits the AnySandwich version of prepareBread, then an exception will be thrown. raise is a class method of NSException that takes a name and a message of the exception. We are using NSInternalInconsistencyException defined in the Cocoa Touch framework to imply an unexpected condition within the called code. You can define your own exception name there. It is totally up to you. The message part of the method accepts a string format to construct an NSString. We use _cmd as part of the message. _cmd is an Objective-C object attribute that contains the name of a selector being invoked or forwarded. In Objective-C 2.0, you can use the following:

```
@throw [NSException exceptionWithName:… reason:… userInfo:…];
```

The @throw keyword with NSException does pretty much the same thing. However, it is simpler to use the raise class method of NSException.

If there is no @catch block in the call stack for an exception thrown from the prepareBread method, you will see a message printed in a crash log like the following (for the sake of brevity, a complete call stack printout is omitted):

```
[Session started at 2010-08-01 18:16:59 -0700.]
2010-08-01 18:17:00.632 TemplateMethod[1315:207] *** Terminating app due to uncaught
exception 'NSInternalInconsistencyException', reason: 'You must override prepareBread in
a subclass'
```

Adding an Extra Step to the Template Method

OK, now we know how to implement the Template Method pattern in our previous sandwich-making process. It would be nice if we could add a slight touch to making some sandwiches—for example, grilling our ReubenSandwich a little bit before it's served. But that final touch is optional in general, which means not all sandwiches have to have an extra step. Also the default implementation of the extra step is a no-op. A method in a parent class that a subclass can extend if necessary is called a "hook," and a hook method usually does nothing by default.

Let's go back to our AnySandwich class. We can provide an *optional* hook method called extraStep for any subclassed sandwich to add some final touches if it is necessary before it's served. A newer version of AnySandwich class is like Listing 18–8.

Listing 18–8. *AnySandwich.h with an Extra Step*

```
@interface AnySandwich : NSObject
{
}

- (void) make;

// Steps to make a sandwich
- (void) prepareBread;
- (void) putBreadOnPlate;
- (void) addMeat;
- (void) addCondiments;
- (void) extraStep;
- (void) serve;

@end
```

In the original make method, extraStep is the second-to-last operation right before serve, as shown in Listing 18–9.

Listing 18–9. *The make Method of AnySandwich.m with extraStep*

```
- (void) make
{
  [self prepareBread];
  [self putBreadOnPlate];
  [self addMeat];
  [self addCondiments];
```

```
    [self extraStep];
    [self serve];
}
```

So for any sandwich that needs an extra step or two before it's served, it can override the extraStep method. The method will be called exactly one step before the serve method in the make method. Since the extraStep is optional, it won't hurt the whole sandwich-making process in general if the method is empty. Also, it doesn't need to raise an exception to guarantee it's overridden by any subclass.

We know our ReubenSandwich would taste a lot better if it's grilled a little bit, so we will add some implementation to the Reubensandwich class to support that (Listing 18–10).

Listing 18–10. *ReubenSandwich Overrides* extraStep *and Adds* grillIt *in the Header File*

```
#import "AnySandwich.h"

@interface ReubenSandwich : AnySandwich
{
}

- (void) prepareBread;
- (void) addMeat;
- (void) addCondiments;
- (void) extraStep;

// ReubenSandwich specific methods
- (void) cutRyeBread;
- (void) addCornBeef;
- (void) addSauerkraut;
- (void) addThousandIslandDressing;
- (void) addSwissCheese;
- (void) grillIt;

@end
```

Its implementation with grillIt as an extraStep is shown in Listing 18–11.

Listing 18–11. *ReubenSandwich Has* grillIt *As Its* extraStep

```
 #import "ReubenSandwich.h"

@implementation ReubenSandwich

- (void) prepareBread
{
  [self cutRyeBread];
}

- (void) addMeat
{
  [self addCornBeef];
}

- (void) addCondiments
{
  [self addSauerkraut];
  [self addThousandIslandDressing];
```

```
    [self addSwissCheese];
}

- (void) extraStep
{
    [self grillIt];
}

#pragma mark -
#pragma mark ReubenSandwich Specific Methods

- (void) cutRyeBread
{
    // A Reuben sandwich requires two slices of rye bread
}

- (void) addCornBeef
{
    // ... add tons of corn beef
}

- (void) addSauerkraut
{
    // ... and sauerkraut.
}

- (void) addThousandIslandDressing
{
    // ... don't forget to put Thousand Island dressing
}

- (void) addSwissCheese
{
    // ... as well as some good Swiss cheese.
}

- (void) grillIt
{
    // finally it needs to be toasted.
}

@end
```

If you have more extra steps for your own version of a Reuben sandwich, feel free to add them to the extraStep method. When the method is invoked, whatever is in it will be invoked as well. So there is no need for modifying AnySandwich for more optional extra steps. From now on, when we make our Reuben sandwich again, it will be grilled. However, our Hamburger doesn't need to do any extra steps like our ReubenSandwich does. The modified algorithm in our AnySandwich class won't affect other sandwiches at all, as the extraStep is optional.

NOTE: A hook method often does nothing by default and is optional for subclasses.

Using the Template Method in the Cocoa Touch Framework

The Template Method pattern is quite common in framework designs. Template methods are a fundamental technique for code reuse. They allow any designer of a framework to leave out some application-specific elements of an algorithm to an application. They are the means for factoring out common behavior in framework classes. This approach can help extensibility and reusability (with the same "recipe") yet maintain loose coupling between different classes (the framework classes vs. yours). The Cocoa Touch framework has also adapted the Template Method patterns. You can find those framework classes here and there within the framework, though they may not be as common as Delegation. In this section, we are going to explore a couple of common template methods in the framework.

Custom Drawing in the UIView Class

Since iOS 2.0, there is a method in the UIView class that allows an application to perform custom drawing by overriding its method:

- (void)drawRect:(CGRect)rect

The default implementation of the method does nothing. Subclasses of the UIView override this method if they actually need to draw their own views. So the method is a hook method.

When there is a need to change the view on the screen, this method will be invoked. The framework handles all the low-level, dirty work to make it happen. Part of the drawing process handled by UIView is to invoke drawRect:. If there is any code in that method, it would be invoked as well. Subclasses can use Quartz 2D function UIGraphicsGetCurrentContext to get the current graphics context for any available 2D elements in the framework.

The client application can also activate the drawing process manually by invoking a UIView's method.

- (void)setNeedsDisplay

It notifies an instance of UIView so that it redraws its entire rectangle on the screen. You can also specify a particular region on the view as a rectangle to be redrawn by using another instance method:

- (void)setNeedsDisplayInRect:(CGRect)invalidRect

invalidRect is the rectangular region of the receiver to mark it as invalid; it means that's the only region needs to be redrawn but nowhere else.

Let's see another framework class that also implements the Template Method pattern.

Other Template Method Implementations in Cocoa Touch

We cannot cover every Template Method adaptation in the framework, but the last one that is worth mentioning is `UIViewController`. It defines some methods that let user applications handle the different orientations of the device. The following is a list of messages that appear when different orientation is changed.

```
shouldAutorotateToInterfaceOrientation:
rotatingHeaderView
rotatingFooterView
willAnimateRotationToInterfaceOrientation:duration:
willRotateToInterfaceOrientation:duration:
willAnimateFirstHalfOfRotationToInterfaceOrientation:duration:
didAnimateFirstHalfOfRotationToInterfaceOrientation:
willAnimateSecondHalfOfRotationFromInterfaceOrientation:duration:
didRotateFromInterfaceOrientation:
```

They are pure hook methods that are waiting to be overridden for some real action. Each one of them will be invoked during specific moments of the device's orientation changes. Subclasses can override selected methods to augment specific behavior during the screen rotation process at different steps and times.

Summary

The Template Method pattern is a fundamental technique for code reuse. Template methods are important in framework class designs, as they are the means for factoring out common behavior in framework classes.

Template methods can be found in many places in the Cocoa Touch framework. We have discussed only a few of them in the previous sections. You can find more in the iOS developer's documentation.

In the next chapter, we are going to discuss another way to encapsulate algorithms in objects as different strategies.

Chapter 19

Strategy

Do you remember the last time you stuffed a bunch of different algorithms in the same block of code and used spaghetti of `if-else` / `switch-case` conditional statements to determine which one to use? The algorithms could be a bunch of functions/methods of similar classes that solve related problems. For example, I have a routine that validates some input data. The data itself can be of any data type (e.g., `CGFloat`, `NSString`, `NSInteger`, etc.). Each of the data types requires a different validation algorithm. If we can encapsulate each algorithm as an object, then we can eliminate a bunch of `if-else` / `switch-case` statements for data type checking in order to determine what algorithm to use.

In object-oriented software design, we can segregate related algorithms into different classes as strategies. A design pattern related to the practice is called the Strategy pattern. In this chapter, we are going to discuss the concepts and key features of the Strategy pattern. We will also design and implement some data validating classes as different strategies to validate the input of `UITextField` objects later in the chapter.

What Is the Strategy Pattern?

One of the key roles in the Strategy pattern is a strategy class that declares an interface common to all supported or related algorithms. There are also concrete strategy classes that implement the related algorithm using the strategy interface. An object of a context class is configured with an instance of a concrete strategy object. The context object uses the strategy interface to call the algorithm defined by the concrete strategy class. Their static relationships are illustrated in a class diagram shown in Figure 19–1.

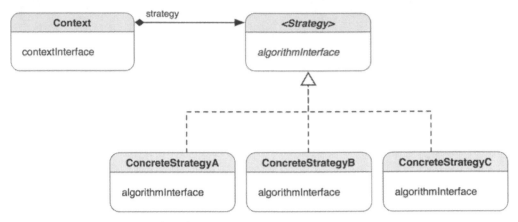

Figure 19–1. *A class structure of the Strategy pattern*

A group or hierarchy of related algorithms in a form of `ConcreteStrategy` (A, B, and C) classes is sharing the common `algorithmInterface` so `Context` can access variants of the algorithm with the same interface.

> **THE STRATEGY PATTERN:** Define a family of algorithms, encapsulate each one, and make them interchangeable. Strategy lets the algorithm vary independently from clients that use it.*
>
> *The original definition appeared in *Design Patterns*, by the "Gang of Four" (Addison-Wesley, 1994).

An instance of `Context` can be configured with different `ConcreteStrategy` objects at runtime. It can be considered changing the "guts" of the `Context` object as the changes appear inside the object. Decorators (see the Decorator pattern, Chapter 16), on the other hand, change the "skin" of the object, as the modifications are stacked up from outside. Please see the "Changing the 'Skin' vs. 'Guts' of an Object" section in Chapter 16 for more detailed discussion about the differences.

THE STRATEGY PATTERN IN MODEL-VIEW-CONTROLLER

In the Model-View-Controller pattern, a controller determines the behavior of a view about what and when to display the data from a model. The view itself knows *how* to draw something but doesn't know *what* until the controller tells it what to display. With a different controller to work with the same view, the format of how to output the data could be the same but the types or formats of the data could be different due to different outputs from a different controller. So the controller in that case is a strategy for the view. As we have mentioned in the previous chapters, the relationship between a controller and a view is based on the Strategy pattern.

When Would You Use the Strategy Pattern?

You'd naturally think about using the pattern when

- A class uses multiple conditional statements in its operations to define many behaviors. You can move related conditional branches into their own strategy class.

- You need different variants of an algorithm.

- You need to avoid exposing complex and algorithm-specific data structures to clients.

Applying Validation Strategies in UITextField

Let's make a simple example of implementing the Strategy pattern in an app. Assume we need to have some UITextField in our app that takes a user's input; then we will use the input later down in the application process. We have a text field that takes only letters, i.e., a–z or A–Z, as well as a field that takes only numerical values, i.e., 0–9. In order to make sure an input is valid in each of the fields, each of them needs to have some validation in place after the user is finished editing the text fields.

We can put some data validation in a UITextField delegate method, textFieldDidEndEditing:. An instance of UITextField invokes that method every time its focus is lost. In that method, we can check that the input of a numeric text field contains only numeric values as well as only letters in an alpha-character text field. The delegate method provides an input reference to the active text field (as textField) in question, but how do we know that one is for numeric or letter inputs?

Without the Strategy pattern in place, we would end up with the code shown in Listing 19–1.

Listing 19–1. *A Typical Scenario of Examining the Content of* UITextField *in Its* textFieldDidEndEditing *Delegate Method*

```
- (void)textFieldDidEndEditing:(UITextField *)textField
{
  if (textField == numericTextField)
  {
    // validate [textField text] and make sure
    // the value is numeric
  }
  else if (textField == alphaTextField)
  {
    // validate [textField text] and make sure
    // the value contains only letters
  }
}
```

The conditionals can go on if we have more text fields for different types of inputs. Our code could be more manageable if we can eliminate all those conditional statements, which would make our lives a lot easier in the long run when we maintain the code later.

HINT: If there are many conditional statements in your code, then it may indicate that they need to be refactored into different Strategy objects.

Now our goal is to yank those validation checks into different Strategy classes so they can be reused in the delegate and other methods as well. Each one of our validations takes an input value from a text field, then validates it based on the required strategy, and finally returns a BOOL value and an instance of NSError if it fails the validation. A returned NSError can help explain what exactly failed the validation. Since both the numeric and alpha input checks are somewhat related (they share the same input/output types), they can be factored into a common interface. Our class design is shown in a class diagram in Figure 19–2.

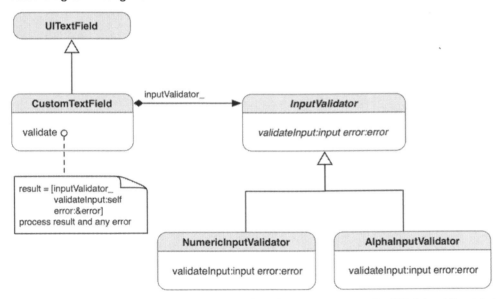

Figure 19–2. *A class diagram shows the static relationships between* `CustomTextField` *and its related* `InputValidator` *strategies.*

We will not declare that interface in a protocol but in an abstract base class. An abstract base class is more convenient for this solution because it is easier to refactor some common behavior among different concrete strategy subclasses later. Our abstract base class of InputValidator should look something like Listing 19–2.

Listing 19–2. *A Class Declaration of Abstract* `InputValidator` *in* `InputValidator.h`

```
@interface InputValidator : NSObject
{
}

// A stub for any actual validation strategy
- (BOOL) validateInput:(UITextField *)input error:(NSError **) error;

@end
```

The validateInput: error: method takes a reference to UITextField as an input so it can validate whatever is in the text field and returns a BOOL value to indicate the outcome of a validation. The method also accepts a reference to a pointer of NSError. When there is an error (i.e., it fails to validate the field), the method will construct an instance of NSError and assign it to the pointer so whatever context is using the validator can have more elaborated error handling from it.

The default implementation of the method only sets the error pointer to nil and returns NO to a caller, as shown in Listing 19–3.

Listing 19–3. *A Default Implementation of Abstract* InputValidator *in* InputValidator.m

```
#import "InputValidator.h"

@implementation InputValidator

// A stub for any actual validation strategy
- (BOOL) validateInput:(UITextField *)input error:(NSError **) error
{
  if (error)
  {
    *error = nil;
  }
  return NO;
}

@end
```

Why don't we use NSString as an input parameter instead? In this case, if it takes only an NSString value, then any action taken inside a strategy object will be one-way. It means that a validator will just do the check and return a result without modifying the original value. With the input parameter set to UITextField, we will have the best of both worlds. Our validators can have an option to change the original value of a text field (e.g., removing invalid values) or just examine the value without modifying it.

Another question is, why don't we just raise an instance of NSException if the input value failed? It is because raising your own exception and catching it in a try-catch block in the Cocoa Touch framework is very resource-intensive and it's not recommended (but try-catch system–raised exceptions are a different story). It's relatively cheaper to return an NSError object, which is recommended in the *Cocoa Touch Developer's Guide*. When we take a look at documentation of the Cocoa Touch framework, we will notice that there are a lot of APIs that return an instance of NSError when anomalies occur. A common example is one of NSFileManager's instance methods, (BOOL)moveItemAtPath:(NSString *)srcPath toPath:(NSString *)dstPath error:(NSError **)error. If there is an error occurring when NSFileManager tries to move a file from here to there for you, it will create a new instance of NSError that describes the problem. The calling method can use the information embedded in the returned NSError object for any further error handling. So the purpose of the NSError object output in our stubbed method provides information about the failure situation.

Now we've defined how a good input validator should behave. Then we can move on to make a real input validator. Let's make a numeric one, as shown in Listing 19–4.

Listing 19–4. *The Class Declaration of* `NumericInputValidator` *in* `NumericInputValidator.h`

```objc
#import "InputValidator.h"

@interface NumericInputValidator : InputValidator
{
}

// A validation method that makes sure the input contains only
// numbers, i.e., 0-9
- (BOOL) validateInput:(UITextField *)input error:(NSError **) error;

@end
```

`NumericInputValidator` subclasses the abstract `InputValidator` base class and overrides its `validateInput: error:` method. We are re-declaring the method here to emphasize what this subclass implements or overrides. It's not necessary but it's a good practice.

Its implementation of the method is shown in Listing 19–5.

Listing 19–5. *The Implementation of* `NumericInputValidator` *in* `NumericInputValidator.m`

```objc
#import "NumericInputValidator.h"

@implementation NumericInputValidator

- (BOOL) validateInput:(UITextField *)input error:(NSError**) error
{
  NSError *regError = nil;
  NSRegularExpression *regex = [NSRegularExpression
                       regularExpressionWithPattern:@"^[0-9]*$"
                       options:NSRegularExpressionAnchorsMatchLines
                       error:&regError];

  NSUInteger numberOfMatches = [regex
                       numberOfMatchesInString:[input text]
                       options:NSMatchingAnchored
                       range:NSMakeRange(0, [[input text] length])];

  // if there is not a single match
  // then return an error and NO
  if (numberOfMatches == 0)
  {
    if (error != nil)
    {
      NSString *description = NSLocalizedString(@"Input Validation Failed", @"");
      NSString *reason = NSLocalizedString(@"The input can contain only numerical
                                                    values", @"");

      NSArray *objArray = [NSArray arrayWithObjects:description, reason, nil];
      NSArray *keyArray = [NSArray arrayWithObjects:NSLocalizedDescriptionKey,
                      NSLocalizedFailureReasonErrorKey, nil];

      NSDictionary *userInfo = [NSDictionary dictionaryWithObjects:objArray
                                                    forKeys:keyArray];
      *error = [NSError errorWithDomain:InputValidationErrorDomain
                          code:1001
```

```
                                    userInfo:userInfo];
        }
      return NO;
   }

   return YES;
}
@end
```

The implementation of the `validateInput:error:` method does mainly two things:

1. It checks the number of matches of numerical values in the text field
    with a configured NSRegularExpression object. The regular expression
    we use there is `"^[0–9]*$"`. It means from the beginning of a whole line
    (denoted as "^") till the end of it (denoted as "$"), there should be zero
    or more characters (denoted as "*") of a set that contains only digits
    (denoted as [0–9]).

2. If there is no match at all, then it creates a new NSError object that
    contains a message that says, "The input can contain only numerical
    values" and assigns it to the input NSError pointer. Then it finally returns
    a BOOL value that indicates the outcome of the validation. The error is
    associated with a custom error code of 1001 and a custom error domain
    value defined in the header of InputValidator as follows:
    ```
    static NSString * const InputValidationErrorDomain =
    @"InputValidationErrorDomain";
    ```

A brother of NumericInputValidator that validates only letters in the input, called
AlphaInputValidator, has a similar algorithm to validate the content of the input field.
AlphaInputValidator overrides the same method as NumericInputValidator does.
Apparently, its validation algorithm checks only if the input string contains only letters,
as shown in its implementation file in Listing 19–6.

Listing 19–6. *The Implementation of AlphaInputValidator in AlphaInputValidator.m*

```
#import "AlphaInputValidator.h"

@implementation AlphaInputValidator

- (BOOL) validateInput:(UITextField *)input error:(NSError**) error
{
  NSError *regError = nil;
  NSRegularExpression *regex = [NSRegularExpression
                       regularExpressionWithPattern:@"^[a-zA-Z]*$"
                       options:NSRegularExpressionAnchorsMatchLines
                       error:&regError];

  NSUInteger numberOfMatches = [regex
                       numberOfMatchesInString:[input text]
                       options:NSMatchingAnchored
                       range:NSMakeRange(0, [[input text] length])];

  // If there is not a single match
```

```
    // then return an error and NO
    if (numberOfMatches == 0)
    {
      if (error != nil)
      {
        NSString *description = NSLocalizedString(@"Input Validation Failed", @"");
        NSString *reason = NSLocalizedString(@"The input can contain only letters", @"");

        NSArray *objArray = [NSArray arrayWithObjects:description, reason, nil];
        NSArray *keyArray = [NSArray arrayWithObjects:NSLocalizedDescriptionKey,
                            NSLocalizedFailureReasonErrorKey, nil];

        NSDictionary *userInfo = [NSDictionary dictionaryWithObjects:objArray
                                                            forKeys:keyArray];
        *error = [NSError errorWithDomain:InputValidationErrorDomain
                                      code:1002
                                  userInfo:userInfo];
      }

      return NO;
    }

    return YES;
  }
@end
```

Our `AlphaInputValidator` also is a type of `InputValidator` that implements its `validateInput:` method. It has a similar coding structure and algorithm as its sibling, `NumericInputValidator`, except it uses a different regular expression in the `NSRegularExpression` object and the error code and message are specific to letters-only validation. The regular expression we use for checking letters is "^[a-zA-Z]*$". It is similar to the one for its brother for numeric validation, except that a set of valid characters contains both lower- and uppercase letters. As we can see, there is a lot of duplicated code in both versions of the method. Both algorithms share a common structure; you can refactor the structure into a template method (see Chapter 18) in the abstract parent class. Concrete subclasses of `InputValidator` can override primitive operations defined in `InputValidator` to return unique information to the template algorithm—for example, a regular expression and various attributes for constructing an `NSError` object, etc. I will leave this part for you as an exercise.

Up to this point, we have our input validators in place, ready to be used in our client app. However, `UITextField` doesn't know them, so we need to have our own version of `UITextField` that understands. We will create a subclass of `UITextField` that has a reference to `InputValidator` as well as a method—namely, `validate`, as shown in Listing 19–7.

Listing 19–7. *A Class Declaration for* `CustomTextField` *in* `CustomTextField.h`

```
#import "InputValidator.h"

@interface CustomTextField : UITextField
{
  @private
  InputValidator *inputValidator_;
}
```

```
@property (nonatomic, retain) IBOutlet InputValidator *inputValidator;

- (BOOL) validate;

@end
```

CustomTextField has a property that retains a reference to any InputValidator. When its validate method is invoked, it will use the InputValidator reference to start an actual validation process. We can see how they can be put together in an implementation shown in Listing 19–8.

Listing 19–8. *An Implementation of* CustomTextField *in* CustomTextField.m

```
#import "CustomTextField.h"

@implementation CustomTextField

@synthesize inputValidator=inputValidator_;

- (BOOL) validate
{
  NSError *error = nil;
  BOOL validationResult = [inputValidator_ validateInput:self error:&error];

  if (!validationResult)
  {
    UIAlertView *alertView = [[UIAlertView alloc]
                                  initWithTitle:[error localizedDescription]
                                        message:[error localizedFailureReason]
                                       delegate:nil
                              cancelButtonTitle:NSLocalizedString(@"OK", @"")
                              otherButtonTitles:nil];
    [alertView show];
    [alertView release];
  }

  return validationResult;
}

- (void) dealloc
{
  [inputValidator_ release];
  [super dealloc];
}

@end
```

In the validate method, it sends a message of [inputValidator_ validateInput:self error:&error] to the inputValidator_ reference. The beauty of the pattern is that the CustomTextField doesn't need to know what type of InputValidator it is using as well as any detail of the algorithm. So in the future if we add some new InputValidator, a CustomTextField object will use the new InputValidator the same way.

All of the plumbing is connected. Let's assume the client is a UIViewController that implements UITextFieldDelegate and has two IBOutlets of CustomTextField, as shown in Listing 19–9.

Listing 19–9. *A Class Declaration of StrategyViewController in StrategyViewController.h*

```
#import "NumericInputValidator.h"
#import "AlphaInputValidator.h"
#import "CustomTextField.h"

@interface StrategyViewController : UIViewController <UITextFieldDelegate>
{
  @private
  CustomTextField *numericTextField_;
  CustomTextField *alphaTextField_;
}

@property (nonatomic, retain) IBOutlet CustomTextField *numericTextField;
@property (nonatomic, retain) IBOutlet CustomTextField *alphaTextField;

@end
```

We have decided to let the controller implement one of the delegate's methods, (void)textFieldDidEndEditing:(UITextField *)textField, and put the check in that area. That method will be invoked every time the value of a text field is changed and its focus is lost. When a user input is done, our CustomTextField will call that method against its delegate, as shown in Listing 19–10.

Listing 19–10. *Client Code Defined in the textFieldDidEndEditing: Method That Validates an Instance of CustomTextField with Its Own Embedded Strategy Object (InputValidator)*

```
@implementation StrategyViewController

@synthesize numericTextField, alphaTextField;

// ...
// other methods in the view controller
// ...

#pragma mark -
#pragma mark UITextFieldDelegate methods

- (void)textFieldDidEndEditing:(UITextField *)textField
{
  if ([textField isKindOfClass:[CustomTextField class]])
  {
    [(CustomTextField*)textField validate];
  }
}
@end
```

When the textFieldDidEndEditing: is hit when one of the text fields is done editing, it checks if the textField is our CustomTextField class. If so, it sends a validate message to it to invoke a validation process against the text input field. As we can see, we don't need those conditional statements anymore. Instead, we have a much simpler statement to do the same data validation. Except for an extra check above it to make sure the type of the textField object is CustomTextField, there shouldn't be anything more complicated.

Hey, wait a minute. Something doesn't look right. How we could assign correct concrete InputValidator instances to numericTextField_ and alphaTextField_ defined in StrategyViewController? Both *TextFields are declared as IBOutlet in Listing 19–9. We can hook them up with the view controller in the Interface Builder through the IBOutlets like we do with other buttons and whatnot. Likewise, in the class declaration of CustomTextField in Listing 19–7, its inputValidator property is also an IBOutlet, which means that we can assign an instance of InputValidator to the *TextField in the Interface Builder the same way. So everything can be actually constructed through the use of reference connections in the Interface Builder if you declare certain attributes or properties of class as IBOutlet. For a more detailed discussion on how to use custom objects in Interface Builder, see "Using the CoordinatingController in the Interface Builder" in Chapter 11, about the Mediator pattern.

Summary

In this chapter, we have discussed the concepts of the Strategy pattern and how we can utilize the pattern to have client (context) classes use variants of related algorithms. The example of implementing input validators for a custom UITextField showcases how various validators can change the "guts" of the custom UITextField. The Strategy pattern is somewhat similar to the Decorator pattern (Chapter 16). Decorators extend the behavior of an object from outside while different strategies are encapsulated inside an object. So it is said that decorators change the "skin" of the object while strategies change its "guts."

In the next chapter, we are going to see another pattern that is related to algorithm encapsulation. An encapsulated algorithm is mainly used for deferring an execution of a command as an object.

Chapter 20

Command

In a battlefield, generals hand out timed instructions in sealed envelopes to soldiers or others, who then open the envelopes and execute the instructions in them. The same instructions can be one-timed or re-executed by different persons at given times. Since instructions are kept in envelopes, passing them around different areas for different purposes is easier than other means of instructions—for example, verbal instruction on the phone or other communication channels.

We borrow a similar idea of encapsulating instructions as different command objects in object-oriented design. Command objects can be passed around and reused at given times by different clients. A design pattern that is elaborated from the concept is called the Command pattern.

In this chapter, we are going to discuss the concepts of the pattern. We will also develop an undo infrastructure for our TouchPainter app so the user can redo/undo what he/she has drawn on the screen. The Cocoa Touch adaptation of the pattern will also be discussed later in the chapter.

What Is the Command Pattern?

A command object encapsulates information regarding how to perform instructions on a target, so a client or an invoker doesn't need to know any details of the target but can still be able to perform any available operations on it. By encapsulating a request as an object, clients can parameterize and put it in a queue or log, as well as support undoable operations. The command object binds together one or more actions with a specific receiver. The Command pattern decouples the binding between an action as an object and a receiver that executes it.

Before we dive into the details of the pattern in Objective-C, let's take a brief look at the structure of the pattern as illustrated in Figure 20–1.

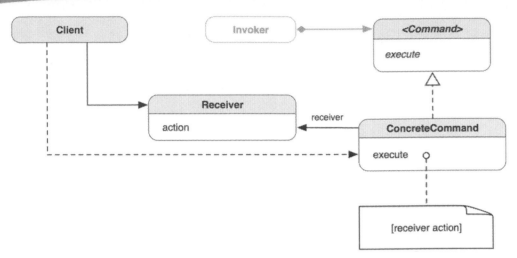

Figure 20–1. *A class diagram that shows the structure of the Command pattern*

So, here is what's happening in the diagram:

- The client creates a ConcreteCommand object and sets its receiver.

- The Invoker asks a generic command (in fact, ConcreteCommand) to carry out the request.

- Command is a generic interface (protocol) that is known to Invoker.

- ConcreteCommand acts as a middleman between Receiver and the action operation for it.

- Receiver can be any object that performs an actual operation with a corresponding request being carried out by a Command (ConcreteCommand) object.

> **COMMAND PATTERN:** Encapsulate a request as an object, thereby letting you parameterize clients with different requests, queue or log requests, and support undoable operations.*
>
> *The original definition appeared in *Design Patterns*, by the "Gang of Four" (Addison-Wesley, 1994).

When Would You Use the Command Pattern?

You'd naturally think about using the pattern when

- You want your application to support undo/redo.

- You want to parameterize an action as an object to perform operations and replace callbacks with different command objects

- You want to specify, queue, and execute requests at different times.

- You want to log changes so they can be reapplied later in case of a system failure.

- You want the system to support transactions with which a transaction encapsulates a set of changes to data. The transactions can be modeled as command objects.

You may ask, "Why can't we just execute a method directly without all the hassles?" Technically, yes, you can call whatever methods or functions you want in your program, and your program still compiles and runs. The problem is every class or method needs to know each other's details in order to work, and it's very complicated to implement any other operations, such as undo. When the program grows larger and larger, it would go to the point where it is very difficult to manage and reuse objects.

Before we get to designing and implementing an undo infrastructure, let's look at some useful resources from the Cocoa Touch framework that we can use for setting up the infrastructure in the next section.

Using the Command Pattern in the Cocoa Touch Framework

Instead of reinventing the wheel, it is a virtue to reuse what is available in the Cocoa Touch framework. The Command pattern is one of cataloged patterns adapted by the framework. By using "off-the-shelf" classes in the framework, we can focus on content development.

NSInvocation, NSUndoManager, and the target-action mechanism are typical adaptations of the pattern in the framework. The target-action mechanism has been covered in many other beginner iOS programming books, so we will go over NSInvocation and NSUndoManager only.

NSInvocation Objects

An instance of the NSInvocation class is just like the original ConcreteCommand class shown in Figure 20–1. An NSInvocation object encapsulates any necessary information to forward an execution message to a receiver at runtime, such as a target object, method selector, and method arguments. So the receiver can be invoked with the embedded selector and other information anytime with the help of the NSInvocation instance. The same invocation instance can repeatedly invoke the same method on the receiver or be reused with different targets and methods signatures.

NSInvocation is a generic layer of abstraction for invocation. Framework designers at Apple apparently didn't know anything about our actual receivers, invokers, selectors, and such when they were designing the infrastructure for the NSInvocation class. So at the creation of an NSInvocation object, we need to provide any necessary information as a form of an NSMethodSignature object. An NSMethodSignature object contains any argument and returns value types of a method invocation. To elaborate from our rather generic example at the beginning of the chapter, we are now going to use NSInvocation in place of the original Command and ConcreteCommand classes as illustrated in Figure 20–2.

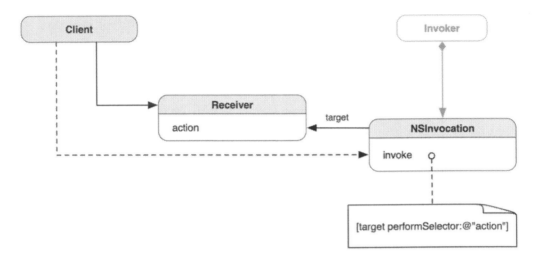

Figure 20–2. *A new class diagram of the Command pattern with the* NSInvocation *class*

We took off the original Command protocol from our first class diagram, and we replaced the ConcreteCommand class with the NSInvocation class provided by the Cocoa Touch framework. The idea is that a client creates a new instance of NSInvocation object with an instance of Receiver and its operation as a selector. Then an Invoker (e.g., a UIButton object) will be set with the NSInvocation object. When the Invoker needs to invoke the action, it will call the invoke method of the NSInvocation object that is stored in the Invoker. Finally, the NSInvocation object will invoke the selector on its target to finish the process.

NSUndoManager

Since the introduction of iOS 3.0, NSUndoManager has been available in the Cocoa Touch framework for iOS application development. NSUndoManager was elegantly designed as a general-purpose undo stack management class, yet it is powerful and versatile enough to use in almost any type of application. We will go over some key features and the idea of NSUndoManager here.

An instance of NSUndoManager manages its own undo and redo stacks. The undo stack maintains all the invoked operations as objects. NSUndoManager can also "reverse" the undo operation (a.k.a. redo) by invoking the operation object that was pushed from the undo stack. A registered undo operation can be an action that reverses a previous action invoked by a client. Instead of home-brewing our own undo stack, NSUndoManager saves us all the hassle of dealing with undo as well as redo operations by using various delayed invocation forwarding mechanisms. An undo manager object collects all registered undo operations that occur within a single-run loop cycle, so that an undo can reverse all changes within the cycle. When an NSUndoManager object is requested to undo the last operation, it will invoke the operation object at the top of the undo stack. When it is done, it will pop the operation object and push it to the redo stack. Likewise when redo is finished, it will move the operation object from the redo stack to the undo stack for the next undo. So NSUndoManager exchanges operation objects between two stacks to manage the whole command history.

Registering Undo Command Operations

Initially, the undo stack is empty. Registering an undo operation adds an invocation object to the undo stack. To add an undo operation to the undo stack, you need to register it with the object that performs the undo operation. There are two ways to register undo operations with an NSUndoManager object:

- Simple undo registration
- Invocation-based registration

Registering a simple undo operation requires a selector that identifies an undo operation with a receiver as arguments. The state is passed to the undo manager prior to any changes. When the undo operation is invoked, the receiver will be reset with the previous state or attributes.

The invocation-based undo involves an NSInvocation object. Using an NSInvocation object means it can take a method with any number and type of parameters. This approach is very useful when a state change requires multiple parameters.

In most cases, a client object that contains or manages other objects in an application owns an instance of NSUndoManager. Since NSUndoManager doesn't retain its invocation target receivers, the client object needs to make sure the receivers being pushed in the NSUndoManager's undo stack have a reference count of at least 1. Otherwise, the undo manager may crash the application if one of its receivers is released when performing an undo/redo. Sometimes, there are cases where an object being modified can have its own undo manager and perform its own undo and redo operations—for example, a drawing app that has multiple drawing views, each of which keeps track of all individual strokes and their colors. Each new stroke added to an active drawing view will register a new undo operation with the view's undo manager. If an undo operation is requested on a particular view, the corresponding undo manager will perform the registered undo operation on the receiver so that the last stroke will be removed.

Implementing Undo/Redo in TouchPainter

As we described in the previous sections, one of the highlighted uses of the Command pattern is to support undo/redo operations in an application.

We are about to design and implement an undo/redo architecture for the TouchPainter app. In the preceding sections, we have discussed using NSInvocation to encapsulate an execution as a command object. We have also explored the possibility of borrowing the NSUndoManager's undo architecture for our own use.

In this section, we will have two sections for different approaches to implement that. In the first one, we will use NSUndoManager for the design. After that, we will discuss how to build our own version of undo/redo from scratch.

Implementing Drawing/Undrawing with NSUndoManager

We've already learned some key concepts and features of NSUndoManager in the preceding sections. In the subsections that follow, we will walk through the process of using NSUndoManager to manage actionable NSInvocation objects for drawing and undrawing strokes and dots against the main Scribble object.

Adding Methods for Generating Drawing/Undrawing Invocations

We need a new NSInvocation object each time when we need the NSUndoManager to register an undo/redo operation. It is handy to have a method or two that can generate prototype NSInvocation objects with which we can just modify a couple of parameters of them with some particular Stroke or Dot objects on the go. Listing 20–1 shows two methods just for that purpose.

Listing 20–1. *Methods That Generate NSInvocation Objects for Performing Drawing and Undrawing Operations Later*

```
- (NSInvocation *) drawScribbleInvocation
{
  NSMethodSignature *executeMethodSignature = [scribble_
                                      methodSignatureForSelector:
                                      @selector(addMark:
                                                shouldAddToPreviousMark:)];
  NSInvocation *drawInvocation = [NSInvocation
                                  invocationWithMethodSignature:
                                  executeMethodSignature];
  [drawInvocation setTarget:scribble_];
  [drawInvocation setSelector:@selector(addMark:shouldAddToPreviousMark:)];
  BOOL attachToPreviousMark = NO;
  [drawInvocation setArgument:&attachToPreviousMark atIndex:3];

  return drawInvocation;
}

- (NSInvocation *) undrawScribbleInvocation
{
  NSMethodSignature *unexecuteMethodSignature = [scribble_
                                      methodSignatureForSelector:
                                      @selector(removeMark:)];
  NSInvocation *undrawInvocation = [NSInvocation
                                    invocationWithMethodSignature:
                                    unexecuteMethodSignature];
  [undrawInvocation setTarget:scribble_];
  [undrawInvocation setSelector:@selector(removeMark:)];
```

```
    return undrawInvocation;
}
```

The `drawScribbleInvocation` method generates an `NSInvocation` object that will be used for adding a `Mark` object to `scribble_`. It requires an `NSMethodSignature` object for a selector that will be invoked to instantiate an `NSInvocation` object. In this case, we need a method signature for the `addMark:shouldAddToPreviousMark:` method of a `Scribble` object. After we create an `NSInvocation` object, we set the second argument (at index 3 from 0) of a `BOOL` value default to `NO` because we undo/redo only complete strokes and dots, not vertices. User arguments collected in the `NSInvocation` object begin at index 2 because the first one (at index 0) is the receiver and the second one is `_cmd` that contains the name of the selector being invoked.

Likewise, the `undrawScribbleInvocation` method creates an `NSInvocation` object the same way except that its selector for the invocation is now `removeMark:` from a `Scribble` object. The invocation object is for undoing a complete stroke or dot later. When we get to the actual drawing code, we'll see how we can assign a real `Mark` object to each of invocation objects generated from the methods.

Adding Methods for Registering Undo/Redo Operations in NSUndoManager

We've seen how to generate `NSInvocation` objects for drawing/undrawing strokes and dots in action, but we also need to register them with the `NSUndoManager` to make those invocations undoable. Listing 20–2 shows the implementation of the methods that are used for registering undo/redo operations with the `NSUndoManager` of `CanvasViewController`.

Listing 20–2. *Methods for Executing and Unexecuting NSInvocation Objects with Help from NSUndoManager*

```
#pragma mark Draw Scribble Command Methods

- (void) executeInvocation:(NSInvocation *)invocation
        withUndoInvocation:(NSInvocation *)undoInvocation
{
  [invocation retainArguments];

  [[self.undoManager prepareWithInvocationTarget:self]
    unexecuteInvocation:undoInvocation
    withRedoInvocation:invocation];

  [invocation invoke];
}

- (void) unexecuteInvocation:(NSInvocation *)invocation
        withRedoInvocation:(NSInvocation *)redoInvocation
{
  [[self.undoManager prepareWithInvocationTarget:self]
    executeInvocation:redoInvocation
    withUndoInvocation:invocation];

  [invocation invoke];
}
```

Both the executeInvocation:withUndoInvocation: and unexecuteInvocation: withRedoInvocation: methods look very similar and somewhat confusing. The first method takes an invocation object to execute straightaway and registers another invocation object as an undo operation. The latter method uses an invocation object in the first parameter to execute *undo* operations and registers the second one for *redo*.

In the executeInvocation: method, we send a prepareWithInvocationTarget: method to CanvasViewController's NSUndoManager to register an undo operation. We pass in unexecuteInvocation:undoInvocation withRedoInvocation:invocation as a complete invocation message for an event of undo. The unexecuteInvocation: method registers the invocation object in executeInvocation: as a redo operation. If you look closely, you will notice that they are crisscrossing with an invocation object that draws and another invocation object that undraws what has been drawn.

Modifying Touch Event Handlers for Invocations

Now we are getting to change the original touch event handlers in CanvasViewController to create invocation objects to prepare all the drawing actions for undo/redo. Listing 20–3 shows the required modifications. We'll break it up into two parts to discuss.

Listing 20–3. *Modifications to the Original Touch Event Handlers in* CanvasViewController *That Accommodate the* NSInvocation-*Based Undo/Redo Operations with* NSUndoManager

```
#pragma mark -
#pragma mark Touch Event Handlers

- (void)touchesBegan:(NSSet *)touches withEvent:(UIEvent *)event
{
  startPoint_ = [[touches anyObject] locationInView:canvasView_];
}

- (void)touchesMoved:(NSSet *)touches withEvent:(UIEvent *)event
{
  CGPoint lastPoint = [[touches anyObject] previousLocationInView:canvasView_];

  // add a new stroke to scribble
  // if this is indeed a drag from
  // a finger
  if (CGPointEqualToPoint(lastPoint, startPoint_))
  {
    id <Mark> newStroke = [[[Stroke alloc] init] autorelease];
    [newStroke setColor:strokeColor_];
    [newStroke setSize:strokeSize_];

    [scribble_ addMark:newStroke shouldAddToPreviousMark:NO];

    // retrieve a new NSInvocation for drawing and
    // set new arguments for the draw command
    NSInvocation *drawInvocation = [self drawScribbleInvocation];
    [drawInvocation setArgument:&newStroke atIndex:2];

    // retrieve a new NSInvocation for undrawing and
```

```
    // set a new argument for the undraw command
    NSInvocation *undrawInvocation = [self undrawScribbleInvocation];
    [undrawInvocation setArgument:&newStroke atIndex:2];

    // execute the draw command with the undraw command
    [self executeInvocation:drawInvocation withUndoInvocation:undrawInvocation];
  }

  // add the current touch as another vertex to the
  // temp stroke
  CGPoint thisPoint = [[touches anyObject] locationInView:canvasView_];
  Vertex *vertex = [[[Vertex alloc]
                      initWithLocation:thisPoint]
                     autorelease];

  // we don't need to undo every vertex
  // so we are keeping this
  [scribble_ addMark:vertex shouldAddToPreviousMark:YES];
}
```

The touch event handlers in this listing are discussed in the "Updating Strokes on the CanvasView in TouchPainter" section of Chapter 12. So we will not repeat ourselves with its details here but will highlight some key areas of the touch handling processes and the changes we make for undo/redo.

In the touchesMoved: method, the type of Mark object is determined by two situations:

- If the previous touch was the first touch on the screen, then we will create an instance of Stroke and attach it to scribble_ under the main parent.

- Other touches in the method will be treated as vertices of a stroke. So we will create an instance of Vertex and attach it to scribble_ under that last child Mark (i.e., a Stroke we added before) in the main parent.

At the point where it identifies the beginning of a Stroke object, we removed the original message statement of addMark:shouldAddToPreviousMark: for scribble_ for adding a new Stroke object. Instead, we use the *scribbleInvocation methods (* here is a general purpose wildcard character, not a notation for a pointer) defined previously to generate template invocation objects for adding and removing the new Stroke object.

After setting appropriate arguments for the drawInvocation and undrawInvocation objects, we set them for executeInvocation: to start executing the drawing operation. drawInvocation will be invoked in the method, and at the same time undrawInvocation will be registered as an undo operation.

```
- (void)touchesEnded:(NSSet *)touches withEvent:(UIEvent *)event
{
  CGPoint lastPoint = [[touches anyObject] previousLocationInView:canvasView_];
  CGPoint thisPoint = [[touches anyObject] locationInView:canvasView_];

  // if the touch never moves (stays at the same spot until lifted now)
  // just add a dot to an existing stroke composite
  // otherwise add it to the temp stroke as the last vertex
  if (CGPointEqualToPoint(lastPoint, thisPoint))
```

```
{
  Dot *singleDot = [[[Dot alloc]
                        initWithLocation:thisPoint]
                      autorelease];
  [singleDot setColor:strokeColor_];
  [singleDot setSize:strokeSize_];

  [scribble_ addMark:singleDot shouldAddToPreviousMark:NO];

  // retrieve a new NSInvocation for drawing and
  // set new arguments for the draw command
  NSInvocation *drawInvocation = [self drawScribbleInvocation];
  [drawInvocation setArgument:&singleDot atIndex:2];

  // retrieve a new NSInvocation for undrawing and
  // set a new argument for the undraw command
  NSInvocation *undrawInvocation = [self undrawScribbleInvocation];
  [undrawInvocation setArgument:&singleDot atIndex:2];

  // execute the draw command with the undraw command
  [self executeInvocation:drawInvocation withUndoInvocation:undrawInvocation];
}

// reset the start point here
startPoint_ = CGPointZero;

// if this is the last point of stroke
// don't bother to draw it as the user
// won't tell the difference
}

- (void)touchesCancelled:(NSSet *)touches withEvent:(UIEvent *)event
{
  // reset the start point here
  startPoint_ = CGPointZero;
}
```

When it comes to drawing a dot in the touchesEnded: method, we follow the same procedure we did for drawing a stroke. We use the same singleDot object for the executeInvocation: method.

So far we have implemented the undo/redo infrastructure with the help of NSUndoManager. In the following sections, we are going to discuss how to build our own undo/redo from the ground up. Free feel to read on if you are interested in knowing how a bare-bones undo/redo can be implemented with the Command pattern in Objective-C. Otherwise, you can skip to the "Allowing the User to Activate Undo/Redo" section toward the end of the chapter.

Home-Brewing Your Own Drawing/Undrawing Infrastructure

Congratulations! You have made it to the point where we are about to brewing our own undo/redo architecture. Before we get to the design, let's look at how we can collect and put together all the commands executed in an application. Executed command objects can be collected and queued as a list of command history, as shown in Figure 20–3.

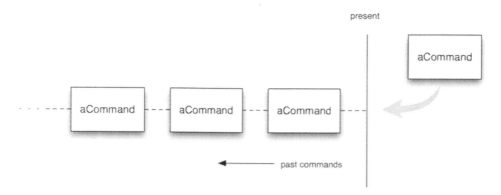

Figure 20–3. *A sequence of executed commands forms a linear command history*

As long as there is a new command object executed and added to the list, the list can keep growing in one direction. In a traditional sense, you can perform undo or redo operations with any one of them by traversing the command history list. There are many approaches to implementing a command history. One of the common ways is to use an index to keep track of the current command objects in the list. By increasing or decreasing the index value, you can navigate to a particular command object for either undo or redo. In fact, using indexing to navigate for either undo or redo operations can be quite tricky. There is a simpler and less error-prone way. Instead of using a single command list for both undo and redo, we can have one stack for undo and another one for redo just like NSUndoManager. Executed command objects are pushed to the undo stack. The one at the top is always the last command executed. When an application needs to undo the last execution, it will pop the last command off the undo stack and then undo it. When it's done, the application will push the command to the redo stack. Until all the command objects have been undone, the redo stack is already filled up with all the undone command objects. A similar procedure applies to redo, just in a different direction. A diagram that illustrates this mechanism is shown in Figure 20–4.

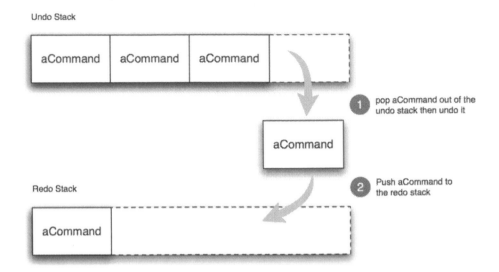

Figure 20–4. *Transferring* aCommand *from the top of the undo stack to a redo stack during an undo operation*

Command objects are just being popped and pushed between the two stacks without using any complex indexing scheme to navigate the list.

Designing a Command Infrastructure

We are going to implement undo/redo operations with the two-stack approach for our faithful TouchPainter app. When a user touches the canvas, either a stroke or a dot shows up on the screen. First of all, we need to make a "drawing" action as a command object. After it draws something, the app will push it to the undo stack until we need it back to undraw what it did. We call that command for drawing DrawScribbleCommand, as shown in a class diagram in Figure 20–5.

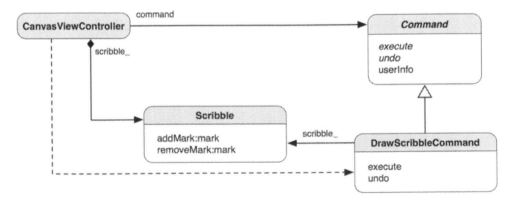

Figure 20–5. *A class diagram of* DrawScribbleCommand *and related classes*

Command is the parent abstract class for DrawScribbleCommand. It declares some common abstract operations of execute and undo. Command also has a concrete userInfo property that allows clients to provide any extra parameters for a Command object. DrawScribbleCommand has a reference to a Scribble object so it can add or remove any Mark objects from it. CanvasViewController here is both a client and invoker. The overall class structure is quite similar to the original class diagram for the Command pattern in Figure 20–1.

Implementing the Command Classes

So, how can we implement it in Objective-C? Let's take a look at the abstract Command class in Listing 20–4.

Listing 20–4. *A Class Declaration of Command in Command.h*

```
@interface Command : NSObject
{
  @protected
  NSDictionary *userInfo_;
}

@property (nonatomic, retain) NSDictionary *userInfo;

- (void) execute;
- (void) undo;

@end
```

Besides the execute and undo methods, Command declares the userInfo property as NSDictionary. Objects of Command's subclasses can use what's in the userInfo to perform any operations in an overridden execute method. The implementation of Command is shown in Listing 20–5.

Listing 20–5. *The Implementation of Command in Command.m*

```
#import "Command.h"


@implementation Command
@synthesize userInfo=userInfo_;

- (void) execute
{
  // should throw an exception.
}

- (void) undo
{
  // do nothing
  // subclasses need to override this
  // method to perform actual undo.
}

- (void) dealloc
{
```

```
    [userInfo_ release];
    [super dealloc];
}

@end
```

There is not much going on in the implementation of Command as both the execute and undo methods are abstract operations. Its subclasses should put some actions in them. Now let's take a look at DrawScribbleCommand in Listing 20–6.

Listing 20–6. *A Class Declaration of DrawScribbleCommand in DrawScribbleCommand.h*

```
#import "Command.h"
#import "Scribble.h"

@interface DrawScribbleCommand : Command
{
  @private
  Scribble *scribble_;
  id <Mark> mark_;
  BOOL shouldAddToPreviousMark_;
}

- (void) execute;
- (void) undo;

@end
```

It declares some private member variables to help perform some operations on a Scribble object later. We are also re-declaring the execute and undo methods in the subclass, so when we look at this class again in the future we won't get lost. The implementation of execute and undo methods is shown in Listing 20–7.

Listing 20–7. *The Implementation of DrawScribbleCommand in DrawScribbleCommand.m*

```
#import "DrawScribbleCommand.h"


@implementation DrawScribbleCommand

- (void) execute
{
  if (!userInfo_) return;

  scribble_ = [userInfo_ objectForKey:ScribbleObjectUserInfoKey];
  mark_ = [userInfo_ objectForKey:MarkObjectUserInfoKey];
  shouldAddToPreviousMark_ = [(NSNumber *)[userInfo_
                                    objectForKey:AddToPreviousMarkUserInfoKey]
                      boolValue];

  [scribble_ addMark:mark_ shouldAddToPreviousMark:shouldAddToPreviousMark_];

}

- (void) undo
{
  [scribble_ removeMark:mark_];
}
```

@end

The overridden execute method is dependent on the information embedded in the userInfo property. If there is no userInfo provided, the method will just bail out. OK, so what's in the userInfo that is so important to DrawScribbleCommand? The userInfo dictionary package contains three key elements that are crucial for using a Scribble object—first of all, a target Scribble object. Without that, nothing else matters. Then there is an instance of Mark that should be added to the Scribble object. Finally, a BOOL value tells how the Mark instance should be attached in the Scribble object. For a detailed discussion of Scribble and its operations, see the Observer pattern, Chapter 12.

The undo method simply tells the stored Scribble object to remove a stored Mark reference.

Modifying CanvasViewController for the Commands

Now we know how a DrawScribbleCommand performs actual drawing with a Scribble object. Let's see how a bunch of DrawScribbleCommand objects are involved in undo/redo operations defined in CanvasViewController, as shown in Listing 20–8.

Listing 20–8. *Methods That Manage Command Objects That Draw Scribbles in CanvasViewController*

```
#pragma mark -
#pragma mark Draw Scribble Command Methods

- (void) executeCommand:(Command *)command
          prepareForUndo:(BOOL)prepareForUndo
{
  if (prepareForUndo)
  {
    // lazy-load undoStack_
    if (undoStack_ == nil)
    {
      undoStack_ = [[NSMutableArray alloc] initWithCapacity:levelsOfUndo_];
    }

    // drop the bottom one if the
    // undo stack is full
    if ([undoStack_ count] == levelsOfUndo_)
    {
      [undoStack_ dropBottom];
    }

    // push the command
    // to our undo stack
    [undoStack_ push:command];
  }

  [command execute];
}
```

The executeCommand:prepareForUndo: method is responsible for executing an incoming Command object as well as pushing it in undoStack_. The method also maintains the size of undoStack_ by dropping the one at the bottom if the stack is already full.

```
- (void) undoCommand
{
  Command *command = [undoStack_ pop];
  [command undo];

  // push the command to the redo stack
  if (redoStack_ == nil)
  {
    redoStack_ = [[NSMutableArray alloc] initWithCapacity:levelsOfUndo_];
  }

  [redoStack_ push:command];
}
```

When the undoCommand method is invoked, it first tries to retrieve a reference to the last command from the top of undoStack_, and then sends it to an undo message to undraw the Mark object that it preserved, as discussed in Listing 20–7. Then it will instantiate redoStack_, if it's not done so, and push the Command object that was popped from undoStack_ half a second ago (it shouldn't take that long, by the way).

```
- (void) redoCommand
{
  Command *command = [redoStack_ pop];
  [command execute];

  // push the command back to the undo stack
  [undoStack_ push:command];
}
```

The redoCommand is even simpler than undoCommand. The first half is almost the same as undoCommand except that the last Command object is now popped from redoStack_ instead, and command invokes execute rather than undo. After that, it pushes command back to undoStack_. So when the undoCommand method is invoked again, the process will be repeated.

So how can we connect DrawScribbleCommand objects with the actual drawing events? We are going explain with a bunch of touch event handlers defined in CanvasViewController in Listing 20–9. The mechanism of drawing different types of Mark based on the touch events are discussed in Chapter 12 as well as the previous "Modifying Touch Event Handlers for Invocations" section. So we will only highlight changes specific to our home-brewed infrastructure. Like in the last part, we will break the listing up into two chunks to discuss.

Listing 20–9. *Touch Event Handlers in* CanvasViewController *That Manipulate* DrawScribbleCommand *Objects*

```
#pragma mark -
#pragma mark Touch Event Handlers

- (void)touchesBegan:(NSSet *)touches withEvent:(UIEvent *)event
{
```

```
    startPoint_ = [[touches anyObject] locationInView:canvasView_];
}

- (void)touchesMoved:(NSSet *)touches withEvent:(UIEvent *)event
{
    CGPoint lastPoint = [[touches anyObject] previousLocationInView:canvasView_];

    // add a new stroke to scribble
    // if this is indeed a drag from
    // a finger
    if (CGPointEqualToPoint(lastPoint, startPoint_))
    {
        id <Mark> newStroke = [[[Stroke alloc] init] autorelease];
        [newStroke setColor:strokeColor_];
        [newStroke setSize:strokeSize_];

        [scribble_ addMark:newStroke shouldAddToPreviousMark:NO];

        NSDictionary *userInfo = [NSDictionary dictionaryWithObjectsAndKeys:
                            scribble_, ScribbleObjectUserInfoKey,
                            newStroke, MarkObjectUserInfoKey,
                            [NSNumber numberWithBool:NO],
                            AddToPreviousMarkUserInfoKey, nil];
        DrawScribbleCommand *command = [[[DrawScribbleCommand alloc] init] autorelease];
        [command setUserInfo:userInfo];
        [self executeCommand:command prepareForUndo:YES];
    }

    // add the current touch as another vertex to the
    // temp stroke
    CGPoint thisPoint = [[touches anyObject] locationInView:canvasView_];
    Vertex *vertex = [[[Vertex alloc]
                        initWithLocation:thisPoint]
                    autorelease];

    [scribble_ addMark:vertex shouldAddToPreviousMark:YES];
}
```

Now instead of using `addMark:shouldAddToPreviousMark:` to add a `Stroke` object, we use a `DrawScribbleCommand` object to handle that. It takes a dictionary of `userInfo` with values associated with three dictionary keys, `ScribbleObjectUserInfoKey`, `MarkObjectUserInfoKey`, and `AddToPreviousMarkUserInfoKey`. These keys are defined in Scribble as follows:

```
NSString *const ScribbleObjectUserInfoKey = @"ScribbleObjectUserInfoKey";
NSString *const MarkObjectUserInfoKey = @"MarkObjectUserInfoKey";
NSString *const AddToPreviousMarkUserInfoKey = @"AddToPreviousMarkUserInfoKey";
```

We add `scribble_`, `newStroke`, and a `BOOL` value of `NO` as an instance of `NSNumber` to the dictionary with the associated keys. Then we create an instance of the `DrawScribbleCommand` object and initialize it with the `userInfo` dictionary that we've just created. Instead of executing it right away, we pass it to a `CanvasViewController`'s instance method, `executeCommand:command prepareForUndo:`, to execute and prepare for undo as described in Listing 20–8. After that, the `DrawScribbleCommand` object is pushed to our previously defined undo stack (i.e., `undoStack_`), and it's ready to be undone.

```
- (void)touchesEnded:(NSSet *)touches withEvent:(UIEvent *)event
{
  CGPoint lastPoint = [[touches anyObject] previousLocationInView:canvasView_];
  CGPoint thisPoint = [[touches anyObject] locationInView:canvasView_];

  // if the touch never moves (stays at the same spot until lifted now)
  // just add a dot to an existing stroke composite
  // otherwise add it to the temp stroke as the last vertex
  if (CGPointEqualToPoint(lastPoint, thisPoint))
  {
    Dot *singleDot = [[[Dot alloc]
                        initWithLocation:thisPoint]
                      autorelease];
    [singleDot setColor:strokeColor_];
    [singleDot setSize:strokeSize_];

    [scribble_ addMark:singleDot shouldAddToPreviousMark:NO];

    NSDictionary *userInfo = [NSDictionary dictionaryWithObjectsAndKeys:
                              scribble_, ScribbleObjectUserInfoKey,
                              singleDot, MarkObjectUserInfoKey,
                              [NSNumber numberWithBool:NO],
                              AddToPreviousMarkUserInfoKey, nil];
    DrawScribbleCommand *command = [[[DrawScribbleCommand alloc] init] autorelease];
    [command setUserInfo:userInfo];
    [self executeCommand:command prepareForUndo:YES];

  }
```

The touchesEnd: method determines if the touch ends at the same spot where it was first landed on the screen. If so, it will create a new Dot object and attach it to the main Mark parent in scribble_. We construct a similar userInfo with the same types of elements associated with the user keys for a new DrawScribbleCommand object. Then we pass it to the executeCommand: again like drawing a stroke with vertices.

```
  // reset the start point here
  startPoint_ = CGPointZero;

  // if this is the last point of stroke
  // don't bother to draw it as the user
  // won't tell the difference
}

- (void)touchesCancelled:(NSSet *)touches withEvent:(UIEvent *)event
{
  // reset the start point here
  startPoint_ = CGPointZero;
}
```

The rest of the code is basically intact. Now you would ask, "Have we forgotten to push the operation for adding vertices into the undo stack in the touchesMoved: method?" We haven't, but we left that out for a reason. We've designed our undo infrastructure around undoing/redoing only a complete stroke or dot, not vertices. If it undoes every "step" when the user creates a stroke, the user experience as well as performance may suffer. So we keep the original addMark: message for scribble_ there.

Allowing the User to Activate Undo/Redo

Up to this point, we seem to have everything in place for our undo infrastructure to roll out. But how does the user actuate an undo/redo process in TouchPainter? On the main canvas view of TouchPainter, there are undo and redo buttons on the right-hand side of the toolbar, as shown in Figure 20–6.

Undo　Redo

Figure 20–6. *A screenshot of the main canvas view showing the undo and redo buttons on the toolbar*

Each of the buttons is tagged. When the user taps either one of them to actuate the process, we can capture and identify it in the onBarButtonHit: method, as shown in Listing 20–10.

Listing 20–10. *An IBAction Method for an Undo/Redo Button Hit in CanvasViewController*

```
#pragma mark -
#pragma mark Toolbar button hit method

- (IBAction) onBarButtonHit:(id)button
{
  UIBarButtonItem *barButton = button;

  if ([barButton tag] == 4)
  {
    [self undoCommand];
  }
  else if ([barButton tag] == 5)
  {
    [self redoCommand];
  }
}
```

The code itself is self-explanatory based on what tag the button has to determine, whether it is for undo or redo.

For the version of `NSUndoManager`, the undo statement is changed to the following:

```
[self.undoManager undo];
```

as for redo:

```
[self.undoManager redo];
```

We have concluded the examples on implementing undo/redo operations in our TouchPainter. The Command pattern is commonly found in many object-oriented software designs.

What Else Can a Command Do?

The Command pattern allows executable instructions encapsulated in command objects. It makes the pattern a natural choice for implementing an undo/redo infrastructure. But it doesn't stop right there. Another well-known use of command objects is for delaying executions in an invoker. Invokers can be a menu item or a button. It's quite common to use command objects to link up operations crossing between different objects—for example, hitting a button in a view controller can execute a command object to perform some operations on another view controller. The command object hides any details related to the operations.

From the sample project of this chapter, you can find a few more `Command` classes used in some other areas in the TouchPainter app for different purposes. The source project files contain a lot more information than we can cover in here, so free feel to check them out and explore what you can find in them!

Summary

This chapter has introduced the Command pattern and how we can implement it in Objective-C. We have designed and implemented an undo infrastructure for the TouchPainter app so the user can undo/redo any strokes and dots drawn on the screen. We have also illustrated how the Cocoa Touch framework has adapted the pattern with different invocation and undo/redo strategies that can be applied in any iOS applications.

The benefits of decoupling between command, invoker, receiver, and client in an application are apparent. If a particular command needs to be changed in the implementation, then most of the other components in the architecture remain intact. It is very easy to add new command classes because we don't need to modify the existing classes in order to do so.

This is the end of this part about encapsulating algorithms. In the next part, we will discuss some design patterns that are related to performance and object access.

Performance and Object Access

Chapter 21

Flyweight

Public transportation, such as buses, has been around for over a century. A lot of passengers can share the expenses of owning and operating vehicles (e.g., buses) when they all go in the same direction. There are multiple stops/stations in public transport. People just hop on and off along the route close to the place where they want to go. The expenses of getting to the place are limited to just the trip. Compared to the costs of owning a vehicle, taking public transport is a lot cheaper. That is the beauty of sharing common resources.

In object-oriented software design, sometimes sharing common objects not only saves resources but also increases performance. For instance, we need one million instances of a class for a particular task, but if we can make an instance of the class sharable by externalizing some unique information, the saved cost could be significant (one unique instance vs. one million of it). A sharable object contains only some intrinsic information that doesn't identify it. A design pattern that focuses on designing sharable objects is called the Flyweight pattern.

In this chapter, we are going to discuss the concepts of the pattern. We will also implement the pattern with a sample app that displays hundreds of flower images with only six unique instances.

What Is the Flyweight Pattern?

There are two key components to implement the Flyweight pattern. They are usually sharable flyweight objects and a pool that keeps them. Some sort of centralized object is crucial for maintaining the pool and returning appropriate instances from it. A factory (either an abstract or a concrete one—see Abstract Factory pattern, Chapter 5) is a perfect candidate for this role. It can return various types of concrete flyweight objects based on their parent type through a single factory method. That kind of factory is commonly referred to as a "manager" in different frameworks (The name "Manager" seems to sound cooler than "Factory" anyway). No matter what it's called, its primary objectives are to maintain flyweight objects in a pool and return any of them appropriately.

What makes flyweight objects "flyweight" in the first place? It doesn't refer to the size of them but the sheer amount of space they can save by sharing. Some (or most) of the object's unique state (extrinsic state) can be taken out and managed elsewhere, and the rest of it is shared. Let's say that you originally needed a million objects of a class, but because objects of that class are flyweights, now one is enough. That's what makes the whole system lightweight thanks to the sharable flyweight objects. With a careful design, memory savings can be significant. In iOS development, saving memory means boosting overall performance.

A class diagram in Figure 21–1 depicts their static relationships.

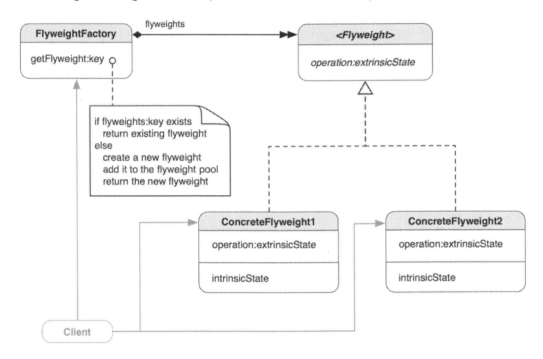

Figure 21–1. *A class diagram of the Flyweight pattern*

Flyweight is the parent interface (protocol) for two concrete flyweight classes, ConcreteFlyweight1 and ConcreteFlyweight2. Each ConcreteFlyweight class maintains its own intrinsicState that doesn't make any object of it unique. Flyweight declares the operation:extrinsicState method, which is implemented by both ConcreteFlyweight classes. IntrinsicState is something that can be shared in a flyweight object, while extrinsicState supplements any missing information that makes a flyweight object unique. Clients provide extrinsicState to an operation: message to let the flyweight object complete its tasks with the unique information from extrinsicState.

Figure 21–2 shows how an instance of FlyweightFactory manages flyweight objects in its pool at runtime.

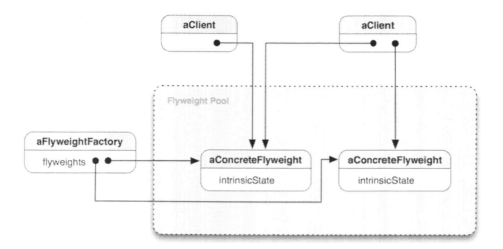

Figure 21–2. *An object diagram that shows how flyweights are shared at runtime*

THE FLYWEIGHT PATTERN: Uses sharing to support large numbers of fine-grained objects efficiently.*

*The original definition appeared in *Design Patterns*, by the "Gang of Four" (Addison-Wesley, 1994).

When Would You Use the Flyweight Pattern?

You'd naturally think about using it when all of the following are true:

- Your app uses a lot of objects.

- Keeping objects in memory can affect memory performance.

- Most of the object's unique state (extrinsic state) can be externalized and lightweight.

- Relatively few shared objects can replace the original bunch of objects after the objects' extrinsic state is removed.

- Your app doesn't depend on object identity since shared objects cannot have unique identities.

We are going to develop an app that draws hundreds or more flower patterns from a pool of shareable flowers to illustrate the concepts of the pattern.

Creating a Hundred-Flower Pool

We are going to create a small app that displays a lot of random flower images on the screen. There are six types of flowers we want to display, as shown in Figure 21–3.

Figure 21–3. *From left to right, top row: anemone, cosmos, and gerberas; bottom row: hollyhock, jasmine, and zinnia*

After many of these flowers have been drawn, the screen will be filled up with them like the one in Figure 21–4.

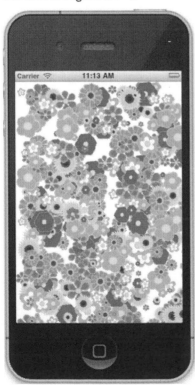

Figure 21–4. *An actual screenshot of our "Hundred-Flower Pool" with only six distinct instances of flower views despite five hundred of them shown onscreen*

Our goal is to draw a lot (hundreds or more) of randomly sized and positioned flowers with just six unique instances of them. If we create one flower instance for each instance drawn on the screen, the app may eat up a lot of memory. Our solution here is to use the Flyweight pattern to restrict our flower instances to no more than the total number of flower types we can choose from.

We need some sort of flyweight factory and some flyweight products for the design as shown in the class diagram in Figure 21–1. `FlowerView` is a subclass of `UIImageView`, with which we can customize drawing a flower image. Our flyweight factory for this app is called `FlowerFactory`, which manages a pool of `FlowerView` instances. Although the objects' class in the pool is `FlowerView`, clients expect instances only of `UIView` returned from `FlowerFactory`. It gives us a more flexible design rather than the factory returning objects of `UIImage` as the ultimate product type. If, for some reason, we also want to have flowers that "draw" themselves instead of display solid images, then we will have to change almost everything—that means we could be in trouble. `UIView` is considered a high-level class for anything that draws on the screen. `FlowerFactory` can return objects of any `UIView` subclass, and it won't break the system. That's one of the benefits of *"program to an interface, not an implementation."*

Designing and Implementing Sharable Flowers

We have six flower images as shown in Figure 21–3: anemone, cosmos, gerberas, hollyhock, jasmine, and zinnia. Each image is maintained in a unique instance of `FlowerView`. The `FlowerFactory` returns only the unique instances of `FlowerView` no matter how many flowers need to be returned. Their static relationships are illustrated as a class diagram in Figure 21–5.

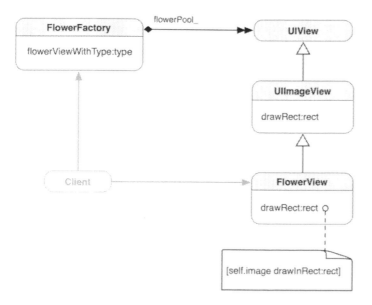

Figure 21–5. *A class diagram of* `FlowerView` *as a sharable flyweight*

FlowerFactory maintains an aggregated reference to a pool of flowers as `flowerPool_`. The `flowerPool_` is a data structure that keeps track of any instances of `FlowerView`. `FlowerFactory` returns an instance of `FlowerView` as `UIView` with its `flowerViewWithType:` method. A new instance of `FlowerView` will be created and returned if a view for a requested flower type does not exist in the pool.

Implementing the FlowerView Class

A class declaration of `FlowerView` is shown in Listing 21–1.

Listing 21–1. *A Class Declaration of FlowerView in FlowerView.h*

```
@interface FlowerView : UIImageView
{

}

- (void) drawRect:(CGRect)rect;

@end
```

Nothing can be simpler than that! It overrides only the `drawRect:rect` method of `UIImageView` and nothing else. We are re-declaring the method here to make it clear about what methods this class implements. The implementation of the method lets only the image stored in `super` (`UIImage`) draw itself separately in a provided rectangular area, as shown in Listing 21–2.

Listing 21–2. *An Implementation of FlowerView in FlowerView.m*

```
#import "FlowerView.h"

@implementation FlowerView

- (void) drawRect:(CGRect)rect
{
  [self.image drawInRect:rect];
}

@end
```

Implementing the FlowerFactory Class

Like what we've seen in Figure 21–5, `FlowerFactory` is declared in Listing 21–3.

Listing 21–3. *A Class Declaration of FlowerFactory in FlowerFactory.h*

```
@interface FlowerFactory : NSObject
{
  @private
  NSMutableDictionary *flowerPool_;
}

- (UIView *) flowerViewWithType:(FlowerType)type;

@end
```

FlowerFactory has a private NSMutableDictionary to keep track of a whole pool of ready-to-return flowers as flowerPool_. It also defines flowerViewWithType:(FlowerType)type as a convenience factory method that returns unique instances of UIView based on the FlowerType parameter. The FlowerType is based on the names of flowers we have in Figure 21–3. Their types are defined as a set of enum values, as shown in Listing 21–4.

Listing 21–4. *The Definition of* FlowerType

```
typedef enum
{
  kAnemone,
  kCosmos,
  kGerberas,
  kHollyhock,
  kJasmine,
  kZinnia,
  kTotalNumberOfFlowerTypes
} FlowerType;
```

It's apparent that the value of kTotalNumberOfFlowerTypes is the total number of flower types we support. So except that value, the FlowerFactory's flowerWithType: method uses any one of these values to determine which flower instance to return.

Let's see how FlowerFactory manages the flower pool in Listing 21–5.

Listing 21–5. *An Implementation of* FlowerFactory *in* FlowerFactory.m

```
#import "FlowerFactory.h"
#import "FlowerView.h"

@implementation FlowerFactory


- (UIView *) flowerViewWithType:(FlowerType)type
{
  // lazy-load a flower pool
  if (flowerPool_ == nil)
  {
    flowerPool_ = [[NSMutableDictionary alloc]
                 initWithCapacity:kTotalNumberOfFlowerTypes];
  }

  // try to retrieve a flower
  // from the pool
  UIView *flowerView = [flowerPool_ objectForKey:[NSNumber
                                        numberWithInt:type]];

  // if the type requested
  // is not available then
  // create a new one and
  // add it to the pool
  if (flowerView == nil)
  {
    UIImage *flowerImage;

    switch (type)
```

```
    {
      case kAnemone:
        flowerImage = [UIImage imageNamed:@"anemone.png"];
        break;
      case kCosmos:
        flowerImage = [UIImage imageNamed:@"cosmos.png"];
        break;
      case kGerberas:
        flowerImage = [UIImage imageNamed:@"gerberas.png"];
        break;
      case kHollyhock:
        flowerImage = [UIImage imageNamed:@"hollyhock.png"];
        break;
      case kJasmine:
        flowerImage = [UIImage imageNamed:@"jasmine.png"];
        break;
      case kZinnia:
        flowerImage = [UIImage imageNamed:@"zinnia.png"];
        break;
      default:
        break;
    }

    flowerView = [[[FlowerView alloc]
                    initWithImage:flowerImage] autorelease];
    [flowerPool_ setObject:flowerView
                    forKey:[NSNumber numberWithInt:type]];
  }

  return flowerView;
}

- (void) dealloc
{
  [flowerPool_ release];
  [super dealloc];
}

@end
```

The flower pool (flowerPool_) is not initiated in FlowerFactory's init method. Instead, it's lazy-loaded in the flowerViewWithType: factory method. The default capacity for the pool is kTotalNumberOfFlowerTypes (i.e., 6). If the requested instance is not in the pool, then the factory will create a new instance of FlowerView with an appropriate flower image and add it to the pool using type as the key and the new instance as the value. Any subsequent requests for a created flower will be returned from the pool. The mechanism of sharing flowers from the pool is pretty straightforward.

How Are FlowerView Objects Shared?

In the original definition of the pattern, flyweight objects usually seem to associate with some sort of intrinsic state that is sharable. Though it may not be the case all the time, our FlowerView flyweight objects do share their internal flower images as intrinsic states. Sharable flyweight objects can also be used as "strategies" (see Strategy pattern,

Chapter 19). Strategies are usually referred to embedded algorithms, by the way. However, regardless of whether a flyweight object has any sharable, intrinsic state, there is still a need for defining some sort of external data structure to keep track of any extrinsic state (unique information) of the flyweight objects. We define a C-struct of `ExtrinsicFlowerState` to serve that purpose, as defined in Listing 21–6.

Listing 21–6. *A Definition of the* `ExtrinsicFlowerState` *Struct*

```
typedef struct
{
  UIView *flowerView;
  CGRect area;
} ExtrinsicFlowerState;
```

The area to display is unique to each flower, so it needs to be treated as an extrinsic state. We need an array to store a bunch of them for flowers created by a client. Figure 21–6 depicts an example of how an array of extrinsic flower states relates to unique instances of `FlowerView` in the flyweight pool of `FlowerFactory`.

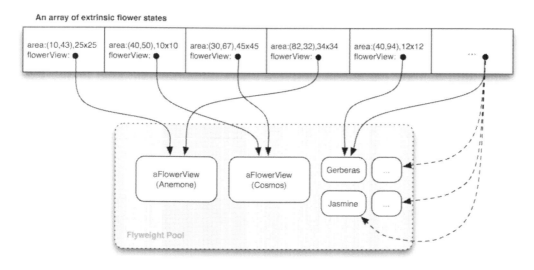

Figure 21–6. *Elements in an array of extrinsic flower states share the same unique instances of* `FlowerView` *objects in the flyweight pool maintained by* `FlowerManager`.

Each unit in an array stores a pointer to a real `FlowerView` object from the pool as well as an area that the flower is supposed to display in. The size of the array doesn't affect the size of the pool at all.

HOW MUCH CAN YOU SAVE?

How much you can save with flyweight objects depends on several factors:

- The reduction of total number of objects that comes from sharing

- The amount of intrinsic state (i.e., sharable state) per object

- Whether extrinsic state is computed or stored

However, transferring, finding, and/or computing the extrinsic state of flyweight objects may induce runtime costs, especially if the extrinsic state was previously stored as an intrinsic state. As more flyweight objects are shared, such costs can be offset by sheering the amount of space savings. So the more flyweights are shared, the greater the storage savings. The savings is directly related to the amount of shared state. The greatest savings occurs when the objects use substantial quantities of both intrinsic and extrinsic states, and the extrinsic state can be computed rather than stored. Then you save on storage in two ways: Sharing reduces the cost of intrinsic state, and you trade extrinsic state for computation time.

Implementing Client Code

Now we have all the pieces in place, and we are ready to see how a client draws 500 flowers using the flyweight infrastructure, as shown in Listing 21–7.

Listing 21–7. *Client Code That Constructs a List of Flowers*

```
- (void)viewDidLoad
{
  [super viewDidLoad];

  // construct a flower list
  FlowerFactory *factory = [[[FlowerFactory alloc] init] autorelease];
  NSMutableArray *flowerList = [[[NSMutableArray alloc]
                                initWithCapacity:500] autorelease];

  for (int i = 0; i < 500; ++i)
  {
    // retrieve a shared instance
    // of a flower flyweight object
    // from a flower factory with a
    // random flower type
    FlowerType flowerType = arc4random() % kTotalNumberOfFlowerTypes;
    UIView *flowerView = [factory flowerViewWithType:flowerType];

    // set up a location and an area for the flower
    // to display onscreen
    CGRect screenBounds = [[UIScreen mainScreen] bounds];
    CGFloat x = (arc4random() % (NSInteger)screenBounds.size.width);
    CGFloat y = (arc4random() % (NSInteger)screenBounds.size.height);
    NSInteger minSize = 10;
    NSInteger maxSize = 50;
    CGFloat size = (arc4random() % (maxSize - minSize + 1)) + minSize;

    // assign attributes for a flower
```

```
    // to an extrinsic state object
    ExtrinsicFlowerState extrinsicState;
    extrinsicState.flowerView = flowerView;
    extrinsicState.area = CGRectMake(x, y, size, size);

    // add an extrinsic flower state
    // to the flower list
    [flowerList addObject:[NSValue value:&extrinsicState
                           withObjCType:@encode(ExtrinsicFlowerState)]];
    }

    // add the flower list to
    // this FlyweightView instance
    [(FlyweightView *)self.view setFlowerList:flowerList];
}
```

In each iteration in the main for loop, a UIView instance (in fact, FlowerView) is returned by an instance of FlowerFactory based on a randomly selected flower type with FlowerType flowerType = arc4random() % kTotalNumberOfFlowerTypes. The integer value of flowerType shouldn't be greater than kTotalNumberOfFlowerTypes. A unique location and size are put in an ExtrinsicFlowerState structure associated with a pointer to an instance of FlowerView. Then the whole extrinsic state structure is added to flowerList, which is an NSArray object. Since ExtrinsicFlowerState is not an Objective-C object, we needed to @encode it in an NSValue object before we can safely add it to the array. When a complete list of 500 flowers is allocated to the array, we will set the list to an instance of FlyweightView (i.e., self.view).

Adding the flower list to FlyweightView is just half of the story; we also need to know how FlyweightView populates and presents all the flowers in the list onscreen, as shown in Listing 21–8. After the flower list is constructed, assign it to a custom view that displays each flower in the list. The list in this example is called flowerList_.

Listing 21–8. *The Custom View is Overriding a UIView's drawRect: Method to Draw the Flowers Onscreen.*

```
- (void)drawRect:(CGRect)rect
{
  // Drawing code

  for (NSValue *stateValue in flowerList_)
  {
    ExtrinsicFlowerState state;
    [stateValue getValue:&state];

    UIView *flowerView = state.flowerView;
    CGRect area = state.area;

    [flowerView drawRect:area];
  }
}
```

In its drawRect: method, the place where you normally define any custom drawing routine, we have a for loop that populates a whole list of previously saved NSValue entries in the flower array. We then retrieve an ExtrinsicFlowerState structure from each NSValue instance in each iteration. Once we get a FlowerView pointer and an area where it should draw into from the ExtrinsicFlowerState structure, we send a drawRect:rect message to the FlowerView instance to perform its drawing operation that we explained in Listing 21–2.

After all 500 flowers are drawn on the view, we will see something like Figure 21–4.

Summary

Sharing is a virtue in humanity. Sharing the same resources to perform a task can be more cost-effective than achieving the same thing with an individual's resources. In this chapter, we have designed an app that can display 500+ flowers on the screen with only six unique instances of different flower images. Those unique flower instances had some uniquely identifiable information (i.e., location and size) stripped off and were left with only the bare-bones operation that displays the flower images. When a unique flower is requested, a client needs to provide some unique information (extrinsic state) to the flower instance so it can draw a unique flower with the provided information. Without using the Flyweight pattern, the app needs to instantiate as many UIImageView instances as required to draw on the screen (i.e., 500+). With a careful design, the Flyweight pattern can save a significant amount of memory by sharing a fraction of the required objects.

In the next chapter, we will see another design pattern that can improve performance as well as provide object access by delaying the operations to the objects with proxy objects.

Chapter 22

Proxy

It's a pretty common marketing strategy that lures people to buy something by offering a trial period without any obligation to pay for it. Sometimes even a 30-day money-back guarantee is not as powerful as a use-it-for-"free" offer. It works particularly well on some expensive items or online subscription services.

We know there are a lot of online dating sites that provide subscriptions to singles who want to find their partners. A lot of them are quite expensive—let's say $100 for three months of unlimited searching and communication with other members. It's expensive, and there is no guarantee that you will definitely find your perfect match after you pay $100 within three months. So a lot of dating sites provide free searches, flirting, or other limited features but not actual communication with other members. This approach is more acceptable than shelling out $100 upfront and hoping for the best. If you really like the service and you get a lot of flirts and messages from other members (both paying and non-paying), then you may feel more comfortable about shelling out that $100 to dive into the game.

So you may ask, "What does this have to do with the Proxy pattern?" One common usage of a proxy is to act as a stand-in, lightweight object that allows clients to access some information or features that are cheap to prepare in the first place. Until the moment when it's worth it or necessary to get the real "deal," the proxy will go ahead and prepare the real, expensive resources for the clients. So a proxy offers you a trial membership at the beginning; when you are ready to pay for the real, expensive membership, the proxy will open that gate for you to access more features available only for paid members.

A design pattern that is elaborated from the idea is called the Proxy pattern. In this chapter, we will discuss its concepts and key features. We will also design and implement a virtual image proxy that displays a placeholder image on the screen while loading a real one in the background.

What Is the Proxy Pattern?

There are several types of proxies:

- A remote proxy provides a local representative for an object in a different address space or in the network.

- A virtual proxy creates heavy-weighted objects on demand.

- A protection proxy controls access to the original object based on different access rights.

- A smart-reference proxy counts the number of references to the real object for memory management. It can also be used for locking the real object so no other objects can change it.

> **THE PROXY PATTERN:** Provides a surrogate or placeholder for another object to control access to it.*
>
> *The original definition appeared in *Design Patterns*, by the "Gang of Four" (Addison-Wesley, 1994).

In general, a proxy acts as a surrogate or placeholder that controls access to another object, objects that are remote, expensive to create, or in need of securing. We can't cover every type of proxy here, so we will focus only on the virtual proxy.

The idea is to have a proxy that basically behaves the same as the real subject. Clients can use the proxy transparently without knowing that what they are dealing with is just a proxy and not the real thing. So when clients request some features that are expensive to create, the proxy will forward the request to the real object and get the features prepared and returned to the clients. The clients have no idea what's going on behind the scenes. Both a proxy and a real subject share the same behavior that clients expect. A class diagram that illustrates this idea is shown in Figure 22–1.

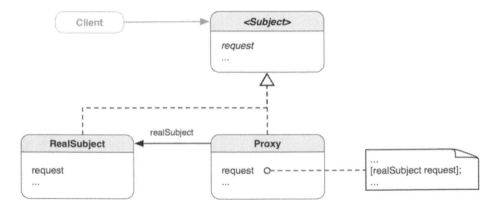

Figure 22–1. *A class diagram of the Proxy pattern*

When a client sends a "request" message to a Proxy object, the Proxy object will in turn forward the same message to a RealSubject object that is sitting in the Proxy object. The RealSubject will carry out any of the real operations to fulfill the request for the client indirectly.

At runtime, you can imagine a scenario of a client who owns a reference to a subject as an abstract type. A reference to it is in fact a Proxy object. The Proxy object itself has a reference to a RealSubject instance that will perform any heavy-duty jobs later if requested. That scenario at runtime is illustrated in Figure 22–2.

Figure 22–2. *A possible object structure of the Proxy pattern at runtime*

When Would You Use the Proxy Pattern?

You'd naturally think about using the pattern when

- You need a remote proxy that provides a local representative for an object in a different address space or in the network.

- You need a virtual proxy to create heavy-weighted objects on demand. We will implement that kind of proxy in a code example later in this chapter.

- You need a protection proxy to control access to the original object based on different access rights.

- You need a smart-reference proxy for counting the number of references to the real object for memory management. It can also be used for locking the real object so no other objects can change it.

Lazy-Loading an Image with a Virtual Proxy

In Chapter 2, we have defined some requirements for the TouchPainter app. One of them was to have a ThumbnailViewController allow the user to browse through all previously saved scribbles in the file system. But loading all of them is not practical, especially when the memory on the device is very limited. Even if we can load all the thumbnail images in the memory at the time when the user enters the view, the performance may suffer if there is very little memory left for the rest of the application.

In the original design discussed in Chapter 2, scribbles are presented as little thumbnails lined up on the screen row by row. Each row is an instance of a customized

UITableViewCell that contains multiple thumbnail placeholders that will present a corresponding thumbnail image of a scribble. Before any actual thumbnail image of a scribble is loaded, a thumbnail placeholder should present a placeholder image that is shared among other thumbnail placeholders on the same viewable area of the view. The framework at runtime will manage UITableViewCell objects. Cells that are viewable (outside of the viewable area of the screen) will be destroyed, while cells that are entering the viewable area will be created or initialized and reused with other off-screen cell resources.

When a real thumbnail image is completely loaded, the original placeholder image will be replaced by the real image. The process continues until all onscreen thumbnail images are completely loaded. The image on the left in Figure 22–3 shows a screenshot of the thumbnail view when it is first being loaded with only placeholder images. The image on the right in Figure 22–3 shows the same view with partially loaded scribble thumbnail images.

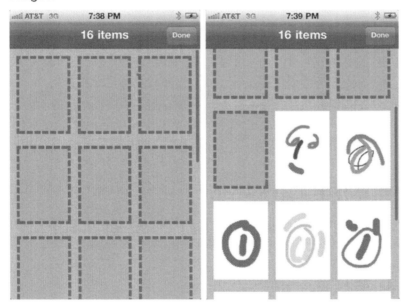

Figure 22–3. *A scribble thumbnail view with only placeholder images vs. the same view with partially loaded scribble thumbnail images*

This type of user interface is used in some iOS applications created by Apple to load thumbnail images while the user is scrolling the view for a whole collection of them. This provides a smooth operation and response to the user while individual small thumbnails are being loaded in the background.

Designing and Implementing a Scribble Thumbnail View

The key elements to make that kind of "magical" thumbnail view are a placeholder image proxy and a mechanism for loading a real image in the background, so that the whole process looks smooth. We can lay out our basic proxy design in a class diagram illustrated in Figure 22–4.

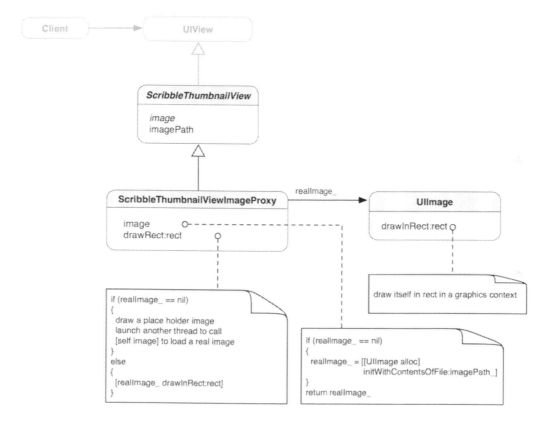

Figure 22–4. *A class diagram of* `ScribbleThumbnail` *proxy structure*

The basic structure of the class diagram for `ScribbleThumbnailViewImageProxy` and a real image object represented by `UIImage` captures the essence of the original Proxy pattern. They are customized to fit what we needed for the TouchPainter app. Both the `ScribbleThumbnailViewImageProxy` and `UIImage` implement pretty much the same `draw*` interface to draw things on a `UIView` object. `ScribbleThumbnailView` itself is a subclass of `UIView`, so subclasses can be used with our `UITableViewCell` that can display them. The complete implementation of the whole user interface involves many other parts. For this example, we will go over only some essential elements that can highlight the concepts of the Proxy pattern. You can check out a copy of the example code for this chapter for the detailed implementation of each piece.

The idea of the image forward-loading mechanism in our ScribbleThumbnailView ImageProxy is that it will load a real image if the real one is not yet loaded and then present it on the screen. But that is just a bottom-line idea. It takes some more tricky moves to make it a working solution for our TouchPainter app. We will get to that later when we discuss the implementation part of the code example.

So far, we've got the big picture of what's going to happen with our proxy design for thumbnails displayed on a view. To visualize what we should expect at runtime with a proxy structure, let's take a look at a diagram that can illustrate that in Figure 22–5.

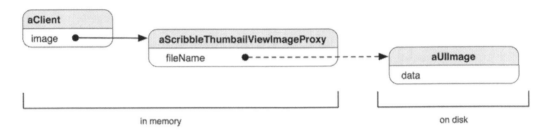

Figure 22–5. *A* ScribbleThumbnailViewImageProxy *object and a* UIImage *object at runtime*

At runtime, aClient is accessing an instance of ScribbleThumbnailView's subclass, in this case, ScribbleThumbnailViewImageProxy. An instance of UIImage is not created until it's requested by aClient. So the real image data is always on disk until the Scribble ThumbnailViewImageProxy object is asked to load it. If the actual loading is never asked to trigger, then only the ScribbleThumbnailViewImageProxy object stays in memory. We can use the similar lazy-loading approach for loading any other expensive resources that need to present on a UIView.

Implementing the ScribbleThumbnailView Class

Listing 22–1 shows a class declaration of ScribbleThumbnailView.

Listing 22–1. *A Class Declaration of* ScribbleThumbnailView *in* ScribbleThumbnailView.h

```
@interface ScribbleThumbnailView : UIView
{
  @protected
  NSString *imagePath_;
}

@property (nonatomic, readonly) UIImage *image;
@property (nonatomic, copy) NSString *imagePath;

@end
```

The only thing that concerns us about the behavior of ScribbleThumbnailView in general is the actual path with which we can load and return a real image. As an abstract base class, ScribbleThumbnailView maintains the abstract image and imagePath properties. These properties are essential for the whole virtual proxy operations we are going to see

later. There is not much going on in the definition of the `ScribbleThumbnailView`
implementation except that there are some property-related directives, as shown in
Listing 22–2.

Listing 22–2. *An Implementation of* `ScribbleThumbnailView` *in* `ScribbleThumbnailView.m`

```
#import "ScribbleThumbnailView.h"


@implementation ScribbleThumbnailView

@dynamic image;
@synthesize imagePath=imagePath_;

@end
```

Implementing the ScribbleThumbnailViewImageProxy Class

Everything seems straightforward so far. Now we are going to get to the trickiest part of
our proxy design—implementing `ScribbleThumbnailViewImageProxy`. Its class
declaration is shown in Listing 22–3.

Listing 22–3. *A Class Declaration of* `ScribbleThumbnailViewImageProxy` *in*
`ScribbleThumbnailViewImageProxy.h`

```
#import "ScribbleThumbnailView.h"

@interface ScribbleThumbnailViewImageProxy : ScribbleThumbnailView
{
  @private
  UIImage *realImage_;
  BOOL loadingThreadHasLaunched_;
}

@property (nonatomic, readonly) UIImage *image;

@end
```

`realImage_` is used for holding a real image reference after it is loaded. A private `BOOL`
member variable, `loadingThreadHasLaunched_`, will be used later for forwarding a loading
process for a real image. The implementation of `ScribbleThumbnailViewImageProxy` is
relatively long. So go get a cup of coffee before we start rolling it.

If you are ready, let's get started and take a look at its implementation in Listing 22–4.

Listing 22–4. *An Implementation of* `ScribbleThumbnailViewImageProxy` *in* `ScribbleThumbnailView`
`ImageProxy.m`

```
#import "ScribbleThumbnailViewImageProxy.h"

// A private category for a forward loading thread
@interface ScribbleThumbnailViewImageProxy ()

- (void) forwardImageLoadingThread;
```

```
@end


@implementation ScribbleThumbnailViewImageProxy

@dynamic imagePath;

// Clients can use this method directly
// to forward-load a real image
// if there is no need to show this object
// on a view.
- (UIImage *) image
{
  if (realImage_ == nil)
  {
    realImage_ = [[UIImage alloc] initWithContentsOfFile:imagePath_];
  }

  return realImage_;
}

// A forward call will be established
// in a separate thread to get a real payload from
// a real image.
// Before a real payload is returned,
// drawRect: will handle the background
// loading process and draw a placeholder frame.
// Once the real payload is loaded,
// it will redraw itself with the real one.
- (void)drawRect:(CGRect)rect
{
  // if is no real image available
  // from realImageView_,
  // then just draw a blank frame
  // as a placeholder image
  if (realImage_ == nil)
  {
    // Drawing code
    CGContextRef context = UIGraphicsGetCurrentContext();

    // draw a placeholder frame
    // with a 10-user-space-unit-long painted
    // segment and a 3-user-space-unit-long
    // unpainted segment of a dash line
    CGContextSetLineWidth(context, 10.0);
    const CGFloat dashLengths[2] = {10,3};
    CGContextSetLineDash (context, 3, dashLengths, 2);
    CGContextSetStrokeColorWithColor(context, [[UIColor darkGrayColor] CGColor]);
    CGContextSetFillColorWithColor(context, [[UIColor lightGrayColor] CGColor]);
    CGContextAddRect(context, rect);
    CGContextDrawPath(context, kCGPathFillStroke);

    // launch a thread to load the real
    // payload if it hasn't done yet
    if (!loadingThreadHasLaunched_)
    {
```

```
        [self performSelectorInBackground:@selector(forwardImageLoadingThread)
                          withObject:nil];
        loadingThreadHasLaunched_ = YES;
      }
    }
    // otherwise pass the draw*: message
    // along to realImage_ and let it
    // draw the real image
    else
    {
      [realImage_ drawInRect:rect];
    }
  }

- (void) dealloc
{
  [realImage_ release];
  [super dealloc];
}

#pragma mark -
#pragma mark A private method for an image forward loading thread


- (void) forwardImageLoadingThread
{
  NSAutoreleasePool *pool = [[NSAutoreleasePool alloc] init];

  // forward loading the real
  // payload
  [self image];

  // redraw itself with the newly loaded image
  [self performSelectorInBackground:@selector(setNeedsDisplay) withObject:nil];

  [pool release];
}

@end
```

Wow! Congratulations, you made it! Since the implementation is huge, we can't cover every bit and piece of it. But we can summarize the whole proxy operation as follows:

- The image property method will load a real image with [[UIImage alloc] initWithContentsOfFile:imagePath_] if realImage_ is not loaded. It eventually returns realImage_.

- ScribbleThumbnailViewImageProxy is a subclass of UIView; its drawRect: method provides a custom drawing algorithm on the screen. In this case, it will draw either a placeholder image or an actual image if it is loaded. If the real image is not loaded, then spawn a new thread to forward the loading process defined in the image property method.

- A thread method, `forwardImageLoadingThread`, is privately defined in an anonymous category. The method will execute the `image` property method so that a real image will be loaded as a `UIImage` object. Then a message of `setNeedsDisplay` to `self` will trigger a view content refresh. Since the real image is completely loaded at this point, the `drawRect:` method will draw the real `UIImage` object by forwarding a `drawInRect:` message to it instead of drawing the placeholder image.

There are a couple of things that are worth mentioning. The private member variable `loadingThreadHasLaunched_` is used to determine if a thread for `forwardImageLoadingThread` is already launched in the `drawRect:` method. If so, it won't do anything except draw the same old placeholder image because the proxy requires loading the real image only once. If the proxy thumbnail view is located outside of the displayable area of the view, `UITableView` will destroy it. When the thumbnail view comes back into the view, then `UITableView` will reuse/construct it and the proxy forward-loading process will start all over again.

Using a Proxy Pattern in the Cocoa Touch Framework

Objective-C doesn't support multiple inheritances. So if your proxy objects are not subclasses of anything specific in the Cocoa Touch framework, you may consider using `NSProxy` for your placeholders or surrogate objects.

The `NSProxy` is a root class in the Cocoa framework just like `NSObject`. The `NSProxy` implements `NSObject` protocol, so an `NSProxy` object is also indeed an `NSObject` type. The `NSProxy` class is an abstract base class so it doesn't have its own initialization method. A call to any method that an `NSProxy` object doesn't know how to respond to will throw an exception.

The main purpose of `NSProxy` is to define an API for objects that act as stand-ins for other objects or for objects that don't exist yet. A message that is sent to a proxy object will be forwarded to the real object or cause the proxy to load or transform itself into the real object. Subclasses of the `NSProxy` can be used to implement lazy instantiation of objects that are expensive to create—for example, a large image from the file system, as in the example in the previous sections.

Even though `NSProxy` is regarded as a type of `NSObject`, its existence has only one purpose – being a proxy. There are two instance methods that are essential to make the whole proxy deal happen, `forwardInvocation:` and `methodSignatureForSelector:`. An `NSProxy` subclass doesn't even need to have other extra methods except, probably, an initialization method and some other useful properties. The key is that when an object of a `NSProxy` subclass doesn't respond to a method that would be available to a real object, then the Objective-C runtime will send a message of `methodSignatureFor Selector:` to the proxy object for a correct method signature of the message being forwarded. The runtime will in turn use the returned method signature to construct an instance of `NSInvocation` and send it with a `forwardInvocation:` message to the proxy object so it will forward the invocation to other object. If the proxy object of NSProxy's subclass can respond to the message, then the forwardInvocation: method will not be invoked at all. Objective-C doesn't support multiple inheritances, but we can achieve that by using NSProxy's message forwarding mechanism to forward tasks that can be handled by other classes' objects.

A common example of the Proxy pattern in an iOS application is the Mail app. Any attachment received in a message will show only some basic information, such as the file name and its size, as shown in a screenshot in Figure 22–6.

Figure 22–6. *An unloaded attachment in a message*

When the user taps the placeholder image to start loading the content of the attachment, the icon will be replaced by a small progress view reporting the actual loading progress, as shown in Figure 22–7.

Figure 22–7. *An attachment is being loaded in the Mail app.*

When the attachment is completely loaded, the actual image will be displayed in the message area, as shown in Figure 22–8.

Figure 22–8. *A completely loaded image attached in a message*

The original attachment placeholder icon is a proxy for loading an actual image across the network when it's asked to do so. If the user never taps the placeholder icon, the attachment will never be loaded and only the basic information of the attachment will be shown. It saves not only network resources, but also memory and the waiting time when the Mail app is still being run.

Summary

Memory usage is always a concern for iOS application development. No matter what kind of iOS device your application is running on, lazy-loading techniques are always recommended for the sake of performance. You can apply the Proxy pattern to an iOS application to lazy-load any expensive data, such as large image files in the file system or large payload from a server through a slow network. A virtual proxy provides some lightweight information to clients that loading an expensive object is not required until it's requested to do so.

In the next part, we will see a different design pattern for abstracting a process of saving the state of an object.

Part **IX**

State Of Object

Chapter 23

Memento

Memento is defined as "an object kept as a reminder or souvenir of a person or event." That really reminds me of "sticky notes." I don't find sticky notes as useful as my buddy does. He keeps track of everything on sticky notes on his desk in his office. They are really short and brief reminders sometimes written in scribbles that only the original author, himself, can understand. Other people, myself included, see them as a bunch of junk flyers on a bulletin board. They just don't mean anything to anybody except the original author. Whenever we need a small, simple, and compact reminder, we write it on a sticky note. After that piece of information is reviewed later and the reminder is no longer valid, we toss it out in a trashcan and forget about it (it's not environmentally friendly at all, I know).

We borrow a similar idea to save the state of an object and restore it later. The state itself is created as a form of object (sticky note). It encapsulates the internal state of the original object (scribbles created by the author). Only the original object that creates the sticky note can understand the saved state and restore the original state with it. A design pattern that is elaborated from the idea is called the Memento pattern.

What's the Memento Pattern?

An application needs to save its own state in some events, such as when the user is saving a document or when the program is exiting. For example, a game may need to save the current state of the current session, such as the game level, number of enemies, types of weapons available, etc. before the game quits. When the game is reopened, the players can pick up where they left off. A lot of times, we really don't need anything super fancy to save the state of the program. Any efficient, simple method should do, but at the same time the saved information should be meaningful only to the original program. The original program should be the only entity that can understand how to decode the saved information in an archive it created. This is how the Memento pattern fits in a software design for programs like games, word processors, or other programs that need to save the snapshot of the complex state of the current context and restore it later.

THE MEMENTO PATTERN: Without violating encapsulation, capture and externalize an object's internal state so that the object can be restored to this state later.*

*The original definition appeared in *Design Patterns*, by the "Gang of Four" (Addison-Wesley, 1994).

There are three key roles in the pattern: originator, memento, and a caretaker. The idea is very simple. The originator creates a memento that contains its state and passes it over to the caretaker. The caretaker doesn't know how to interact with the memento but does keep it in a safe place. Their static relationships are illustrated in a class diagram in Figure 23–1.

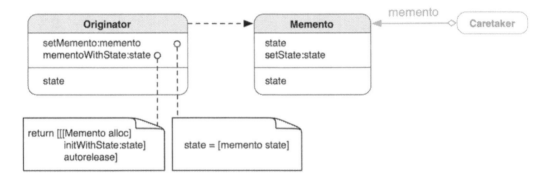

Figure 23–1. *A class diagram of the structure of the Memento pattern*

When a caretaker asks an Originator object to save its state, the Originator object will create a new instance of a Memento object with its internal state. Then the caretaker holds the Memento object for a time or saves it in the file system, and passes it back to the Originator object. The Originator object has no idea how the Memento object is going to be saved. The caretaker doesn't know what's in the Memento object either. A sequence diagram in Figure 23–2 illustrates their interaction.

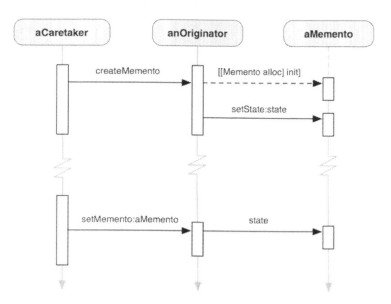

Figure 23–2. *A sequence diagram of the Memento pattern*

The key for this design is to maintain the privacy of a Memento object, so only an Originator object can access the internal state stored in the Memento object (i.e., the Originator's previous internal state). The Memento class should have two interfaces: a wide one for Originators and a narrow one for other objects. In previous diagrams, the setState:, state, and init methods should be private so other objects can't use them, except Originator and Memento.

When Would You Use the Memento Pattern?

You'd think about using the pattern when all of the following applies:

- You need to save the object's state as a snapshot or a portion of it, which can be restored later.

- You need to hide the interface with which obtaining the state would expose the implantation details.

Using the Memento Pattern in TouchPainter

I hope you still remember our faithful little app, TouchPainter. One of the features that we needed to put in is to save a currently active scribble on the CanvasView in the file system. That should be easy. We can just call NSKeyedUnarchiver's class method, archivedDataWithRootObject:, with a Mark composite object as a parameter (NSKeyedUnarchiver is discussed in the "The Memento Pattern in the Cocoa Touch Framework" section). Then we can save a returned NSData object in the file system. Here is a problem: how does a Mark object know where (a path) it should save itself in the file system in the first place? If we really need the Mark know about it, then we need to go back to our Composite pattern chapter (Chapter 13) and make that change. Every time we make any change to our Mark, all of its implementing classes are also affected. Also, we are talking about saving a complete Mark composite structure, not just the individual nodes, as well as other issues like, how can we save a portion of the composite (i.e., some nodes but not all of them)? And how can the composite know where to put the saved nodes back in the structure? We are going to answer these questions in the next sections.

A Mark composite object has primitive operations, so it may not be straightforward to work with structure directly. We need another class called Scribble to manage it at a higher level. In the Observer pattern chapter (Chapter 12), we have discussed how a Scribble object can interact as a model with view controllers like CanvasViewController in the Model-View-Controller paradigm. A Scribble object contains a Mark instance structure that reflects the current state of what's drawn on the CanvasView. The Scribble object's role is not to just contain an instance of Mark but also create a snapshot of it as a memento object and let it be kept safe by another object. The snapshot memento itself could be a complete structure of what the Scribble object has at the moment or a portion of the structure as changes to the internal state. The saving-restore deal is only between the Scribble object and its memento object, but no one else's. The Scribble object doesn't know where its memento will be kept. So we need a caretaker object for keeping and passing around memento objects. A possible class for that role could be ScribbleManager, which we briefly talked about in conjunction with the Façade pattern in Chapter 10. Its role is mainly responsible for managing all the chores related to saving and restoring Scribble objects. Although we will not get into the details of the ScribbleManager class, we'll briefly discuss how it can fit in the picture of the Memento pattern.

Saving a Scribble

Let's recall some of our requirements about saving a scribble in Chapter 2. When the user has tapped a save button, then CanvasViewController will capture what's on the CanvasView as an image. Then it sends a message to an instance of ScribbleManager to save the current Scribble object with the just captured screenshot of the CanvasView. Then the ScribbleManager will take it from there. First of all, it sends a message to the Scribble object to create a ScribbleMemento object that contains a snapshot of its internal state. Once a ScribbleMemento object is created and returned by the Scribble object, the ScribbleManager can have a choice either to save it in a file system or keep it in the memory for a while.

For now we are concerned only about saving the ScribbleMemento object in the file system. The ScribbleManager cannot save the returned ScribbleMemento object just like that. A more convenient way for it to do so is to have the ScribbleMemento appear in a form of NSData, so the ScribbleManager can save it in a file system with some file-related convenience methods available from the NSData object.

We'll not get to all the hocus-pocus of saving thumbnails and whatnot in this chapter, but focus on saving a Scribble object with a simpler method, saveScribble:, from a ScribbleManager object. The big picture of how these mentioned objects interact is illustrated in a sequence diagram in Figure 23–3.

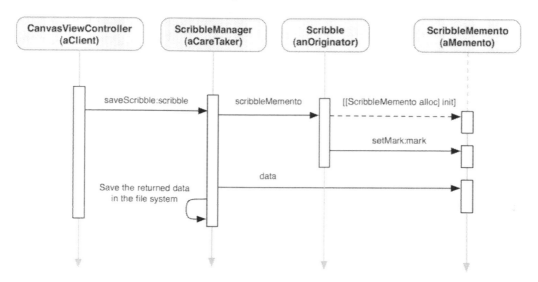

Figure 23–3. *A sequence diagram of the TouchPainter app on storing a* Scribble *object as a memento*

CanvasViewController acts as aClient and sends a saveScribble: message along with a Scribble object in question to a ScribbleManager object. Then inside the method, it will ask the Scribble object to create its ScribbleMemento object for saving. You may wonder why ScribbleManager wouldn't just ask Scribble to pass an NSData object to it directly and save it from there. Using just NSData directly is not enough to solve our problem, as the memento data itself can contain different information about the internal state of the Scribble object. Sometimes we may want the Scribble object just to save changes only. So we need a memento object to give us some clue how to restore a Scribble, whether we need just to attach the saved state to the current one in the Scribble or a complete restoration. The saved state in the memento object can be as complicated as it gets (as long as a Scribble object can understand). Also the same ScribbleMemento objects in memory can be reused in other areas of the application, such as (un)redoing of drawing a stroke or distributing them across the network to share with other users to simulate remote drawing. That said, if we used NSData objects exclusively for a memory-bound state-saving strategy, the performance would suffer as the archiving-unarchiving process takes some extra effort.

Restoring a Scribble

We have just discussed how to save a Scribble object. You might wonder how we can get it back from the file system.

In our earlier sections of this chapter, we have seen that a caretaker will eventually pass a previously saved memento back to an originator to restore one of its previous states. Sometimes it may not be the case. Our scribble saving/loading strategy is a typical example of using a memento without passing it back to its originator.

In Chapter 2, we saw that the user taps a thumbnail in question to open a saved scribble. An object that invokes the process could be a button or a separate command object (see the Command pattern, Chapter 20). The invoker that acts as a client sends a message to an instance of ScribbleManager with all necessary information for it to load and return a Scribble object from an archive (the file system). For an obvious reason, the invoker doesn't know where and how the scribble in question was saved.

Then the ScribbleManager will load the corresponding NSData object with a predefined location in the filesystem. The ScribbleManager passes the data to a ScribbleMemento's class method mementoWithData:data to create an instance of ScribbleMemento. At this point, instead of passing the ScribbleMemento object back to a Scribble originator, we get a brand new instance of Scribble with the ScribbleMemento object because we assume the life of the original Scribble object should have ended before it was saved. Once the invoker gets the new instance of Scribble with a restored state, it will pass it around in the application for further use. A particular use case with a resurrected Scribble object is to ask CanvasViewController to replace its current Scribble object with the resurrected one (i.e., opening a saved scribble).

A sequence diagram of the interaction among all the mentioned classes and roles is shown in Figure 23–4.

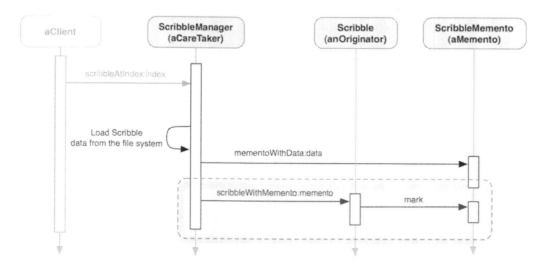

Figure 23–4. *A sequence diagram of the TouchPainter app on retrieving a stored* `Scribble` *object as memento*

You can see that the highlighted part of the diagram is similar to the same area in the sequence diagram for the original Memento pattern in Figure 23–1. The difference is we are not passing the loaded `ScribbleMemento` object back to the very original `Scribble` object that created it. You can, though, use a different operation to "attach" an internal state to an existing `Scribble` object from a `ScribbleMemento` object. We will discuss the details of that operation later in the implementation part of the chapter.

Designing and Implementing ScribbleMemento

When we first introduced the concepts of the Memento pattern, we mentioned that a memento object should have wide interfaces for its originator but narrow interfaces for other objects, such as a caretaker. Wide interfaces (vs. narrow ones) offer more options and freedom to use the object. The Memento pattern suggests that wide interfaces should be available only to originators and mementos. Wide interfaces are usually declared as `private` (operations or constructor) and `friend` in other object-oriented languages like C++. With a `friend` directive for local methods or classes, another class can access them like its own private resources. Everything in Objective-C is public, so we need some other trick to achieve the same thing.

There is a unique feature of Objective-C called categories. Categories allow developers to add extra methods to an existing class without subclassing. How can we use a category to make our wide interfaces private? All we need to do is create a category for `ScribbleMemento`, called `ScribbleMemento (Private)`. The `ScribbleMemento (Private)`'s interfaces will not be exposed to other classes unless they know where to get the declaration. So you can put private (or friend) operations in that category declaration so that they are available only to `Scribble`. The public (narrow) interfaces of `ScribbleMemento` are separated from what's declared in the `ScribbleMemento (Private)` category. In Objective-C 2.0, you can use an anonymous category, e.g.,

ScribbleMemento(), for declaring any private operations. It's called an extension. The main difference between an extension and a regular category is that an extension's operations should be defined in the class's principal implementation but a regular category's implementation can be in a separated file. Also, if the implementation of any operations declared in an extension can't be found, the compiler will give you some warnings. It's considered a better alternative to declare private methods instead of a regular category. But it doesn't mean the original category feature is obsolete. We still need it to extend some framework classes because we cannot modify their original class files.

A class diagram that illustrates idea around the basic design for ScribbleMemento is shown in Figure 23–5.

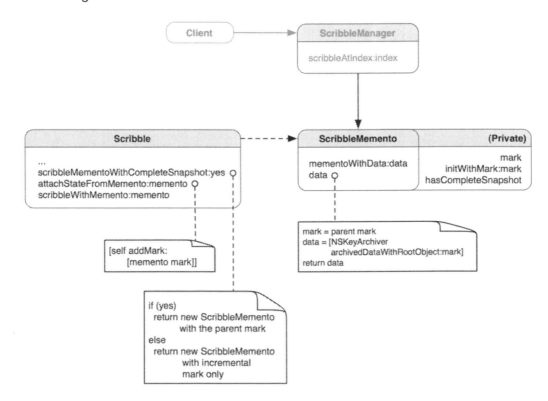

Figure 23–5. *A class diagram of the* ScribbleMemento *and its related classes*

ScribbleMemento offers its narrow functionalities with the mementoWithData:data and data methods. The mementoWithData:data method allows other classes to get an instance of ScribbleMemento by providing an NSData object. The data method does the reverse: it returns an archived form of a ScribbleMemento object as NSData. Other classes should never be able to see the narrow interfaces defined in the private category.

Implementing the ScribbleMemento Class

Let's take a look at some code for what we have designed so far for ScribbleMemento in Listing 23–1.

Listing 23–1. *A Class Declaration of* ScribbleMemento *in* ScribbleMemento.h

```
#import "Mark.h"


@interface ScribbleMemento : NSObject
{
  @private
  id <Mark> mark_;
  BOOL hasCompleteSnapshot_;
}

+ (ScribbleMemento *) mementoWithData:(NSData *)data;
- (NSData *) data;

@end
```

ScribbleMemento keeps a reference to a private Mark object as the internal state for Scribble. It also has a BOOL private member variable, hasCompleteSnapshot_, to tell a Scribble object later whether the stored Mark reference is a complete snapshot or just a fragment of it. The declarations for the narrow operations are in there too. We will get to the narrow operations in its implementation later.

Its extension (private category) declares wider interfaces that should be used by Scribble objects only as shown in Listing 23–2.

Listing 23–2. *A Private Category of* ScribbleMemento *Declared in* ScribbleMemento+Friend.h

```
#import "Mark.h"
#import"ScribbleMemento.h"

@interface ScribbleMemento ()

- (id) initWithMark:(id <Mark>)aMark;

@property (nonatomic, copy) id <Mark> mark;
@property (nonatomic, assign) BOOL hasCompleteSnapshot;

@end
```

A Scribble object can create and initialize a ScribbleMemento object with its own internal Mark reference. The Scribble object can access ScribbbleMemento's mark and hasCompleteSnapshot properties as well.

Listing 23–3 shows its implementation.

Listing 23–3. *An Implementation of* ScribbleMemento *in* ScribbleMemento.m

```
#import "ScribbleMemento.h"
#import "ScribbleMemento+Friend.h"

@implementation ScribbleMemento
```

```objc
@synthesize mark=mark_;
@synthesize hasCompleteSnapshot=hasCompleteSnapshot_;

- (NSData *) data
{
  NSData *data = [NSKeyedArchiver archivedDataWithRootObject:mark_];
  return data;
}

+ (ScribbleMemento *) mementoWithData:(NSData *)data
{
  // It raises an NSInvalidArchiveOperationException if data is not a valid archive
  id <Mark> retoredMark = (id <Mark>)[NSKeyedUnarchiver unarchiveObjectWithData:data];
  ScribbleMemento *memento = [[[ScribbleMemento alloc]
                              initWithMark:retoredMark] autorelease];

  return memento;
}

- (void) dealloc
{
  [mark_ release];
  [super dealloc];
}

#pragma mark -
#pragma mark Private methods

- (id) initWithMark:(id <Mark>)aMark
{
  if (self = [super init])
  {
    [self setMark:aMark];
  }

  return self;
}

@end
```

The instance method, data, sends a message, archivedDataWithRootObject:self, to the NSKeyedArchiver class to get an encoded version of self and then returns it. The class method, mementoWithData:(NSData *)data, creates a new instance of ScribbleMemento with a provided NSData object. data is first being unarchived by the NSKeyedUnarchiver object to decode it back to an instance of ScribbleMemento before the instance is returned.

We @synthesize'd the mark and hasCompleteSnapshot properties in the main implementation of Scribble. We did so because @synthesize'ing properties in a category is not allowed in Objective-C 2.0. Also the compiler enforces an extension, so its implementations should be put in the class's principal @implementation section. As the properties are @synthesize'd in the implementation, it won't break the privacy concerns for ScribbleMemento objects.

Besides the private properties, we also put the `initWithMark:` method definition in the main implementation here.

Something that is worth mentioning here is that the `mark` property is actually copying another `Mark` object, not just retaining it. Why is that? If it just retains it and the original `Mark` object has been modified in other parts of the app, then the state we collected for the `ScribbleMemento` object will be screwed. It seems the difference between copy and retain is small in code, but the impact could be immeasurable. It's similar to copying an instance of `NSString` in a property instead of just retaining it as the string could be modified outside of the class.

Modifying the Scribble Class

We've implemented the `ScribbleMemento` class. In order to let `Scribble` and `ScribbleMemento` work together, we need to make some modifications in the `Scribble` class, as shown in Listing 23–4.

Listing 23–4. *A Modified Class Declaration of Scribble in* `Scribble.h`

```
#import "Mark.h"
#import "ScribbleMemento.h"

@interface Scribble : NSObject
{
  @private
  id <Mark> parentMark_;
  id <Mark> incrementalMark_;
}

// methods for Mark management
- (void) addMark:(id <Mark>)aMark shouldAddToPreviousMark:(BOOL)shouldAddToPreviousMark;
- (void) removeMark:(id <Mark>)aMark;

// methods for memento
- (id) initWithMemento:(ScribbleMemento *)aMemento;
+ (Scribble *) scribbleWithMemento:(ScribbleMemento *)aMemento;
- (ScribbleMemento *) scribbleMemento;
- (ScribbleMemento *) scribbleMementoWithCompleteSnapshot:(BOOL)hasCompleteSnapshot;
- (void) attachStateFromMemento:(ScribbleMemento *)memento;

@end
```

We've added another `Mark` reference to `Scribble` as `incrementalMark_`, which is used for keeping a reference to a complete stroke or dot added to `parentMark_`.

There are several methods for use with `ScribbleMemento` objects exclusively. We've seen some of those in the preceding sections when we were designing the architecture for implementing the pattern. We'll go through the details of each of them in a modified version of the implementation of `Scribble` in Listing 23–5. The code is quite long, so we will break it up into a few chunks and walk through it.

Listing 23–5. *A Modified Implementation of* Scribble *in* Scribble.m

```objc
#import "ScribbleMemento+Friend.h"
#import "Scribble.h"
#import "Stroke.h"

// A private category for Scribble
// that contains a mark property available
// only to its objects
@interface Scribble ()

@property (nonatomic, retain) id <Mark> mark;

@end


@implementation Scribble

@synthesize mark=parentMark_;

- (id) init
{
  if (self = [super init])
  {
    // the parent should be a composite
    // object (i.e., Stroke)
    parentMark_ = [[Stroke alloc] init];
  }

  return self;
}
```

We import the private category that we have defined in Listing 23–2 with which we can create a ScribbleMemento object inside Scribble. A Scribble object contains a reference to a Mark object, which is considered the main parent of a Mark composite structure. The Mark property is an internal state of a Scribble object, and it is exposed only to itself.

Please refer to Chapter 12 for a detailed discussion about operations related to Mark objects in the Scribble class.

```objc
#pragma mark -
#pragma mark Methods for Mark management

// please refer to Chapter 12 for the detail of
// the methods related to Mark management.

- (void) addMark:(id <Mark>)aMark shouldAddToPreviousMark:(BOOL)shouldAddToPreviousMark
{
  // manual KVO invocation
  [self willChangeValueForKey:@"mark"];

  // if the flag is set to YES
  // then add this aMark to the
  // *PREVIOUS*Mark as part of an
  // aggregate.
  // Based on our design, it's supposed
  // to be the last child of the main
```

```
   // parent
   if (shouldAddToPreviousMark)
   {
     [[parentMark_ lastChild] addMark:aMark];
   }
   // otherwise attach it to the parent
   else
   {
     [parentMark_ addMark:aMark];
     incrementalMark_ = aMark;
   }

   // manual KVO invocation
   [self didChangeValueForKey:@"mark"];
}

- (void) removeMark:(id <Mark>)aMark
{
   // do nothing if aMark is the parent
   if (aMark == parentMark_) return;

   // manual KVO invocation
   [self willChangeValueForKey:@"mark"];

   [parentMark_ removeMark:aMark];

   // we don't need to keep the
   // incrementalMark_ reference
   // as it's just removed in the parent
   if (aMark == incrementalMark_)
   {
     incrementalMark_ = nil;
   }

   // manual KVO invocation
   [self didChangeValueForKey:@"mark"];
}
```

We have added a statement in the addMark:shouldAddToPreviousMark: method to save aMark as incrementalMark_ when it is being attached directly to the main parent mark (i.e., a stroke or a dot).

If we're deleting a Mark object that is also being referenced in incrementalMark_, then we need to set it to nil afterward. Otherwise, it may crash the whole application if it will be used again.

```
#pragma mark -
#pragma mark Methods for memento

- (id) initWithMemento:(ScribbleMemento*)aMemento
{
   if (self = [super init])
   {
     if ([aMemento hasCompleteSnapshot])
     {
       [self setMark:[aMemento mark]];
```

```
  }
  else
  {
    // if the memento contains only
    // incremental mark, then we need to
    // create a parent Stroke object to
    // hold it
    parentMark_ = [[Stroke alloc] init];
    [self attachStateFromMemento:aMemento];
  }
}

return self;
}
```

A Scribble object can be initialized with a ScribbleMemento object with which the Scribble object can restore its own state with access to the private mark property of the ScribbleMemento object.

```
- (void) attachStateFromMemento:(ScribbleMemento *)memento
{
  // attach any mark from a memento object
  // to the main parent
  [self addMark:[memento mark] shouldAddToPreviousMark:NO];
}
```

The attachStateFromMemento: method allows a Scribble object to add any Mark object from a ScribbleMemento object. Since our design deals only with incremental Mark objects that were attached to the main parent before, we add the memento's Mark object to the main parent here as well.

```
- (ScribbleMemento *) scribbleMementoWithCompleteSnapshot:(BOOL)hasCompleteSnapshot
{
  id <Mark> mementoMark = incrementalMark_;

  // if the resulting memento asks
  // for a complete snapshot, then
  // set it with parentMark_
  if (hasCompleteSnapshot)
  {
    mementoMark = parentMark_;
  }
  // but if incrementalMark_
  // is nil then we can't do anything
  // but bail out
  else if (mementoMark == nil)
  {
    return nil;
  }

  ScribbleMemento *memento = [[[ScribbleMemento alloc]
                                initWithMark:mementoMark] autorelease];
  [memento setHasCompleteSnapshot:hasCompleteSnapshot];
```

```
    return memento;
}

- (ScribbleMemento *) scribbleMemento
{
    return [self scribbleMementoWithCompleteSnapshot:YES];
}

+ (Scribble *) scribbleWithMemento:(ScribbleMemento *)aMemento
{
    Scribble *scribble = [[[Scribble alloc] initWithMemento:aMemento] autorelease];
    return scribble;
}


- (void) dealloc
{
    [parentMark_ release];
    [super dealloc];
}

@end
```

In the scribbleMementoWithCompleteSnapshot: method, if the hasCompleteSnapshot parameter is YES, then it will create an instance of ScribbleMemento with parentMark_, otherwise incrementalMark_.

scribbleMemento is a convenience method that uses the scribbleMementoWith CompleteSnapshot: method with a BOOL parameter set to YES to create and return a ScribbleMemento object that contains a complete snapshot of the current state.

Another method, scribbleWithMemento:, is a class method that creates a new Scribble object with a ScribbleMemento object.

We've seen using incrementalMark_ to keep a reference to a particular Mark object added to parentMark_ in a Scribble object. A Scribble object can create a ScribbleMemento object with incrementalMark_ for keeping particular changes that were only *added* to its own internal state. How would you modify the implementation in the preceding example to provide another option for a Scribble object, so that it can also save a Mark object that was *removed* from the parent?

Putting Everything Together with a Caretaker

We've got everything set up except that we're still missing the part where a caretaker manages ScribbleMemento objects. In the earlier part of the chapter, we assumed that we could use ScribbleManager to play the caretaker role for us. It offers a simple operation called saveScribble: to let clients save any Scribble object they have. It also provides a scribbleAtIndex: method that takes an index that identifies a particular Scribble object with which a ScribbleManager object will load and return.

Let's take a look at some implementation code that is simplified for the saveScribble: method and see how it captures the internal state of a Scribble object and saves it in the file system in Listing 23–6.

Listing 23–6. *Simplified Code for* saveScribble: *That Saves a* ScribbleMemento *Object in the File System*

```
// get a memento from the scribble
ScribbleMemento *scribbleMemento = [scribble scribbleMemento];

// get an NSData object from the memento
// so we can use it to save itself in the
// file system
NSData *mementoData = [scribbleMemento data];

NSString *mementoPath;
// ...
// construct the path for saving
// the memento and perform any other
// operations before actually saving it
// in the file system
// ...
[mementoData writeToFile:mementoPath atomically:YES];
```

We first ask a Scribble object to get us a ScribbleMemento instance with its scribbleMemento method. But we can't save the ScribbleMemento object in the file system as-is. So we need it to package itself as an NSData object with a data message call to the ScribbleMemento object. Then we save the NSData object with a path in the file system.

The resurrection operation is pretty much like the saving one, as shown in Listing 23–7. Likewise, it is also a simplified version of the scribbleAtIndex: method.

Listing 23–7. *Simplified Code for* scribbleAtIndex: *That Retrieves a* ScribbleMemento *Object from the File System, and Then Restores It As a* Scribble *Object*

```
NSString *scribbleMementoPath;

// ...
// use the provided index to retrieve
// the path that was used for saving
// the memento before. We will use the
// path to load the memento later
// ...

// use NSFileManager to load the memento file
// as NSData with the path that we just reconstructed
NSFileManager *fileManager = [NSFileManager defaultManager];
NSData *scribbleMementoData = [fileManager contentsAtPath:scribbleMementoPath];

// we create a ScribbleMemento from
// the NSData object. Then we use the
// memento to resurrect a Scribble object
// based on what's saved in the memento
ScribbleMemento *scribbleMemento = [ScribbleMemento
                                mementoWithData:scribbleMementoData];
Scribble *resurrectedScribble = [Scribble scribbleWithMemento:scribbleMemento];
```

First we use the provided index to locate the path that points to the saved data file in the file system. Then we load the NSData object back from its archive file and use the data object to create a ScribbleMemento object with a class message mementoWithData:. Finally, we use the ScribbleMemento object to resurrect a Scribble object with scribbleWithMemento:.

The Memento Pattern in the Cocoa Touch Framework

The Cocoa Touch framework has adopted the Memento pattern with archiving, property list serialization, and core data. Property list serialization and core data are outside the scope of this book. We will focus only on archiving and briefly go through its key features and how it can be applied to our example in the previous sections.

Cocoa archiving encodes objects, along with their properties and relationships with other objects, in an archive that can be stored in the file system or transmitted between processes or across a network. The relationships of the objects with other objects are treated as a network of object graphs. The archiving process captures the object graph as an architecture-independent byte stream that preserves the identity of the objects and relationships among them. The objects' types are also stored along with their data. Objects decoded from the byte stream are normally instantiated with the same classes of objects that were originally encoded.

When we want to archive an object, most of the time we think about saving the program's state. In the Model-View-Controller paradigm, the program's states are usually maintained in model objects. You encode a model object in an archive, and you read it back by decoding it. The encoding and decoding operations are performed using an NSCoder object at runtime. NSCoder itself is just an abstract class. Apple suggests using the keyed archiving technique with NSKeyedArchiver and NSKeyedUnarchiver classes, which are concrete classes of NSCoder. The object being encoded and decoded must conform to the NSCoding protocol and implement the following methods:

```
- (id)initWithCoder:(NSCoder *)coder;
- (void)encodeWithCoder:(NSCoder *)coder;
```

These methods are related to encoding and decoding the object during the archiving and unarchiving processes. We'll discuss the methods in a little bit.

In the example of the ScribbleMemento, we have implemented the archiving and unarchiving processes with the NSKeyedArchiver and NSKeyedUnarchiver classes. The object being encoded was a Mark composite object. You can go to Chapter 13 for the discussion on Mark and its composite related operations. In order to make NSKeyedArchiver and NSKeyedArchiver happy to do the job for us, we need to make sure all Mark classes conform to the NSCoding protocol and its required methods. So first of all, we need the Mark protocol to adopt NSCoding so other classes will follow, as shown in Listing 23–8.

Listing 23–8. *Mark Implements the NSCoding Protocol*

```
@protocol Mark <NSObject, NSCopying, NSCoding>

@property (nonatomic, retain) UIColor *color;
@property (nonatomic, assign) CGFloat size;
@property (nonatomic, assign) CGPoint location;
@property (nonatomic, readonly) NSUInteger count;
@property (nonatomic, readonly) id <Mark> lastChild;

- (id) copy;
- (void) addMark:(id <Mark>) mark;
- (void) removeMark:(id <Mark>) mark;
- (id <Mark>) childMarkAtIndex:(NSUInteger) index;

// some other methods defined in other chapters
@end
```

So all Mark's implementers should be NSCoding-compliant until they all implement the required methods. Let's look at Vertex's implementation of these methods in Listing 23–9.

Listing 23–9. *NSCoding's Method Implementation in Vertex*

```
- (id)initWithCoder:(NSCoder *)coder
{
  if (self = [super init])
  {
    location_ = [(NSValue *)[coder decodeObjectForKey:@"VertexLocation"] CGPointValue];
  }
  return self;
}

- (void)encodeWithCoder:(NSCoder *)coder
{
  [coder encodeObject:[NSValue valueWithCGPoint:location_] forKey:@"VertexLocation"];
}
```

coder is provided at runtime by an archiver or unarchiver with which we need to instruct it how to encode/decode an object with the same key. In the case of Vertex, when the encodeWithCoder: method is invoked at runtime when it is saving its object, it sends an encodeObject: message to encode its location_ attribute as a key, @"VertexLocation". And it uses the same key to decode the same attribute in the initWithCoder: method with a message, decodeObjectForKey:, to an unarchiver.

Dot follows pretty much the same procedure, except its objects have a couple more attributes to take care of, as shown in Listing 23–10.

Listing 23–10. *NSCoding's Method Implementation in Dot*

```
- (id)initWithCoder:(NSCoder *)coder
{
  if (self = [super initWithCoder:coder])
  {
    color_ = [[coder decodeObjectForKey:@"DotColor"] retain];
    size_ = [coder decodeFloatForKey:@"DotSize"];
  }
```

```
    return self;
}

- (void)encodeWithCoder:(NSCoder *)coder
{
    [super encodeWithCoder:coder];
    [coder encodeObject:color_ forKey:@"DotColor"];
    [coder encodeFloat:size_ forKey:@"DotSize"];
}
```

The reason we don't forward the same message to super in the initWithCoder: and encodeWithCoder: methods of Vertex is that Vertex is a direct subclass of NSObject and NSObject does not implement those methods.

The implementation for Stroke looks very similar to Vertex's and Dot's, as in Listing 23–11.

Listing 23–11. *NSCoding's Method Implementation in* Stroke

```
- (id)initWithCoder:(NSCoder *)coder
{
    if (self = [super init])
    {
        color_ = [[coder decodeObjectForKey:@"StrokeColor"] retain];
        size_ = [coder decodeFloatForKey:@"StrokeSize"];
        children_ = [[coder decodeObjectForKey:@"StrokeChildren"] retain];
    }

    return self;
}

- (void)encodeWithCoder:(NSCoder *)coder
{
    [coder encodeObject:color_ forKey:@"StrokeColor"];
    [coder encodeFloat:size_ forKey:@"StrokeSize"];
    [coder encodeObject:children_ forKey:@"StrokeChildren"];
}
```

The children of a Stroke object can be encoded recursively as well. We just toss the whole children attribute in coder during encoding, and we can get it back in one piece from the coder of an unarchiver in the initWithCoder: method.

Summary

So far, we have discussed the concepts of the Memento pattern and how we can apply it to an iOS application development with the TouchPainter app example. ScribbleMemento can also be reused for implementing (un)redo operations by keeping a list of small changes to the internal state of a Scribble object. A list of ScribbleMemento objects that carry only small changes of the Scribble can be useful for sharing strokes across the network. So the other remote user who is sharing the same drawing session can see a simulated remote drawing, one stroke at a time.

This marks the end of the catalog for all the design patterns presented in this book. Now, you should feel quite comfortable using any of them for your real projects. I do hope that you can find them useful in many aspects of your software design ventures!

Index

W

X

Made in the USA
Lexington, KY
02 May 2012